Lead Like an Entrepreneur

Lead Like an Entrepreneur

Neal Thornberry, Ph.D.

McGraw-Hill
New York   Chicago   San Francisco   Lisbon
London   Madrid   Mexico City   Milan   New Delhi
San Juan   Seoul   Singapore   Sydney   Toronto

The **McGraw-Hill** Companies

Library of Congress Cataloging-in-Publication Data is on file.

2 3 4 5 6 7 8 9 0   FGR/FGR   0 1 9 8 7 6

ISBN 0-07-226235-4

The sponsoring editor for this book was Roger Stewart and the production supervisor was David Zielonka. It was set in Fairfield Medium by Patricia Wallenburg.

Printed and bound by Quebecor Fairfield.

Contents

vi   Contents

Introduction

In almost all the large corporations with whom I have worked, several individuals stand out. They are frequently pointed to as having done something exceptional to move the company along, change its direction or, most important, put the company or a significant part of it on a new path of growth, renewed energy, and profitability.

Sometimes, they outlast the disruption and creative destruction that often accompanies their tenure, and sometimes they do not. They are generally spoken about respectfully and are often held in awe, because they do not appear to be the average manager or organizational leader. Not many exist in large organizations, but the few who do have proven that with strong passion, a clever mind, bureaucracy-avoidance skills, determination, and sometimes help from a mentor or two, they can bring significant value to the organization—not only through their abilities to inspire and lead but more importantly because they are significant new-value creators known as *entrepreneurial leaders.*

This book is about those entrepreneurial leaders: who they are, what they do, and how large companies can benefit significantly from identifying, developing, and supporting these new corporate leaders. Entrepreneurial leaders share many traits with start-up entrepreneurs, yet they are different. They want to ply their trade within an already existing company. Rather than beginning from scratch, they prefer to be given a "head start." They are able to think and act in ways that are similar to start-up entrepreneurs, but have the added talent that I call "corporate radar." Often, they are able to run the corporate gauntlet better than their peers, and they know how to get things done despite bureaucratic rules and regulations. Few of these entrepreneurial leaders go outside their companies to start a brand-new business. Rather than going it alone, they prefer to push and prod their current organizations into action, often in directions about which the organization is ambivalent.

Entrepreneurial leaders create economic value for the organization because their drive and energy is focused on identifying, developing, and capturing new business opportunities. Sometimes this energy is focused externally, on market opportunities, and sometimes it is focused internally on creative asset management (which in turn results in growth and the creation of economic value). But creative they are—often doing and seeing things that others have missed.

Leading like an entrepreneur does not require some gift from heaven or the right genes at birth. Most managers who want to act in more entrepreneurial ways can learn to do so. The key is *wanting to*. Without the desire, leading like an entrepreneur is a nonstarter. But with desire, the entrepreneurial mindset and skill set can be learned and applied in a corporate environment. This book examines people who have the natural inclination to lead like entrepreneurs and people who have developed into entrepreneurial leaders despite their own self-perception of having not one entrepreneurial bone in their body.

Whether these talents are natural or learned, organizations derive huge benefit from finding, developing, and supporting this kind of leadership behavior, because it directly affects the organization's ability to survive, thrive, and create economic value. As companies get larger, they often lose sight of their entrepreneurial origins and become suffocated by their own process and procedural weight. Entrepreneurial leaders are the perfect antidotes to this kind of organizational stagnation because they bring to the table risk taking, bureaucracy busting, opportunity focus, and a passion for making money that most organizations wish all their managers had.

The personal profiles included in this book should give hope to every organizational employee who ever said, "Well, that could never happen here." Organizations don't make things happen—people do. And entrepreneurial leaders make *significant* things happen. If you are a CEO, look for and develop more people who can lead like entrepreneurs. As you will see, it doesn't take many of these people to make a significant difference to both the top and bottom lines.

Managers, take heart: As you read this book, you will see that many ways exist to outwit, outmaneuver, and overcome the bureaucratic impediments that get in the way of your success. There is no need to wring your hands, curse the gods—or blame senior management. This book will show you examples and techniques used by successful entrepreneurial leaders to get around, through, in between, or over these types of hurdles. Cleverness is also a key entrepreneurial trait, and you will see much of it in my examples.

Education does make a difference. In this book, you will learn about an educational investment of about $2 million in entrepreneurial leadership that led to first-year new business worth $250 million—not a bad return on investment. You will also see several examples of an educational program developed at Babson's School of Executive Education that involves education wrapped around real-time new business development. It was designed to teach managers to become entrepreneurial leaders and has shown some spectacular successes.

These programs not only demonstrate the amount of entrepreneurial leadership than can be learned by corporate managers, they also demonstrate that, when this education is integrated with the identification and pursuit of real opportunities, both the organization and the individual benefit. If this type of behavior is supported and replicated, it provides the best defense against organizational lethargy, stagnation, and eventual decline.

Acknowledgments

Writing a book is quite an undertaking, one that could lead you to the undertaker. It has been an interesting experience. I think the real test of knowing something is your ability to communicate it to others. I hope my book will do this clearly, logically, and compellingly. While my name is on the book, a cast of characters behind the scenes always must be given credit as well. Without their help, insights, knowledge, and support, this book would never have been accomplished. Among the cast, I would like to thank and acknowledge the following:

- *Meg Thornberry*—Thanks to my lovely wife, without whose support, confidence, caring, and, yes, even nagging, this book would not have been possible. She pushed me when I needed it, kept silent when I did not, and always supported me with her confidence that I had something valuable to say.
- *My Babson colleagues*—Special thanks to Tom Moore, former Dean at Babson's Executive Education, and Stephen Flavin, Associate Dean. Tom gave me both the emotional and financial support to pursue writing this book, and Stephen has done the same. In addition, Stephen has been a stalwart supporter and architect of our corporate entrepreneurship brand at Babson. Also, I wish to thank Allan Cohen, faculty member, and Steve Spinelli, Provost, for their support of this project. Both, authors in their own right, gave me some great advice.
- *Mark Maletz*—Mark is both a friend and colleague who helped Babson with our first foray into corporate entrepre-

neurship when, as a McKinsey consultant, he introduced us to Siemens and helped design our first-ever corporate entrepreneurship management development program. Over the years, he has been an ambassador for Babson, telling others about our capabilities in this field. I probably would not have written this book without Mark's involvement in the program and his inclusion of me.

- *My Siemens colleagues*—I have a great deal of affection and admiration for this company. Siemens was our first real test case to see if the magic of start-up entrepreneurship could be infused into a large company, and Siemens was willing to take the trip with us, despite the risk. I have been associated with the company for over 8 years and have met some wonderful people and traveled to exotic locations as a result. Special thanks go to Udo Dierk, former head of Siemens Management Learning, and all his colleagues in that department, especially Toni Jakubetzki, head of the S3 General Manager's Program for Europe, and Alf Keough, the acting head of Siemens Management Learning and the architect of their Senior Management Program.
- *John Kilcullen*—John's insights and emotional support have been very important to me during the course of writing *Lead Like an Entrepreneur*. John started the Dummies series of books at IDG, and he was our first Babson Executive Education–developed case study on corporate entrepreneurship. John has graciously helped us over the years as the "mystery speaker" who hides behind glasses as an anonymous faculty member while we discuss the case about him called "Corporate Entrepreneurship for Dummies." Eventually, an unwitting participant makes a negative comment about him (which I usually provoke) and then the trap is sprung. John comes to front of the room and shakes hands with the victim who made the negative remark. It is great theater and great fun (if perhaps a little sadistic on our part); the class loves it, and the learning is enhanced tenfold.
- *Sam Perkins*—I've singled out Sam for special acknowledgment. He is our superb case writer at Babson, and his insights, writing acumen, and the ability to learn the com-

plexities of things quickly impresses all of us. Sam has been incredibly helpful in developing many of the entrepreneurial leader profiles that you will read in this book. Reading business articles and cases can be deadly boring but, in Sam's hands, the profiles come alive. He not only describes the businesses scenarios well, but we also get to know a lot about the people through his perceptive lens.

· *Roger Stewart and McGraw-Hill*—I found out after I wrote about 80 percent of the book that I had done things the wrong way. Most authors write a proposal and one or two chapters and then shop the book around to either agents or publishers. This allows the publisher to have more direction over the chapters to come. Very fortunately for me, Roger and McGraw-Hill saw the value in my material and agreed to publish it despite my unorthodox approach.

Chapter One

In Search of Entrepreneurial Spirit

About 10 years ago, we began to notice that something new was happening with many of our executive education clients at Babson College (which has a reputation as one of the world's leading educational institutions in the field of start-up entrepreneurship). We started getting calls from top executives at large companies wanting our help in figuring out how to take the widely perceived "magic" of start-up entrepreneurship and infuse it into their managers and the fabric of their organizations. They wanted to make their managers more entrepreneurial as leaders and their organizations more entrepreneurial as entities. These first few requests, which grew into a steady stream by the end of the 1990s, were our introduction to the realm of "applied corporate entrepreneurship."

In all honesty, we didn't really know where to start at the time. The whole notion of corporate entrepreneurship and the development of entrepreneurial leaders within large companies had only been introduced to the business world in 1985, when Gifford Pinchot wrote a groundbreaking work on something labeled "intrapreneurship."[1] This concept was broadly characterized as an attempt to apply those entrepreneurship principles derived from research on start-ups to already existing medium- and large-sized companies.

For the most part, only other academics read this work; thus, little in the way of real implementation of the concept was apparent in large established companies. Some of my colleagues in the start-up side of entrepreneurship actually told me there was no such thing as corporate entrepreneurship. They said it was an oxymoron, like "jumbo shrimp." And they were right: *oxymoronic* is a perfect term to describe the concept of corporate entrepreneurship.

The words *corporate* and *entrepreneurship* seem somehow incompatible. We often associate *corporate* with words like *large, organized, bureaucratic, formal, stiff,* and *hierarchical. Entrepreneurial,* in contrast, conjures up associations like *creative, inventive, small, quick, driven, winning.* These associations have a positive connotation in our society; whereas corporate, as in corporate headquarters, seems to have a more negative aura around the water cooler.

But corporate entrepreneurship, or something like it, was the perceived solution many of our corporate clients were requesting. While several forms of corporate entrepreneurship have since evolved, in the early days, what most of these companies actually wanted was for their managers to act more like entrepreneurs in their leadership roles.

So, what stops companies from staying entrepreneurial? Most were started by entrepreneurs, but somewhere along the way, this essential spirit was eroded, sometimes to the point of disappearing completely. And the erosion process often is not obvious. It can be slow, happening over years of policy making, structure building, and the development of an increasingly risk-averse culture. In the remainder of this chapter, we look at this erosion process to understand why many companies need to rekindle their entrepreneurial roots.

Symptoms of Corporate Inertia

One of the first questions we posed to those pioneers who sought our help in making their corporations more entrepreneurial was, "If you think corporate entrepreneurship is the answer, what's the problem?" Before recommending a dose of entrepreneurship or to help managers lead like entrepreneurs, we needed to know exactly what organizational ills they thought this medicine might help them cure.

In many respects, their answers were similar to what a doctor hears when the patient says, "I don't know exactly what's wrong, but I just don't feel well." And, as with many patients, these companies had myriad presenting symptoms. We heard things like:

- "Our employees just don't seem to take initiative."
- "Our managers usually wait for someone higher up to make decisions."
- "Our growth has been flat for the past 2 years."
- "Competitors are kicking our butt."
- "We just don't seem to be able to attract the bright young graduates anymore."
- "We have gone through so many cost-cutting exercises that people are worn out and very cynical about the overused mantra of doing more with less."
- "We need our managers and our employees to think and act more like owners."

The underlying systemic disease that these symptoms revealed was, of course, a lack of both sustained profitable growth and the creation of economic value for the owners. Organizations that are not able to grow or create economic value don't last very long.

That Lost Entrepreneurial Spirit

It was ironic that many of the struggling companies who came to us for help were founded by entrepreneurs—people who had an innovative idea, saw an opportunity in the marketplace, and turned their dreams into a shining reality.

But, at some point in the growth process, these same companies became overlarge, multilayered, highly structured, and bureaucratic. The founding entrepreneurs were no longer present, and these companies started to evolve into entities in which the ability to nurture new ideas into real products and customer-attracting services was often hindered by processes, procedures, structures, systems, executive perks, and the maintenance of power. In many respects, these organizations were increasingly trapped by their own success. Often, people in these organizations agreed that they needed more entrepreneurial spirit, increased cleverness, and enhanced innovation, but feared that their company could not get out of its own way to accomplish these things.

Over time, these established organizations often get so focused on doing things the *right way* that they lose sight of doing the *right things*. For instance, in bad economic times, opportunity focus gives way to cost focus, with companies bringing in "hired guns" famous for management styles steeped in deconstruction. DEC's Robert Palmer, Robert Allen at AT&T, "Chainsaw" Al Dunlap at Sunbeam, and others have brought their gunslinger's approach to the top seats in organizations. (A few leaders—longtime GE chairman and CEO Jack Welch and Lou Gerstner at IBM—have been able to rekindle entrepreneurial spirit in their organizations from the ashes of deconstruction, but most have been unable to find or sustain a new spark of innovation.)

While gunslingers can be effective at cutting costs, they usually are not equally effective in creating sustained value. For example, Procter & Gamble (P&G) went through a major cost-cutting program and found that, while it improved the bottom line, it did not really help them with new product development. As a result, they created a department called Corporate New Ventures,[2] which was well-funded and reported to the highest levels in the company. This department was able to foster greater innovation and had an entrepreneurial orientation aimed at finding the next million-dollar hit product.

The Cost of Cost Savings

A brief story from my own experience illustrates the kind of decisions often made by many large, bureaucratized organizations when they become more concerned with cost savings than with seizing new business opportunities.

Several years ago, I was about to begin a new fall semester teaching my college's required organizational behavior (OB) class. Book salespeople often visit faculty members to showcase their latest textbooks. So, it was not unusual that Rich, a salesman from a prominent publisher, visited my office regularly with updates on his company's latest entries into the field. In mid-August—only a few weeks from the start of the semester—he showed me a new OB textbook, one that I was quite keen to use in the upcoming semester. I had several sections of this course, as did my colleagues. We agreed to use the book and asked Rich to order it for us.

Several days later, he called to tell us that there was a problem. The book was new and was being printed. It would be ready just before classes started, but the book would have to be shipped via overland truck—it would be approximately 2 to 3 weeks late for the start of the semester. This was, of course, a real problem considering the fact that it was a 14-week course. So, I suggested to Rich that he send the books by air freight. He told me that the company had a policy against air shipments.

I patiently explained that, if we did not get the books in time for the start of the course, I would have to choose a more readily available text from another publisher. Rich appealed to his manager and to his manager's manager to countermand the policy in this case—but to no avail. Both higher-level managers agreed that this was an unfortunate policy, but both said their hands were tied. Clearly, at this company, efficiency and expense control had "evolved" to the degree at which they stood in the way of business growth and value creation.

The upshot of all of this was that the publisher lost a significant order, as well as the potential for ongoing future orders, as a direct result of a rigid cost-containment policy. And, the lost opportunity goes much further than our book orders. The academic world is very small, and I have told many of my peers outside the school's walls about this incident. Perhaps worst of all, the company also lost a dynamic salesperson when Rich left in disgust shortly after this incident.

This vignette illustrates how a company can lose sight of its real purpose and how managers and employees can become so distant from this purpose that they fail to act in ways that actually help protect their long-term employment. Following the "ship only by truck" rule kept these managers out of trouble today, but will surely put them in harm's way tomorrow. Thus, the absence of an entrepreneurial viewpoint and the failure of managers to lead like entrepreneurs can have dire consequences for large organizations struggling to survive in an increasingly turbulent and competitive environment.

The Challenge of Turbulent Environments

In addition to the tendency for long-established companies to be suffocated by their own processes and procedures, living in turbulent times and environments only exacerbates the problems. Figure 1.1 shows a scale that I frequently use in my corporate entrepreneurship courses and speaking engagements. As you can see, it is really a five-point scale that moves from *Steady and stable* (1) to *Chaotic and unpredictable* (5). I ask course participants to use this scale to rate for their particular companies the turbulence in the industry or marketplace. By "turbulence," I mean the speed at which market conditions change, the frequency of the arrival of new competitors on the scene, and the rate of change in the technology involved in their particular business.

Over the last 10 years, in my executive development programs and speeches, only two people have rated the turbulence of their company's environment as stable or changing slowly. One of these people worked for the Registry of Motor Vehicles (no surprise there!) and the other for the India Coal Company.

The India Coal Company manager actually shocked the class when he described his organization as a huge bureaucracy hoping to grow even larger and more cumbersome. I had just finished sermonizing about the need for speed in large companies when he told us that 500,000 people were working directly and indirectly for the company and that it hoped to add as many employees as possible. In fact, he informed us, he and his co-workers wanted to have a bloated bureaucracy with many

Environmental Turbulence

- Steady and stable

- Slowly changing, predictable, trends are evident

- Increasing rate of change with some predictability, unforeseen trends appear

- Rapid change, little predictability, many surprises

- Chaotic and unpredictable

FIGURE 1.1   Rating scale for environmental turbulence.

layers of management, and were not the least bit interested in being more entrepreneurial.

The explanation for the company's rampant bureaucracy? It is government-supported and directed more toward creating employment than making money. The government subsidizes the company, the manager explained, as a means of employing thousands of people, keeping crime under control, and feeding hungry mouths.

Notwithstanding these two exceptions, everyone else I've asked this question of in the past 10 years has rated their industries at 3 or higher, ranging from *Some predictability* to *Chaotic and unpredictable.*

Why should this state of affairs drive companies to seek out and develop entrepreneurial leaders? Well, as environments become less predictable, some of our most favored and widely hyped models of strategic planning and control become less effective, perhaps even obsolete. It is interesting to note that many large companies use very static planning and diagnostic models—like Michael Porter's "Five Forces"[3]—even when operating in dynamic environments. It is almost as if their "genetic code" forces them into yet another process-oriented approach with the hope that this will somehow stabilize an unstable environment.

EVA as an Innovation Driver

> Simply put, EVA is a company's net operating profit after
> taxes and after deducting the cost of capital. The capital is
> all the money tied up in such things as heavy equipment,
> real estate, and computers, plus so-called working capital—
> mainly cash, inventories, and receivables. The cost of capi-
> tal is the minimum rate of return demanded by lenders and
> shareholders, and it varies with the riskiness of the compa-
> ny. When you are making more money than your cost of
> doing business plus your cost of capital, you are creating
> wealth for your shareholders.[4]

With the arrival of EVA (economic value added), the playing field
has become both more level and more visible. The formula can be
applied unemotionally and uniformly. The advent of EVA has put
tremendous pressure on companies to demonstrate that they are
adding value. Cost cutting does not do this any more than downsizing does. Only the development of new products, services, and
markets achieves this added value for shareholders. And—as anyone who follows the markets knows—the vast number of options
open to investors means they will not spend a single cent on a
company that is not consistently adding value to its shares.

It is no wonder then, that large, publicly traded companies
increasingly stress the importance of EVA to their managers
and ask them to focus their activities around this concept.
Although increasing numbers of critics now question whether
the search for EVA has become too limiting and shortsighted,
it seems that this concept is here to stay. Value creation is and
always will be the domain of entrepreneurs, because they know
they must accomplish it for themselves, their investors, and for
society. Thus, developing a cadre of entrepreneurially focused
organizational leaders seems a prudent action in today's EVA-
driven, turbulent environment.

Strategic Plans or Strategic Handcuffs?

Consultants and academics have made an awful lot of money
creating a science out of strategic planning. Managers and

executives are fully immersed in the lingo of strategic planning. They know about competitor analysis, Porter's "Five Forces," scenario planning, and so on. Most organizations follow some sort of strategic thought process. In many cases, large companies have found that strategic plans, and the budgeting process that often accompanies this sort of planning, also can create strategic handcuffs. This is largely because static models aren't valuable tools in planning for dynamic markets. They can certainly help to identify a company's strengths and weaknesses and outline certain current opportunities and threats. But building an inflexible three- to five-year plan based on current realities could become a very dangerous approach in a rapidly changing and chaotic environment.

Companies can be so thoroughly engaged in planning that they miss real opportunities. Managers at a well-known global conglomerate with over 400,000 employees often lament that, by the time the budgeting process has been completed, they have to wave bye-bye to some good new opportunities because they no longer have the time, resources, or energy to go after them. Perhaps this is one of the reasons why this company is now investing so heavily in innovation and entrepreneurial leadership development, and they are seeing a return on this investment.

Strategic planning can, in fact, limit opportunities unless the strategy builds in opportunity focus. Some companies are actually creating internal venture capital funds so that they can exploit unforeseen opportunities as they arise or are identified. Not all these efforts have been successful, mostly due to the "business as usual" bureaucratic handling of internal venture capital funds, but this is a move in the right direction. Entrepreneurial leaders recognize the importance of having an opportunistic mindset, and they push and prod their organizations to be ready when a good opportunity comes along. Often, these entrepreneurial leaders seek outside funds if their own budgeting and planning processes get in the way. We will see some good examples of this in later chapters.

I am not advocating the elimination of plans or budgets. Without them, a corporation's finances would be sheer chaos.

Rather, I suggest building flexibilities into the planning and budgeting processes, to make room for unanticipated opportunities.

In increasingly turbulent environments, companies must learn to blend the disciplines of planning and budgeting with opportunity focus if they are to survive and thrive. Entrepreneurial leaders know how to work with these processes and how to circumvent or modify them if necessary. Large, bureaucratically oriented companies must find a counterbalance or antidote to keep them from suffocating under their own weight. I recently worked with senior managers of a large company who were wringing their hands over the processes that often got in the way of their ability to capture the new business opportunities that their smaller competitors were gleefully gobbling up. They spent a full day debating the problem, and then came to the conclusion that they needed rules about not following the rules. Bureaucracies, like viruses, tend to spread. They create more and more rules, which only add weight, slowness, and lethargy to an already overburdened organization.

I told this forlorn group of executives that the answer did not lie in more rules, but in encouraging people to break, circumvent, and eventually change or eliminate those rules that get in the way of doing business. In short, they needed more entrepreneurially oriented leaders at all levels within the organization. It's people, not rules, who make money. It's people, not rules, who create the relationships that grease the wheels of value creation. Shipping books by air costs money, but it makes even more money. Companies need more of this type of thinking, and it is what this book is ultimately about.

In the next chapter, we examine the different kinds of corporate leadership, look at how entrepreneurial leadership differs from other kinds of leadership, and note that many corporations do not seek out this type of leadership skill despite its shown effectiveness in promoting growth and value creation.

Summary

The world is not nearly as safe and predictable as when I was a child. On the other hand, it is pretty exciting. New technologies allow us to do things that my grandparents would never have dreamed possible, and global communications are at our fingertips. With all that is going on, it is no wonder that so many good companies have trouble staying on top. Being big and fast can be difficult, but that is required in today's global and turbulent environment. Rekindling that lost entrepreneurial spirit can be a major shot in the arm for many a struggling company. The entrepreneurial spirit is an inherently creative one and, when released, it can provide a powerful antidote to a large company's stagnation and complacency.

Chapter Two

What They Forgot to Remember

Leading like an entrepreneur requires a different view of leadership. It requires that managers integrate both an entrepreneurial mindset and an entrepreneurial skill set into their daily lives as organizational leaders and managers. In short, they need to view their jobs through an entrepreneurial lens. Doing so helps them focus their activities on the really important stuff and gives them a solid platform for making the right decisions. Very few managers are ever fired for consistently generating profitable growth, adding new customers, or making the organization both more effective and efficient. Wearing an entrepreneurial hat also helps managers manage their time—a very difficult thing in today's complex and fast-paced business environment. It is easy to get caught up spending time in non–value-creating activities. Entrepreneurs know that their time is best spent with customers, trying innovative things, and managing cash flow. It isn't spent in worrying about who gets the biggest office, counting paper clips, or sitting in endless internally focused meetings.

To better understand the nature of entrepreneurial leadership, we must look at each of the components that make up the term: *entrepreneurial* and *leadership*. In this chapter and the next, we examine both these elements in detail, in an attempt to understand how their combination results in a 1 + 1 = 3 formula that can help many large organizations reignite their entrepreneurial flame.

Leadership versus Management

Figure 2.1 represents the model or set of roles that many companies increasingly ask their managers to play. These companies not only want their managers to be good managers and good leaders, they want them to think and act like entrepreneurs; that is, to demonstrate creative use of assets, grow the business, make it run better, innovate, and, in the end, create greater economic value for the company's owners. This is asking a lot. Integrating these roles is no easy matter. In fact, a great deal of tension, if not outright conflict, can be generated among them.

John Kotter,[1] a researcher at Harvard, has drawn a fairly strong distinction between managing and leading. In his view, management is more akin to administration, whereas leadership is about change and transformation. Of course, this is somewhat confusing when you get into details like doing a performance review. Is that management or leadership? It may be

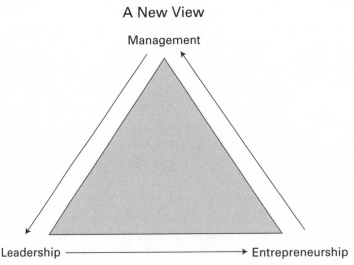

FIGURE 2.1   The entrepreneurial leadership model.

a management tool, but if an employee is inspired to change her behavior, then it must involve leadership (from Kotter's perspective), as well. Nonetheless, some of his points are cogent. Often, managers are rewarded for keeping the ship running smoothly and on an even keel. Leaders, Kotter would argue, are focused on changing things—potentially pointing the ship in a totally different direction, possibly changing the crew, and refitting the entire ship. As Kotter points out, some inherent discord exists between running the ship smoothly and dramatically changing direction, which could set all matter of other changes in motion.

Regardless of whether you buy the distinction between management and leadership, it is a moot issue when one leads like an entrepreneur. You cannot be a successful entrepreneurial leader unless you simultaneously manage assets and inspire people, while also consistently focusing on value-creating activities. Leading like an entrepreneur always involves the creation of value through some change or rearrangement of assets for the purposes of developing a new business or venture. Entrepreneurial leadership always involves inspiring and motivating employees to capture that new business opportunity.

In observing effective entrepreneurial leaders, it is clear that they are able to blend the roles of manager, leader, and entrepreneur, but their entrepreneurial bent tends to outweigh or highly influence how they practice their other roles. Since they are always focused on (some would say obsessed by) their pursuit of new business opportunities, they dislike performing management or leadership activities that get in the way of pursuing opportunities. For example, their management role may reward them for following corporate policies, as in the publisher example mentioned in Chapter 1. But, if company policies get in the way of developing and capturing new business opportunities, then entrepreneurial leaders try to ignore, avoid, change, defy, finesse, or manipulate those policies so that they do not become an obstacle to value creation.

Entrepreneurial leaders are also less interested in leading and inspiring subordinates to do across-the-board financial cuts in the name of fairness, when they know instinctively that money should be taken from one group to fund a significant new business opportunity sought after by another group. "To hell with fairness over value creation" would be their refrain. Yet, company after company applies across-the-board cuts in the name of fairness rather than redirecting that money to seize opportunities.

Entrepreneurial leaders still require good general management skills and the ability to motivate and inspire. Would-be entrepreneurial leaders with no understanding of cash flow, net present value, or market dynamics won't be around long. They either will not be able to convince others that their idea is an opportunity or they will underestimate the risk profile of a potential new venture. They also need leadership skills if they are to persuade and influence others to get on board with a new entrepreneurial venture. So, to be an effective entrepreneurial leader, you need good management skills and good leadership capabilities, but the compass setting is on E for "entrepreneurial focus."

Entrepreneurial Orientation—The Missing Link

To understand the leadership side of entrepreneurial leadership, it is important for us to take a little sojourn through some of the key research findings on business leadership. It is almost impossible to visit a bookstore, go online, or walk through an airport without seeing an advertisement or other promotion for the latest book on leadership. Leadership gurus make millions selling themselves and their theories, and legends like Jack Welch are constantly sought for their leadership secrets. Despite the hype, it is clear that the buyers of these books, primarily managers and business professionals, are truly seeking help. Many of these readers find themselves in leadership roles and looking for the manual. It can be a rather confusing maze.

Consultants, business school professors, training and development professionals, and human resources (HR) managers stand at the ready to help in this process. The help often comes in some sort of leadership package or model against which managers can assess themselves and then develop an action plan for improving their leadership capabilities. A company can spend several hundred thousand dollars developing a set of these capabilities or competencies, which they then expect their managers to practice.

Most of these approaches provide valuable feedback and developmental information to both the individual and the organization. Unfortunately, however, most of the models tend to focus on the manager's internal interactions with his or her direct subordinates and rarely provide feedback on how clever, creative, or entrepreneurial that manager is in creating value for the company.

I have yet to see any 360-degree survey items that focus primarily on the value-creating competencies of a leader, yet the purpose of any business is the creation of value for its owners (and, by extension, for society in general). This is a significant oversight. The entrepreneurial mindset, or competency if you will, so prevalent at the organization's founding, seems to have been overlooked.

I was asked by the spin-out of a large well-known telecommunications company to help it with the development of an internal leadership program for the new company. I met with the head of HR and several of his staff to discuss the possibility of working together. They brought with them a very well thought out and researched leadership competency program that they had taken from the parent company—which, like many large telecoms, was quite bureaucratized. As you would expect, this competency model mirrored the parent company's large-company orientation, with its emphasis on following rules, regulations, and procedures. Needless to say, risk taking, innovation, acting like an owner, and encouraging employees to think about new ways to do their jobs were not elements of this scheme. Yet, the HR people were insistent in applying this large-company competency model to the spin-out.

I told them that this competency model was completely inappropriate for a start-up organization trying to work in the highly competitive and volatile area of information technology. I also suspected that this type of model was one reason why the parent company had to create the spin-out in the first place— only outside the parent's bureaucratic structure and processes would it have a chance of surviving. The spin-out strategy was a good idea, but here were HR managers from the parent company trying to bring in an old leadership model and force it on the new offspring.

Ultimately, I was asked to step off the project because I had the audacity to question the logic and appropriateness of the parent company's model. In private, several of the HR staff told me that my comments were spot on, but they were afraid to disagree with their boss. Here was a perfect example of nonentrepreneurial leadership. Entrepreneurial leaders question the status quo and often buck the system, because they see a better way. And, they are willing to fight for their views. It is ironic that, in this case, this type of competency, which was really the most important for their future, was nowhere to be found in their corporate list of leadership competencies, nor in the behaviors of the people working with the spin-out.

Leadership Theories: The Trait Approach

It is important to understand something about the various approaches to leadership research and theory to see why we have missed this link and why entrepreneurial leadership's time has come. So, I have included a short historical trip through "Leadership Land" to help put the concept of entrepreneurial leadership in context.

Throughout the centuries, people have been interested in what makes leaders tick. From Julius Caesar to Jack Welch, the search for finding the "right stuff" seems insatiable. Unfortunately, the prospecting and mining of "right stuff" has yielded very little high-grade ore. When I teach leadership courses, one of the first things I do is ask the group to list the key characteristics that make a successful leader. I collect all these items, and usually wind up with a list of at least 15 to 18 characteristics that include such generalities as courage, good listening skills, charisma, decisiveness, honesty, integrity, knowledge, sensitivity, aggressiveness, and the like. I am always surprised that no one objects to this list until I have pointed out to them that they have just built a competency model that no one in the room, not even Jack or Julius, could live up to.

They grudgingly agree that that's true, and then often have a great deal of difficulty when I tell them that these characteristics do not explain more than about 20 percent of a business leader's success. Figure 2.2 shows the results of one of the more scientific studies of personality traits and their relationship to leadership success. This study was written up by Edwin Ghiselli, a noted organizational psychologist, in his book *Explorations in Managerial Talent*.[2] Each of the characteristics in this list shows some relationship to leadership success. They are presented in descending order of importance, with the first item, Supervisory Abilities (empathy), being the most important. But, all combined, statistically, they do not explain more than 20 percent of a leader's success.

While Ghiselli's study used the term *management*, much of the book dealt with what we think of as the *leadership* compo-

Some relation to
managerial success

Supervisory abilities

Need for achievement

I.Q.
Need for self-actualization
Self-assurance

Decisiveness

Lack of need for security

Lack of working-class affinity

Initiative

Lack of need for high financial reward

Need for power

Maturity

No relation to
managerial success

Masculinity–femininity

FIGURE 2.2   Ghiselli study on personality characteristics.

nent of managerial work. Statistically, the multiple correlations of all of these traits combined only explain about 20 percent of the leader's success. While some of my participants are a little shocked, and even somewhat depressed, that their favorite trait did not make the list, I think the news is good. The really important question is: What explains the rest of the leader's success? The answer clearly involves learning, experience, adaptability, and perhaps knowing oneself enough to make the right choices. Thus, much of what we call leadership can be learned, and this applies equally to leading like an entrepreneur.

Since the Ghiselli work dates back to the 1960s, it is important to do a little translation of characteristics in the above figure. Ghiselli defined "supervisory abilities" as innate empathy. Interestingly, the trait of empathy is a little bit like old wine in new bottles. We saw it pop up again in the recent work on "emotional intelligence," but Ghiselli discovered it 40 years ago.

And the phrase "lack of working-class affinity" sounds a little old-fashioned, but Ghiselli was referring to the ability of effective leaders to distance themselves emotionally and socially from their direct reports. This ability allows them to make some of the tough people decisions that we often have to make when we manage people with whom we are also friendly. Ask anyone who has ever been promoted over their peers, and they will tell you how important and valid this characteristic is.

Behavioral Leadership

Because corporations are always searching for managers with the right stuff, and because they are always looking for ways to instill those traits into their managers, many researchers have turned to a search for observable, measurable, learnable behaviors that lead to what we now think of as leadership competency. This approach cares less about what you are made of or what you inherited genetically, and focuses instead on how you act. It focuses on the concept of leadership *style*, which is inherently more malleable than personality.

Over 30 years ago, studies at Ohio State University and the University of Michigan identified two key sets of behaviors (often referred to as "leadership style") that leaders demonstrate or don't demonstrate when they are trying to lead or influence.[3] These two sets of behaviors, or competencies, are most widely known as "task-oriented" and "people-oriented" behaviors. Thus, any manager can be assessed on his leadership style by observing how often he engages in either task-oriented behaviors or people-oriented behaviors when trying to inspire or motivate his employees.

As you would expect, leaders who demonstrate a lot of "production" or task orientation spend much of their time focusing on the measurement of goal attainment, giving directions and instructions, work planning, adherence to standards, and so forth. So, most of their conversations with subordinates focus on how the work is going. By contrast, leaders whose style is described as more "people" oriented are also concerned with task accomplishment, but spend more time on creating good human relations, with the assumption that good relations and interpersonal warmth will facilitate performance. Style research indicates that these two sets of behaviors or general leadership competencies are independent; thus, a leader could be high on one dimension and low on the other, low on both, or high on both.

Most 360-degree leadership surveys have at their core these two sets of dimensions. So, while this type of survey may purport to measure eight different competencies, most of those competencies will fall within either one or both of the two "buckets" of either task- or people-orientation. It is interesting to note that neither the original research nor the subsequent development of very sophisticated 360-degree survey data has ever focused significantly on a leader's entrepreneurial orientation or competencies.

Situational Leadership

Continuing research on leadership style evolved into the concept of situational leadership theory.[4] This approach encourages managers to develop a repertoire of both people and task competencies, so that they can be effective in various situations. Thus, some situations require different combinations and different frequencies in the use of these style components.

So, if a leader is working with a very capable group of people who know what to do and have the skills, motivation, and self-confidence to do it, then the leader should get out of their way and reduce the intensity and frequency of leadership interventions. If the group is low in job knowledge or competencies, less motivated and less confident, then the situational theory suggests that the leader focuses more on a task or production orientation.

The situational approach, and the behavioral research on which it is based, advises managers to "flex" with the situation. The leader adapts her style in accordance with the current leadership context in which she find herself. The focus on behavior and style flexibility is sometimes referred to as "transactional" leadership, because of the emphasis on daily interpersonal interactions or transactions that occur between leaders and their subordinates. This type of leadership advice sounds pretty good for day-to-day leadership interactions, but it may be just the wrong advice when a leader is asked to bring about significant organizational change or engage in serious entrepreneurial activity. That type of leadership is generally referred to as "transformational."

Transformational Leadership

Leaders charged with significant organizational change must take a somewhat different leadership stance. Instead of aspiring to change their style to fit the situation, they actually need to make the situation conform to their vision of the desired state. According to Warren Bennis,[5] a leadership expert, transformational leaders do three things very well. They "paint, communicate, and anchor" a vision for their organization. This is the type of leadership for which people like Jack Welch, Lou Gerstner, and others are praised.

These leaders bring about significant change in their organizations and do so by inspiring, motivating, and sometimes scaring employees into getting on board with the new direction. In sharp contrast to situational leadership theory, these people are often inflexible, single-minded, obstinate, and stubborn in their views of where the organization has to go. If their vision is wrong, or they are unable to get enough people to go along with it, they are often chucked out, and the search for another leader begins.

In most organizations, the kind of leadership on which a manager focuses is usually associated with their supervisory level. For example, at the first level of supervision, leaders are often more valued for their technical knowledge. Middle managers are often encouraged to be good transactional or situational leaders. Senior managers are often paid to bring about significant changes in the organization, to make it more competitive, efficient, and effective (Fig. 2.3).

Both leadership risks and rewards increase as managers move up the organizational hierarchy. Transformational leadership is inherently more risky, because the stakes are higher when significant organizational changes are undertaken. Figure 2.4 shows the differences between what we call transactional or situational leadership and transformational leadership.

Interestingly, entrepreneurial leadership can be practiced at all levels. It is not level-dependent—opportunities are opportunities. Some are realized by internal focus and some by external focus, but level is important only in terms of how much

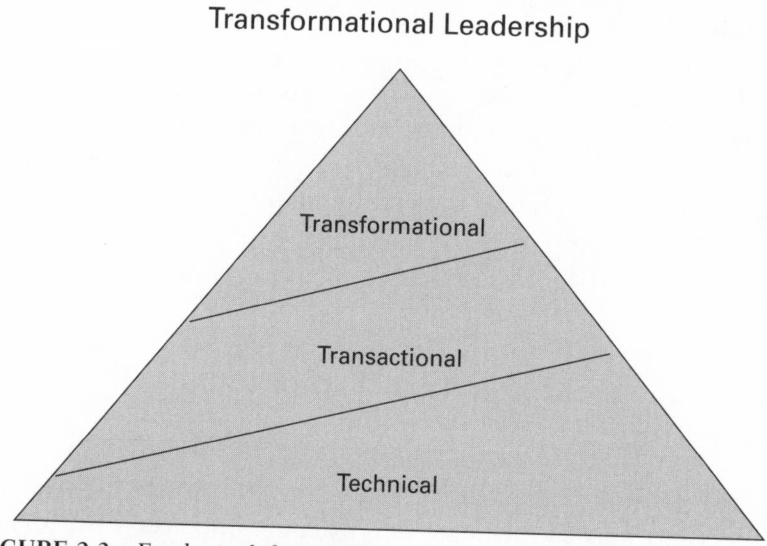

Transformational Leadership

FIGURE 2.3 Emphasis shifts to different leadership capabilities as individuals move up the organizational hierarchy.

Critical Differences

Transactional/Situational	Transformational
• Leader adapts to various situations	• Organization adapts
• Focus is on day-to-day activities	• Focus is on the organization, not the individual
• Development of task and people behaviors	• Consistency, not adaptability
• Situational analysis decides emphasis	• Symbolic influence
	• Strategic emphasis

FIGURE 2.4   Transactional/situational versus transformational leadership.

power a manager has within the organization. One of the best entrepreneurial pieces of advice that CEO Scott Cook of Intuit (the company that makes Quicken) ever got regarding one of its financial software packages came from a janitor at the company. All humans are inherently creative, and opportunities identification does not depend on where one sits in the organizational hierarchy.

In my seminars, I try to get managers to understand that leadership is a complex phenomenon. No one type of leadership exists, but rather, several types requiring different competencies, different philosophies, and different applications. Not all good transactional managers are good transformational leaders, and vice versa. In fact, in many respects, these two types of leadership have key opposing elements—especially around whether the leader adapts or the organization adapts.

Entrepreneurial and Transformational Leadership

Entrepreneurial leadership is more like transformational leadership than it is like transactional leadership, yet it differs in some fundamental ways. Much of the research and study of transformational leaders suggests that, after creating and communicating a vision, the really good leaders are able to make the vision a reality. "Anchoring" the vision means changing things within the organization so that the vision is implemented. Thus, great transformational leaders, such as Jack Welch, focus a great deal of their energy on aligning people behind the vision and then reorganizing, restructuring, outsourcing, hiring, and firing, so that the vision becomes a reality.

These leaders often develop far-reaching "culture change" programs and spend a great deal of time being the spokesperson, cheerleader, salesperson, and head motivator who gets people to line up behind the new direction. Most researchers and consultants estimate that it takes years, not months, to finally realize the cultural changes often necessary for effective organizational transformation. So, the transformational leader's focus is both long-term and internal. Rearranging attitudes and organizational components so that a real change is realized takes time, focus, energy, and persistence.

Many things can derail or undermine organizational change, so transformational leaders need the courage of their convictions and willingness to stay the course. They also require a critical mass of employees to buy into and help implement the details of change. Meetings, meetings, meetings, and intense internal debate often accompany significant organizational transformation. Thus, much of the transformational leader's time and energy is inherently internally focused.

Entrepreneurial leadership, on the other hand, is inherently opportunity-focused—and therefore external—even if it involves a rearrangement of internal assets. Entrepreneurial leadership is not about endless internal debates. It is not about marathon meetings or total organizational alignment. Rather, as can be seen in Figure 2.5, it is about sharp, externally or internally focused, action-oriented opportunity identification, development, and capture.

The fundamental difference between transformational leadership and entrepreneurial leadership is focus. But, other differences exist as well. Transformational leaders spend a lot of time trying to change people's attitudes, to get them convinced of the

Visionary Leadership

Transformational	Entrepreneurial
• Focus on the organization	• Focus on the opportunity
• Changing attitudes	• Finding like-minded people
• Focus on change	• Focus on building/creating
• Passion	• Passion
• A stake in the ground	• A moving stake
• Creative rearrangement	• Creative destruction/rearrangement
• Committed investment	• Staged investment
• Symbolic communications	• Intimate, personal communications
• Long-term, stay the course	• Medium-term, exit strategy

FIGURE 2.5   Similarities and differences between transformational and entrepreneurial leadership.

wisdom of a new direction—and they need to change a lot of people's minds. Entrepreneurial leaders do not have the time or the patience to change a lot of people's minds. Opportunities do not wait for years; opportunities have windows that open and close. Missing the window means lost opportunity. Instead, entrepreneurial leaders seek out and recruit like-minded individuals who share their understanding and passion for the opportunity and are interested in taking quick, decisive action. They use this core team of people to influence others in the organization to support their opportunity, but only those who are necessary. They do not try to convince everyone to support their ideas, but they do try to neutralize those who would derail the opportunity. Entrepreneurial leaders are not interested in convincing the whole organization, but only their close-knit, focused entrepreneurial team and key opportunity stakeholders.

While transformational leaders try to bring about a change in existing order, entrepreneurial leaders try to develop a new order. Entrepreneurial leaders create something that did not exist before, and new learning is always involved. Instead of changing things, they often have to destroy things in order to shepherd in the new. Transformational leaders often are happy with transforming, whereas entrepreneurial leaders often have to discard, destroy, rearrange, or reinvent structures, processes, and models to make way for their opportunity. The opportunity comes first. (Later in this book, you will see several examples of where creative destruction was necessary in the pursuit and capture of real value-creation activities.)

For transformational leaders, their vision is a stake in the ground around which they try to rally the organization. Jack Welch, for example, is renowned for saying that GE will be number one or two in all the markets that they serve, or they will get out of that business. This is clearly a measurable stake and one that can be used to hold both individuals and groups accountable. When Zaki Mustafa, head of Corning's Serengeti Eyewear Division,[6] said the company would change from a product- to a market-focused organization, he planted a stake in the ground. Transformational leaders make a commitment to their vision and typically stay the course until proven wrong or deselected. These commitments generally come from some well thought out and formulated strategy that requires long-range planning. They are not just whims or based on gut feelings. Once the company is committed to being number one, as in the case of GE, or becoming market-focused, like Corning's sunglass division, then quixotic changes or impulsive redirections of resources from the primary goal are not welcome, since they can derail the company from its new vision.

Entrepreneurial leadership, on the other hand, often involves a dynamic, rather than a static, stake. The development of new opportunities is a dynamic process. As any entrepreneur will tell you, an original idea is rarely the same as the finally realized opportunity. As the entrepreneur learns more about the potential customer, emerging technology, market dynamics, or what have you, this learning starts to change how the entrepreneurial leader sees the opportunity. True entrepreneurial opportunities require shaping and reshaping. Failures almost always happen along the way, and entrepreneurial leaders learn from these failures to further hone and refine their opportunity.

For entrepreneurial leaders, the stake is constantly moving, especially when they are charting waters that few others have navigated. A road map exists for cutting costs, reorganizing, and changing incentive schemes. But, no road map is available for believing that calling people dummies will make them buy hundreds of thousands of books. Nor is there a road map for believing that JetBlue could become a viable airline within its first year of ownership in one of the worst environments for airlines. Zoots, the dry cleaning franchise, had no chart to tell them that trying to create a national brand for dry cleaning would be a good idea.

Tremendous risk often exists in these types of entrepreneurial situations, because the need to change things midstream, based on new data, is a requisite for any entrepreneurial leader and his team. The stake moves, and the entrepreneurial leader must get his small band of like-minded team members to move with it.

Because transformational leaders tend to be in it for the longer term, they ask for the reassignment of capital and resources for the longer term. They tend to think in capital-budgeting terms. Moving resources to promote greater sales in Europe or Asia generally requires some longer-term planning and capital investment decisions. Thus, transformational leaders usually are actively involved and engaged in the capital-budgeting process. They ask for large sums of capital or the redirection of capital to bring about the desired organizational transformation. And, because in large companies budgeting cycles can be up to a year or longer, this necessitates some deep discussions and planning.

Entrepreneurial leaders have a "pay as you go" or "pay later" mentality. They do not think in capital-budgeting terms because they cannot do the kind of long-term planning often necessitated by major organizational change. They seek staged investment or self-funding strategies: "Pay a little, learn a lot."

In other words, entrepreneurial leaders understand the effects of cash flow and the ownership of assets on the creation of economic value. They understand the importance of proving their business idea and the use of gating (qualifying) procedures to force "go, no-go" decisions. And, they believe that you must leverage resources whenever possible. Once organizations have made a significant capital investment in projects, it is hard for them to pull the plug on these projects.

Entrepreneurial leaders, on the other hand, make smaller, staged bets, thus allowing them to disengage if they discover that their new business idea is not viable. They may ask for large investments, but only after they have proved that their new business idea is not just an idea but a real opportunity.

John Kilcullen of IDG Books was down to his last $200,000 before the Dummies concept hit him (more on this in Chapter 5). He credits much of his creativity to the pressure he felt as his staged investment money was running out. For IDG, the original $1.5 million investment was a drop in the bucket, but for Kilcullen it was enough to prove or disprove the viability of a potentially huge opportunity.

Entrepreneurial leaders and transformational leaders also tend to communicate somewhat differently. Transformational leaders need a big stage and often use symbolic communications to great benefit. Jack Welch supposedly promoted a middle manager by two levels, even though he lost a lot of money trying to grow a business, because Welch wanted to reinforce the value of risk taking. Clearly, this was a powerful symbolic message as well as a real one.

Good transformational leaders leverage symbolism because they know it travels well. Dramatic stories can spread through organizations like wildfire. A small biopharmaceutical company with whom I worked fired one of its senior executives who was extremely popular with his employees and many others within the organization. It did this because, despite his popularity, he was bad-mouthing the new strategy the organization was taking. The president of the company fired him as a way to communicate that the organization was taking a new direction and, regardless of popularity or past success, employees needed to decide to either get on the train or jump off. This firing created quite a stir around the company and made it crystal clear that people had to commit to the new direction or face the consequences.

Entrepreneurial leaders prefer to discuss their opportunities in one-on-one or small-group settings. They build alliances one ally or stakeholder at a time. They not only use these smaller settings to showcase their ideas, they tend to welcome criticism if it is well thought out, because it helps them avoid mistakes and therefore manage risks. In contrast, at the pharmaceutical company, criticism was clearly not welcome: Once the captain had charted the course, he countenanced no mutinous sailors.

Entrepreneurial leaders also plan exit strategies. When a venture or an opportunity has peaked in value or is not working, they want to get out—either to cash in on the value or to stop the bleeding.

Similar, Yet Different

But entrepreneurial leaders and transformational leaders are also alike in several significant ways. First, they are passionate. The transformational leader is passionate about the changes he thinks the organization must make in order to survive and thrive, and he is willing to go down with the ship if wrong. Entrepreneurial leaders are equally passionate, but they are passionate about their opportunities. The passion generally comes from giving birth to the baby. It is their idea, or they stimulated its birth. It is their ego, and thus they feel personally and emotionally committed to nurturing, protecting, and buffing their baby. They are known for vociferously defending their baby as well. Transformational leaders can be equally passionate because it is usually their head on the block. Entrepreneurial leaders are passionate because the idea or opportunity usually sprang from their head.

Second, they both must be visionaries: The transformer about the new direction of his organization, the entrepreneur about his opportunity. They both must paint, communicate, and anchor their visions. The transformer has to anchor by managing a broad array of organizational levers, like strategy, structure, processes, assets, HR policies, and the like, while the entrepreneur must anchor opportunity by recruiting like-minded team members, staging investment, managing risk profiles, getting and leveraging limited assets and resources, focusing on the check writers, and defending against the corporate antibodies that try to destroy his new ideas.

Third, they both tend to be somewhat stubborn and single-minded. Once the entrepreneurial leader has enough information and experience to believe that her idea is not just an idea but a real opportunity, she becomes obsessed with seeing it through and only listens to counteradvice if it is extremely well-grounded and she hears it from multiple sources. Even then, she might ignore the advice based on her intuition. Intuition plays a very important role for both entrepreneurial leaders and for transformational leaders, although it is more prevalent in entrepreneurial leaders. Intuition, of course, comes from gut feelings and either years of experience or rock-solid knowledge building. It also comes from developing confidence over time, in the veracity of hunches. Transformational leaders often have a gut feeling about those things that their organizations have to do to get on a better track, but they also rely heavily on tried-and-tested management techniques, like competitor analysis and strategic planning. They are also expected to do the proper analysis before they commit their organization to a significant new direction.

Entrepreneurial leaders have more freedom in this area. They often put a lot of faith in their hunches, and they only need a couple of potential customers to reinforce their hunches before they start moving. They will figure out the details later. Often, they are successful because their intuition is "counterintuitive."

I mentioned John Kilcullen earlier, the creative genius behind the founding of the Dummies books at IDG. He had an intuition that a need existed to simplify or "dumb down" a lot of information so that the man on the street could get a handle on complex topics. *DOS for Dummies*[7] and *Investing for Dummies*[8] are two examples. When he first had his Dummies inspiration, most respected and experienced publishers and editors within IDG thought he was crazy to call his potential customers dummies, and they were appalled at the idea. Some even tried to torpedo his venture. But his intuition or instincts were right. He also believed that a book could be branded by titles, not just by authors. This was another counterintuitive intuition that led to the successful Dummies brand. And, who would think that people would actually walk out of a bookstore carrying a large, bright yellow book titled *Sex for Dummies*[9]—thus, publicly admitting that they need some help in the sexual skills area? Yet, they do, in record numbers, even in France.

A Little Difference Can Make a Big Difference

In the next chapter, I will go into much more detail regarding the skills, attitudes, capabilities, and, yes, even traits, that show up in the entrepreneurial side of those entrepreneurial leaders with whom we have worked and studied. But, it is interesting to note that perhaps even a little bit of entrepreneurial orientation on the leader's part can reap large benefits.

I recently came across a fascinating, mostly unnoticed study in the *Journal of Business Venturing*[10] that demonstrates how a few more-entrepreneurial leadership behaviors can make a real difference. The authors describe how a large southeastern U.S. utility organization, upon becoming privatized, attempted to infuse entrepreneurial leadership behaviors into its managers. As we all know, government utilities are poster children for inefficient bureaucracies. Their typical motto is, "If we need more money, we'll raise the rates." With privatization, of course, this attitude is severely challenged. In this little study, managers were given a course in how to foster and nurture a more creative climate for their direct reports, in which their subordinates would be challenged to think of new and different ways of doing things. They were taught to push their subordinates to gain new skills and knowledge and to try to circumvent bureaucratic red tape. Figure 2.6 shows the 11 entrepreneurial leadership behaviors, defined by the company, that the managers were asked to practice to create a more innovative and entrepreneurial culture within their own departments.

However, the most fascinating aspects of the study were its results. The authors followed up with the managers to see if they were practicing these behaviors, using a 360-degree management survey that included those 11 specific behaviors along with numerous other generic leadership survey items. They found the managers who consistently practiced these behaviors

Corporate Entrepreneurship Behaviors

- Efficiently gets proposed actions through bureaucratic red tape and into practice
- Displays an enthusiasm for acquiring skills
- Quickly changes course of action when results aren't being achieved
- Encourages others to take the initiative for their own ideas
- Inspires others to think about their work in new and stimulating ways

- Devotes time to helping others find ways to improve products and services
- Goes to bat for the good ideas of others
- Boldly moves ahead with a promising new approach when others might be more cautious
- Vividly describes how things could be in the future and what is needed to get there
- Gets people to rally together to meet a challenge
- Creates an environment where people get excited about making improvements

FIGURE 2.6   Entrepreneurial leadership qualities identified in utilities study.

had significantly higher results in terms of employee satisfaction, customer satisfaction, and financial district margin contributions than their peers who did not practice these behaviors. While these utility company managers were not themselves acting as entrepreneurs, they were creating a more entrepreneurial culture that encouraged innovation from their direct reports.

This little study provides a tantalizing look at the possibilities of training managers to be entrepreneurial leaders. While the behaviors in this study focused more on climate building than on direct value-creating actions, the results are nonetheless intriguing. And, these behaviors are typical of a type of entrepreneurial leader I call an Accelerator, because they accelerate the pace of innovation in their part of the organization. You will meet an Accelerator later, in Chapter 7.

In the next chapter, we will explore in greater depth what we call the entrepreneurial mindset and skill set. The good news is that, despite conventional wisdom, entrepreneurship can be learned. You will discover what it means to truly don the "entrepreneurial hat" in your role as leader and manager.

Summary

Leadership is a complex subject. Everyone has an opinion, and new theories (including mine) pop up on bookshelves every day. But, one truth is undeniable, and that is that leadership effort must ultimately be focused on value-creating activities if an organization is to survive and thrive. In my travels, I am very concerned that company managers and employees are becoming more and more disconnected from this fact. When we are treated badly by a customer service person or an organizational employee, this treatment has negative ramifications, because we won't spend our money there again. And, if the customer representative's bad behavior is supported, perhaps even encouraged, by the organization, then we have a severe disconnect between what people are doing and the fundamental value-creating mission of the organization.

But, when a leader acts in more entrepreneurial ways, no confusion arises about the company's mission or the leader's purpose. All the other stuff is secondary. We have spent far too much time training leaders to be inwardly introspective and organizationally focused. Managers in large companies must be as concerned about leading value creation as they are about self-awareness, presentation skills, coaching, and running effective meetings. And, in today's volatile environment, maybe even more so.

Chapter Three

Breaking the Entrepreneur's Code

So far, we have talked a lot about the leadership side of the entrepreneurship-leadership equation. Now, we need to look in more depth at the entrepreneurial side. Leadership requires passion, vision, focus, and the ability to inspire others. Entrepreneurial leadership requires all these, plus a mindset and skill set that helps entrepreneurial leaders identify, develop, and capture new business opportunities. The leadership part comes in showing vision and passion for the opportunity, focusing people on the opportunity, and then inspiring them to go after it. But, the key for entrepreneurial leaders is the opportunity bit. Their focus is not general. Instead it is laser-like, pinpointed on an opportunity, usually one that has emanated from their own gray matter and from their hearts. What differentiates entrepreneurial leaders from their brethren is this passion—some would say obsession—to go after new, innovative, out-of-the-box, different, unusual, against-the-grain, often counterintuitive new business opportunities. They take the pursuit of these opportunities personally, due to their emotional stake in them, and they hold themselves both responsible for the opportunity's success and accountable for its failure. They are willing to take the heat, and sometimes bet their jobs on their ideas. They also have the discipline to differentiate good ideas from good opportunities.

Some entrepreneurial leaders seem to come with the entrepreneurial mindset already hardwired. Others don't. The good news is that managers who are not already so wired can develop the wiring. Some leaders already have the desire or mindset, but not the skill set. Here again, the entrepreneurial skill set can be developed. Later, we will talk about how this can be done in a planned and systematic way.

Let's look now in more depth at the concept of entrepreneurship, the other half of the entrepreneurial leadership equation. Entrepreneurial leaders seem to have an inherently entrepreneurial bent, whether latent or expressed. So, as with the discussion of leadership, it makes some sense to take a little tour of what we know about this entrepreneurial bent. In some respects, entrepreneurial leaders have the entrepreneur's lineage, but not in all aspects. While most of us think that we know what it means to be entrepreneurial, it has been my experience that some significant misconceptions exist concerning this concept. For example, few people know that 80 percent of new business start-ups fail or that successful entrepreneurs are not great risk takers. Instead, they are excellent risk managers.[1] They are also not lone rangers, at least not the successful and serial ones.

Understanding the Territory

As I have stated, one of the big challenges in working with large companies seeking greater entrepreneurial orientation was getting an answer to the question "Why do you want this?" The second challenge was answering the question "What is the *this*?" Trying to agree on the answer to this question has not only been a great learning experience, it has provided a few laughs, albeit ones of frustration, along the way.

As an example of why this is so important, Colonia Insurance, a German subsidiary of AXA Insurance, was working closely with me and a colleague from McKinsey & Company, trying to change its culture to become more entrepreneurial. Colonia asked us to help create a program on corporate entrepreneurship for it through which traditional insurance managers could learn to lead in more entrepreneurial ways and uncover new business opportunities. The program was entitled the Unternehmer Program. *Unternehmer* is German for *undertaker*. Think about the potential confusion around this title, let alone the meaning of *entrepreneurial*. *Undertaker* can mean "under the ground taker (mortician)," "shopkeeper," or "one who undertakes a task." In working on this program, I interviewed a number of Colonia managers to better understand the company and their understanding of what we were trying to do. One of my most difficult interviews was with a middle manager, who insisted that corporate entrepreneurship was about cost cutting.

I don't think I ever convinced him that entrepreneurial leadership was not about cost cutting (except under some very special circumstances, which we will cover later). He was not alone in his view. I also spent a year with a large European company that had its primary roots in the hospitality industry. This company was very successful, but the executive team believed they needed an infusion of entrepreneurial thinking. While they understood start-up entrepreneurship, it was not clear to them what entrepreneurship meant when practiced by managers inside an already established business. We literally spent a year trying to define the concept for them before they would commit to partnering with us on an educational intervention.

So, some confusion still exists around the general notion of entrepreneurship, let alone entrepreneurial leadership. We have learned a very important lesson over the years: If you ask a manager to think and act like an entrepreneurial leader, then you better be very careful about what you mean by *entrepreneurial*. One of my colleagues is fond of saying, "Be careful what you wish for—you might just get it." This is also true of entrepreneurial leadership. Later, you will see that some companies are not very well prepared to deal with those of their wishes that come true.

The Focus on Opportunity

One thing is certain: Whether you are talking about start-up entrepreneurs or entrepreneurial leaders in a large corporation, their focus, passion, and expertise is in the identification, development, and capture of significant new business opportunities. The word *significant* is key. It is not business as usual; it is business as *unusual*. And these opportunities, when captured, represent a significant increase in economic value either for the start-up entrepreneur and his investors or for the already established enterprise and its shareholders and employees—and ultimately society.

Creativity is a human condition. We demonstrate it when we are children. Depending on what paths we take in life and where we work, we may use more or less of it, but we always retain the capacity for creative thinking. Most managers with whom I work come up with great ideas to improve their business and, with the right stimulation, most of these people can come up with really creative or innovative new business ideas. The problem is that very few of these ideas represent opportunities. Ideas are literally a dime a dozen (probably a dollar now, due to inflation), but a great idea is not necessarily a great opportunity.

Entrepreneurial leaders do several things really well. First, they identify new business opportunities that have significant potential for the larger enterprise. These opportunities generally fit with current organizational strategy and goals, but simultaneously lead the organization down new paths or into new high-potential areas that challenge the status quo. They get their ideas and inspiration from many different sources. Sometimes, they copy what someone else is already doing, but do it so much better that they build a significant new business. Michael Dell took lessons from IBM. Toyota borrowed from W. Edwards Deming. Seiko took cues from the Swiss watch industry. Bill Gates walked by all the unpatented goodies that Xerox left on open display in its Palo Alto lab, and he was inspired to build a company using much of this unprotected property. The products were not necessarily new, but someone thought about how to do it better, quicker, cheaper, or just differently. These people did not think up the idea, they just improved on it. They were innovators, not creators. They were copycats, with a twist. Their real creativity came from their ability to structure their businesses effectively and to give the customer a new value proposition. So, wearing an entrepreneurial hat does not necessarily mean coming up with a brand-new product or service; it can involve creative distribution and delivery, an innovative business model, or merely improving on the better mousetrap someone else actually built first.

Good ideas also come from good solid strategy formulation and market analysis. Good strategic planning with a dose of intuition often can lead an organization down a high-potential new avenue for growth, if the planning process is dynamic and interactive. All too often, however, traditional approaches to strategic planning lead only to minor iterations of what a company is already doing, not to breakthrough thinking.

Great Idea or Great Opportunity?

Ideas come to all of us, but not all good ideas are good opportunities. Entrepreneurial leaders work with their ideas to determine if they are actually good opportunities—opportunity identification is not the same as idea identification. An entrepreneur determines whether her idea is an opportunity through bootstrap market research, interviewing potential customers, or going to work for someone who has relevance to her idea. She gets enough experience and intimacy with her idea to determine whether it is just an idea or truly an opportunity.

In addition, a good idea needs some strong potential financial legs to be considered an opportunity. Steve Spinelli,[2] a colleague, suggests that an idea has to pass the "3 M Opportunity Test." As seen in Figure 3.1, the three Ms are Market demand, Market size and structure, and Margin analysis.

Steve's requirements mirror what most venture capitalists would expect from a start-up venture. Keep in mind that corporations seeking new business ventures may bend some of these requirements because it makes sense to do so—perhaps as a defensive move, to develop some new technologies, or for other important reasons. But the market—its size and structure and the potential margins—must be analyzed and show enough potential to justify the increased risk associated with

Market Demand—An opportunity must have the potential to:
- Provide the company with a market share of at least 20%
- Allow for 20% growth per year for the new venture
- Be durable: lasting for more than 3 years

Market Size and Structure—The market for the new venture needs to have the following characteristics for the venture to be a viable opportunity:
- Fragmented or emerging, since mature markets tend to have more limited opportunity sets
- Total market worth of $50 million with a $1 billion potential
- Not have proprietary barriers to entry

Margin Analysis—
- 40% margins if the new business is striving to be the low-cost provider
- Break-even within 1–2 years
- The company can work with less capital requirements than the competition
- Will result in an overall increase in the company's P/E ratio

FIGURE 3.1   The three Ms of opportunity.

going where the company has not gone before. Venture capitalists must be assured that their money is working well for them, as do shareholders in large companies.

Creating Luck

Luck rarely has anything to do with the identification of good business opportunities. I like to say that luck happens when experience and opportunity collide in the presence of an open mind. Good opportunities rarely happen by accident. Luck may play some part in whether the opportunity is actually captured, but not in its identification. So, entrepreneurs play with an idea—they research it, modify it, and craft it until they are satisfied that it is real.

The second thing entrepreneurs do well is shape the opportunity—crafting it until it can become a commercial reality. They use a variety of tools to do this, including market research, financial analysis, customer investment, and pilot testing. The original idea is rarely the final opportunity. All this shaping changes the entrepreneur's original view, as do other people's comments and criticisms. Shaping is much like taking a raw piece of metal or a clump of wet clay and molding it. We often see in entrepreneurs some similarities to artists. A potter may start with an idea of a vase, but turn it into something quite different by kiln time. As the opportunity progresses, an entrepreneur may change his mind about what he originally wanted. The experience of molding is a stimulus to further learning and creativity.

Another thing that entrepreneurs do is capture the opportunity. They actually marshal the internal (sometimes external) resources and people necessary to make the opportunity a reality. Capturing happens in many ways, but it is always enabled by the passion and persistence of the individual and his ability to impassion and inspire others, especially upper management. This passion probably gives entrepreneurial leaders the toughness to take multiple bureaucratic bashings.

Entrepreneurs also do something else very well: They try to create and maintain a balance or harmony among sometimes competing opportunity mechanisms. One of my colleagues, Jeff Timmons,[3] created a model, shown in Figure 3.2, that he believes represents a very important balancing act that most start-up entrepreneurs manage well.

As you can see from the model, entrepreneurs must be good at this balancing act to bring their opportunity to fruition. The reality only comes about when the opportunity, the resources, and the team are balanced and interacting. A team and an idea that have few or no resources leads to nothing. By the same token, great resources and a good opportunity will go nowhere with a poor team. The entrepreneur must actively juggle all three of these balls simultaneously. The real trouble happens when they start to get out of sync. A successful entrepreneur must act quickly and decisively when this starts to happen. For example, sometimes a start-up entrepreneur will involve family members as both investors and employees at the same time. Many an entrepreneur has discovered that a blood relative cannot hack it, and he must cut the cord quickly. As you might imagine, this is a very painful thing to do, with potential long-term and dramatic repercussions. But a start-up entrepreneur who doesn't act quickly and decisively may no longer have an opportunity. Perhaps the

The Entrepreneurial Process

The Balancing Act

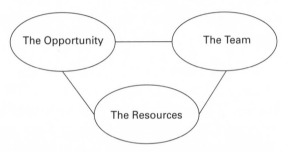

FIGURE 3.2   Timmons' model of the entrepreneurial balancing act.

biggest advantage to having a venture capital partner is that you can blame them for the family member's departure. Clearly, venture capitalists and investors cannot afford to have the success of a great opportunity and their resources resting in the hands of a poor team.

Entrepreneurial Leadership Requires an Even Greater Balancing Act

Entrepreneurial leaders in large companies actually have a more difficult balancing act than those of start-up entrepreneurs, since they often don't have direct control over the elements described in the Timmons model. Start-up entrepreneurs are able to work with a blank slate. They can pursue any idea or opportunity they want—logical, crazy, and even outlandish. No one can say, "No, don't go after that." They have absolute freedom to hit anyone and everyone up for money and resources. And, they can try to recruit anyone they desire to be a team member. Whether they succeed depends on how well they can convince various constituencies of the viability of their opportunity. If one bank turns them down, they can go to another, and another, until they go broke, burn out, or win.

Entrepreneurial leaders in established companies must work within many more boundaries, but they often have access to many more resources as well. Entrepreneurial leaders look for opportunities that leverage the organization's capabilities and are relevant to the company's strategic aims, while at the same time pushing the organization into new and sometimes counterintuitive areas. While we have seen some examples of really far-out stuff that does not follow this general paradigm, that is rare. PepsiCo would probably not encourage airplane building any more than Boeing would try to find opportunities in the soft-drinks market. Why? Because they have little experience, skills, or passion for this very different kind of business. And, they would probably encounter some pretty "bad luck."

The Entrepreneurial Leader's "Turf"

Over the last few years of trying to educate managers to lead like entrepreneurs and companies to be more entrepreneurial, I have evolved a model that differs from the Timmons model; it shows the somewhat trickier *environment* that entrepreneurial leaders in large companies must master to be successful. Figure 3.3 shows this model, alongside the Timmons model.

This model differs from the Timmons model in several very significant ways. First, note the different shapes in each of the models. In the Timmons model, circles and ovals are used, while in my model, I prefer triangles. Triangles are more rigid, more stable, more sturdy, and certainly harder to modify. Timmons' ovals are soft, more fluid. The start-up entrepreneur has a huge effect on these elements, and they are constantly changing as the business grows and changes. Large organizations are rarely so fluid. In fact, companies have worked hard to make sure that things are organized and that systems, strategy, and such fit. They are not so easily changed.

In the Timmons model, the start-up entrepreneur has much say over the opportunity and team and can go to many places

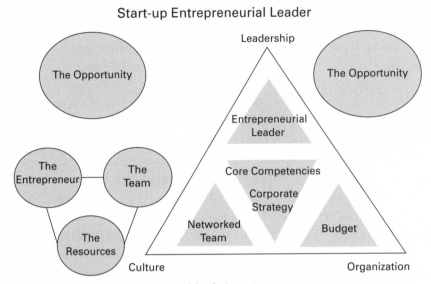

FIGURE 3.3   The entrepreneurial leader's environment.

and many people for resources. The start-up entrepreneur can go after anything he wants, can pick whomever he likes to be on a team, and is the ultimate decision maker and resource allocater.

Entrepreneurial leaders live in a similar but different world; another paradigm. The entrepreneurial leader, usually a line manager, has much less say. She is stuck with a budget and the command structure that is in place, has usually inherited a team, and her ideas can't get too far away from the company's corporate strategy and core competencies if she is to succeed. And, while resources may be vast, the entrepreneurial manager is in constant competition with others to get them. As Figure 3.3 shows, the entrepreneurial leader is already encapsulated by a corporate culture (usually quite strong in a large company), senior executives with an in-place value system, and an organization structure that already has a lot of information telling people how to behave.

In many ways, being an entrepreneurial leader is a lot trickier, albeit less risky, than being a start-up entrepreneur. Political savvy, corporate radar (the ability to see approaching enemies), influencing abilities, and good general management skills are far more important to entrepreneurial leaders in large companies than they are to start-up entrepreneurs. But large companies also have a significant array of resources and talent—if only the corporate entrepreneur can get access to them.

The risk–reward equation also can be quite different for the entrepreneurial leader. Start-up entrepreneurs have unlimited up- and downsides. They can lose everything or make a boatload of money. Most entrepreneurial leaders have a cushion on the downside (they can go back to their old job) and a ceiling on the upside (senior managers hate to see a middle-manager entrepreneur making more money than they do).

Obviously, start-up entrepreneurs and entrepreneurial leaders are different. But they also have a lot in common. For example, the entrepreneurial process of identifying, shaping, and capturing opportunities is the same, and they still have to balance resources, the opportunity, and the team. Later, you will see that entrepreneurial leaders also can focus their entrepreneurial leadership energy inwardly on creative asset management or innovative value chain reconfiguration to give their organizations a real shot in the economic arm. This still involves value creation, but the focus starts at a different place.

Entrepreneurial leaders effectively navigate the waters of the company's current culture, leadership, and organizational processes while simultaneously trying to identify, shape, and capture new opportunities that may strain the way the organization is currently led and managed. If the entrepreneurial leader pushes the status quo too far, he is likely to be perceived as off the wall. If the entrepreneurial leader does not push the organization enough to allow a high-potential opportunity to be captured, then he has failed, and the organization may have lost a huge chance to create economic value.

Effective entrepreneurial leaders appear to have an exceptional ability to push for necessary change while still being perceived as one of the team. They also do their homework meticulously, so that they are hard to dismiss as crackpots, misfits, or just dime-a-dozen idea generators. They know their own company, its strategies, and the values of senior management, and they are able to position their new business opportunities in ways that challenge the organization, yet create the promise of immense top-line success.

Notice too, in the entrepreneurial leader model in Figure 3.3, that the triangles seem to fit quite nicely together. While Timmons talks about *balance* for the start-up entrepreneur, I prefer to use the term *rotation*. If any of the internal triangles is rotated too quickly or at too much of an angle, it can become orthogonal (at a right angle) to an adjacent triangle. If that happens, the organization's internal defenses kick in and mount a serious and often overwhelming attack. Successful entrepreneurial leaders are able to manage the rotation of these elements by reshaping or reframing their opportunities, so that they are or appear to be more in line with organization-al goals and strategies.

The Entrepreneurial Mindset

The entrepreneurial half of the entrepreneurial leadership equation requires the wearing of an entrepreneurial hat on a day-to-day basis. Some people refer to this focus as a "mindset" or "philosophy," or perhaps a lens through which the leader tends to consistently view his corporate world. It is more fruit-ful to view this as a mindset than as an inherent or inborn char-acteristic, since people can learn to wear this hat.

Simply defined, this mindset is a way of thinking and act-ing that is entrepreneurial in nature and manifests itself in a number of outwardly observable behaviors. Unlike a trait, a mindset can be learned (modeled) by most people if they have the desire to do so—and *desire* is the key word. What separates most organizational managers from entrepreneurial leaders is desire. Some people have this desire naturally, but we have seen others, employed in large corporations, get it through a combination of education, personal development, and well-designed compensation and motivational strategies.

The entrepreneurial mindset involves the following 10 qualities. Some of these were discussed by Jeff Timmons in his earlier work on the entrepreneurial mindset, but I have added some and removed others based on my own observations of large-company entrepreneurial leaders in the field.

· Internal locus of control
· Tolerance for ambiguity
· Willingness to hire people smarter than oneself
· A consistent drive to create, build, or change things
· Passion for an opportunity
· A sense of urgency
· Perseverance
· Resilience
· Optimism
· Sense of humor about oneself

Let's look at each of these in more depth and see how these characteristics interact.

Internal Locus of Control

"Internal locus of control" is a fancy term often used by psychologists to describe a person's attitude towards his external environment. Many individuals, and even whole societies, have a view that they are often controlled by the external world, that fate is in charge, that what happens to them is largely in the hands of God, Allah, their boss, or the company. They see themselves as largely controlled, not controlling. This is called an external locus, or center, of control.

With an attitude of "go with the flow," it's in the hands of a higher power, don't swim against the tide may be very helpful for personal serenity, it is not the stuff of which entrepreneurial leaders are made. Most successful entrepreneurial leaders have a strong internal locus of control. They see themselves, rightly or wrongly, as determining much of their own fate. You could call this an egotistical view, but it leads them to believe that they have the power to make things happen, that they are more in control than controlled. This internal locus of control leads them to believe that they can make things happen, that they can overcome obstacles and convince or neutralize naysayers. An internal locus of control is not the same thing as personal confidence. Many start-up entrepreneurs lay awake at night wondering if they have the capabilities to really pull off their creations, but deep down inside, they have a strong belief that with energy, drive, and commitment, they can stack the odds in their favor. This mindset is extremely functional for entrepreneurial leaders in large organizations, since it causes them to believe that they can outwit, outsmart, outmaneuver, and outrun their own organization's bureaucracy.

Tolerance for Ambiguity

Another common characteristic of many entrepreneurial leaders is their tolerance for ambiguity. Opportunity identification, development, and capturing a significant new business opportunity is a messy affair. Zoots: The Cleaner Cleaner is an excellent example of the ambiguity and sometime-chaos that start-up entrepreneurs must not only tolerate, but be comfortable with. Zoots, started by Todd Krasnow, a former executive with Staples, was a new concept in the dry cleaning business. His vision, along with partner Tom Stemberg (founder of Staples), was to consolidate the mom-and-pop dry cleaning industry under a national brand called Zoots. Zoots would offer state-of-the-art logistics, excellent customer service, and 24-hour access, and they would brand themselves by driving around in a fleet of loud purple vans.

Krasnow had never been in this business, but he and his team studied the industry in depth, to the point of Krasnow practically living with an independent local dry cleaner to learn the business. They thought they were superbly prepared for the opening of Zoots' doors in 2000 but, shortly after the doors opened, the roof caved in. They had badly underestimated the complexity and difficulty of managing the operations side of the business. Garments were lost, routing slips misplaced, and special orders were mishandled. They were forced to go through several operations managers before they were finally able to get control of the logistics of the new venture. Krasnow doesn't know if they will ever have complete control, with zero errors, but this is what he and his team are striving for.

Some people would have been unable to cope with this kind of chaos and uncertainty. Todd and his team looked at these problems as opportunities to learn more about the business. They felt that if, over time, they could learn from their mistakes and remain calm, they would ultimately win the operations battle. But, they had many months of living in an uncertain and ambiguous environment before some semblance of certainty emerged.

The old saying "If you can't handle the heat, stay out of the kitchen" is aptly restated for entrepreneurial leaders. For the right person, this is the fun, it's the adrenaline rush that causes the entrepreneurial leader to seek out new opportunities time after time. If you can't handle the uncertainty and ambiguity of starting a new venture, work for the Registry of Motor Vehicles, where there is no ambiguity.

Willingness to Hire People Smarter Than Oneself

Every spring, our college holds a Founder's Day celebration to honor the inception of the school. As part of the tradition, we invite famous entrepreneurs to spend a day with us sharing their success stories and hard-earned lessons. It is the highlight of the year and very well attended by college residents, outsiders, and the press. We have honored such famous entrepreneurs as Barry Gordy (Motown Records), Richard Branson (Virgin Airlines), Ray Kroc (McDonald's), Arthur Blank (Home Depot), and myriad other name brand "entre-lebrities" (celebrity entrepreneurs).

Our students are always looking for the secrets to these famous people's success. All these celebrity entrepreneurs have taken different routes to success, and they each operate in different businesses in different industries, so it is hard for students to find that one resonant and consistent kernel of wisdom. But, one kernel has come out very consistently and predictably over the years: It is the willingness of successful entrepreneurs to hire people smarter than themselves. By smarter, I don't necessarily mean people with higher IQs, but rather that this trait encompasses an ability to recognize personal limitations and a willingness to bring in people who are much more knowledgeable about different aspects of the business.

While this sounds like common sense, many people in existing organizations are frightened or intimidated by having people working for them who know more than they do. Our Founder's Day entrepreneurs say that they recognize that the business would never grow beyond their own capabilities if they did not "hire higher." I know many managers in large corporations who are scared to death to do this because they are afraid that their subordinates will outshine them. Not so with entrepreneurial leaders. In fact, they often look for rebels to hire. Rebels—not complainers. Real rebels disagree, but they come up with a better idea and have the passion and guts to defend their point of view.

Two examples make clear why this entrepreneurial mindset is so important. Ray Kroc told our students that his first model for McDonald's was to have only company-owned stores. In this way, he felt that he could control the image, quality, and operations of each store. But this approach tied up a lot of cash in real estate, and he wasn't really making that much money. He said that McDonald's never really took off until he hired a CFO who was an expert in franchising. The CFO convinced Ray to have both company-owned stores and a large franchise organization. It was only then that McDonald's really caught fire. Had Kroc not been willing to hire someone smarter than himself, McDonald's would probably not be the icon that it is today.

Not long ago, I had the chance to do some educational programs for a small software company specializing in outbound-calling telemarketing software. The founder of the company had grown it to about $250 million in revenues, and he wanted to double the size of the company in 3 years. Unfortunately, he was a somewhat paranoid, control-oriented individual, who had gone through three CEOs and two senior management teams in less that 2 years. He knew he needed help, and he had succeeded in attracting and hiring seasoned executives, but he was afraid to let them manage the business. He was continually going around these people to check their decisions, and he would often countermand them. He refused to follow good advice, and he eventually caused his company's own stock to plummet from double digits to $4 per share. Eventually, the board of directors had to wrest control of the company from its own founder because of his inability to hire and use people smarter than himself.

A Consistent Drive to Create, Build, or Change Things

Entrepreneurial leaders also share another common mindset: their desire to create, build, or change something. Notice that "love of money" is not one of the aspects of an entrepreneurial mindset. One myth about entrepreneurs is that they are in it for the money. Money is important, but the real drive is the creation of something that is a reflection of the individual and his or her potential legacy. If it works well, the money follows. Many of my students challenge me about the "not in it for the money" aspect, so I give them two things to think about. First, if money is the primary motivation, why do so many entrepreneurially minded folks who are wealthy beyond imagination still start new businesses? Why don't they just retire and enjoy their riches? The answer is because it isn't the money, it's the creating or changing. The second thing I tell my doubting students is to go home, sit in a chair, and spend 2 hours trying to think up ways to make tons of money. They come back and tell me they now get the point. They found those 2 hours very frustrating. It doesn't work. The business idea comes first, not the idea of money.

You'll notice that I also said, "*change* things." Many entrepreneurial leaders succeed not by building or creating things from scratch but from changing things. They see opportunities to make existing products, services, or companies better. They can be more innovators than creators, but they are not satisfied with the status quo. John Kilcullen, the founder of the Dummies educational series, was always somewhat of a rebel (albeit a respectful one) with his bosses, because he could see better ways of doing things. It wasn't until he worked with IDG Corporation and its entrepreneur founder Pat McGovern that he found a truly willing ear for his rebellious nature.

Passion for an Opportunity

Perhaps the most enigmatic characteristic of the entrepreneurial mindset may not be a characteristic or mindset at all, but an "emotional" set. Entrepreneurial leaders have a strong passion for their idea or opportunity. In short, they love their baby, and no one better call their baby ugly. Because their baby is a reflection of themselves, their wants and their desires, a personal attachment exists. In large corporations, it is quite usual to find unimpassioned managers who often shepherd the desires and wishes of others. In fact, business schools often teach MBAs to view their work in an analytical, detached, aloof, and objective way. This is the antithesis of an entrepreneurial mindset.

Leading like an entrepreneur clearly requires some objectivity about the opportunity as well, but never total objectivity. Entrepreneurial leaders are no more objective than parents are about their children. You can never be totally objective about your own creations. Thus, leading like an entrepreneur requires the proactive seeking of advice from objective parties like colleagues, consultants, customers, subordinates, and bosses—to keep the entrepreneurial leader from loving her baby to death.

One of the more interesting debates in my area of study is whether passion can be developed in managers who are asked to play the role of entrepreneurial leader. Some companies, like Intel, will ask a manager to consciously adopt this role for a year or two. In this role, they are asked to adopt an already existing idea and develop into it into a highly successful commercial venture. But, can corporate entrepreneurs also adopt the passion that the originator of the idea had? The development of this passion is one of the biggest challenges that large companies face in trying to rekindle their entrepreneurial spirit. Later in the book, I will give you some examples of how companies have either selected for passion or have induced it through reward systems.

A Sense of Urgency

A sense of urgency, sometimes described as impatience, also accompanies the entrepreneurial mindset. Entrepreneurial leaders are described as wanting to get on with it. They push to meet or beat deadlines. This sense of urgency is driven by both the desire to see their idea come to fruition and a fear that, if they don't act first, they miss their window of opportunity—a competitor or rival might get there first and end their dream. This sense of urgency is generally not as evident among traditional large-company managers. However, an urgency often arises in "covering your ass" in some of these companies, where one's tail gets shot off if it is stuck out too far.

This is not to say that all corporate managers lack urgency, but in those who do have it, it is often outwardly motivated. The boss will get on their case if they miss a deadline, the appraisal might be affected, or they could suffer some other short-term consequences, but they don't usually own the urgency—it is delegated.

The entrepreneurial leader's sense of urgency is born from an inward drive. Their deadlines are self-imposed: the cash might run out, a customer might be lost, someone has to constantly mind the store. They are always vigilant and on top of their progress, because they have a very personal stake in it. This type of urgency, I believe, also can be developed in corporate mangers. But like passion, it has to be either selected for or influenced through specific reinforcement strategies, such as equity sharing.

Perseverance

In many respects, perseverance is a by-product of some of the other mindset characteristics. If you love your idea, then it is likely that you will have the drive to see it through. If you have a sense of urgency, and fear the consequences of not getting there first, then you will be spurred to stay the course. Perseverance is also a by-product of having an internal locus of control. Because successful entrepreneurial leaders believe they can make it happen, they believe that all they have to do is stick to it long enough and they will realize their dream. This perseverance is not generalized, but rather opportunity-specific. They may not persevere in all aspects of their life, but they certainly do so with ideas about which they feel passionate.

Many entrepreneurial leaders with whom we have worked can be nonfinishers in other aspects of their lives, but they are typically slaves to their beloved business ideas. Since they are pulled in this direction, rather than pushed, they do not describe their need to persevere as onerous.

Resilience

When I was a child, I was given a toy called a Bobo clown. This toy was like a big balloon, but weighted at the bottom. We would blow it full of air and then punch it in its bright red nose as hard as we could. No matter how hard we hit Bobo, he would bounce right back up to be lambasted again. In short, Mr. Bobo was quite a resilient fellow, and resilience is a key characteristic of the entrepreneurial mindset. Many entrepreneurial leaders fail in their first attempts to sell the organization on their ideas but, like the Energizer Bunny, they keep going. Unlike the Bobo clown, however, successful entrepreneurial leaders rarely bounce back up to get hit in the exact same spot again. They have learned to bob and weave, and to duck when necessary.

This resiliency factor is very important. People who take themselves too seriously, are perfectionists to a fault, and beat themselves mercilessly for making a minor mistake don't usually make good entrepreneurial leaders. Unlike the Bobo doll, they don't bounce back, and they become increasingly deflated with each blow. Leading like an entrepreneur requires an acceptance for making mistakes—but not for making the same mistake twice. Learning from mistakes allows Bobo to appear another day.

Optimism

I have never met one successful entrepreneurial leader who is a pessimist about his business idea. This does not mean that they are not pessimists about the government, taxes, their marriage, or religion, but they are perennially optimistic about the potential success of their opportunity. They truly believe in it, they don't think anything will stop them, and they know they are resilient enough to overcome obstacles and setbacks. If they were not positive thinkers about their own creation, then why on earth would they want to pursue it? This optimism is a very valuable currency when selling their ideas to others.

I am on the board of a small software start-up. The CEO doesn't yet have much of a product, and their current version has a lot of flaws, but he remains perennially optimistic. His optimism is infectious, and he has gotten several large companies to offer him beta sites to test and perfect the product, because they are so caught up in his optimism. They are aware of the flaws as well, but can't help themselves from helping him because of his infectious optimism.

Sense of Humor about Oneself

Most of us enjoy someone with a sense of humor, but this trait is extremely important and functional for entrepreneurial leaders. Following the opportunity process is messy. We don't know if an idea is an opportunity until we dig into it. As we dig, we learn. We realize that what we thought we knew about the opportunity isn't quite accurate. We make mistakes, take wrong turns, back up and take another direction, and often have to admit our own mistakes and omissions. If entrepreneurial leaders take themselves too seriously, then they don't recover well emotionally from these missteps. They need a healthy ability to fall down, get up, dust themselves off, look in the mirror, and have a good laugh at how silly they look. This characteristic also allows them to take some of that bureaucracy bashing I talked about earlier and see it as somewhat humorous. Finally, self-humor probably releases some of those well-publicized endorphins that allow us to feel more serene even in the presence of stress.

Inborn Traits or Learned Behavior?

Most of the research on these characteristics describes them as personality characteristics or inherent traits. If one takes this position, then it requires a big leap of faith to assume that a company can induce or teach someone to have these characteristics. Therefore, if the company wants to become more entrepreneurial, it must identify people who already have the right stuff and put them in key decision-making positions so that they can utilize their "God-given" entrepreneurial talents. Hewlett-Packard (HP) recently created a spin-out e-business segment, and populated it with those rebels from HP who seemed to always challenge the system with better ways of doing things. It assumed that these rebels were entrepreneurial misfits, so it moved them out of HP facilities and put them together in an offsite location with safeguards to prevent HP from stifling this group with its rules and regulations.

But, if you look at the preceding characteristics in depth, you will see that they are actually a mixture of traits, beliefs, emotions, and attitudes. For example, passion is an emotion that is often quite transient. When researchers describe entrepreneurs as passionate, they are describing the entrepreneur relative to the passion she has for a specific idea or opportunity. Likewise, locus of control may be a trait, but it also can be seen as an attitude. We often say people have a chip on their shoulders. This means that they feel they are owed something or have a grudge against something or somebody. But, it is unlikely that they were born with this chip on their shoulders. They had to learn it. Thus, locus of control may be as much a learned attitude or state of mind as an inborn trait. When we discuss attitudes or states of mind, we get into more malleable or coachable characteristics. People can learn to get that chip off their shoulders, and they can learn that they have more control than they think they have. Ask many a battered woman or recovering alcoholic if their attitudes about locus of control have changed, and they will tell you yes. The battered woman has learned that she does not deserve to be beaten and learns to stand up and defend herself, and the recovering alcoholic has learned that he does not have to see himself as a slave to the bottle.

If one takes the view that many of the above characteristics can be modified using the proper experiences, self-motivation, and encouragement, then learning to become an entrepreneur (as opposed to being born one) is quite possible. It becomes an issue of mindset and motivation. In the next chapter, we will show you how the energy emanating from this mindset can be channeled by the entrepreneurial leader into specific new business opportunities. And, we will see that this channeling is a function of both the individual's role in the organization and his personal preferences.

Summary

Entrepreneurship is about opportunity identification, development, and capture. This is the be-all and end-all. This is what entrepreneurs do, and why they are called entrepreneurs. What separates most of us from successful entrepreneurs is that they are willing to spend the time and energy to go through this process. The process is not magic; it can be learned. A clear discipline is involved in turning an idea into an opportunity. This discipline can be taught, and many of our students apply this discipline successfully in starting new businesses. Managers and large companies can do the same thing. But companies who wish to rekindle their entrepreneurial spirit need to create an environment in which managers become impassioned about an idea to the point that they are willing to pursue it even if there are obstacles. And, they need to convince these managers that they have more ability to make things happen than they might think.

Chapter Four

Guiding the Entrepreneurial Laser

In my studies of entrepreneurial leaders, I have found various ways in which they focus their entrepreneurial energy and skills. Earlier, I spoke about the obsessive, almost laser-like nature with which they go after new business opportunities. Some entrepreneurial leaders are directly and externally focused on market opportunities, while others are internally and indirectly focused on market opportunities. Regardless of focus, the goal is the same: the creation of economic value.

I also have found that entrepreneurial leaders can play either an active role as lead entrepreneurs themselves or act as the catalysts who stimulate the entrepreneurial actions and energies of others. While neither the roles, nor the foci, are mutually exclusive, the orientations are different. The nature of the orientation depends both on a person's job or role in the organization and on that person's preferences as to the entrepreneurial roles he chooses to play. In Figure 4.1, we see this interaction between roles and focus.

Activist Orientation

Activist entrepreneurial leaders take a driver- or owner-orientation to value creation. They see themselves as "on the line" for

Focusing Entrepreneurial Energy

	Internal	External
Activist	Miners (Operational)	Explorers (Market)
Catalyst	Accelerators (Unit)	Integrators (Enterprise)

FIGURE 4.1   Entrepreneurial leadership focus and roles.

identifying, developing, and capturing value-creating new business opportunities. Sometimes, these opportunities are in their units or departments, and sometimes the opportunities cross organizational boundaries. Sometimes, activist entrepreneurial leaders need permission from others to pursue their value-creating projects, and sometimes they do not. Much depends on the nature and scope of the opportunities they have identified.

Activists push others within the organization in new directions. These new directions could involve different strategic directions or the rearrangement of assets in the current business, which could give the company significant competitive advantages. Activists tend to be serial—in other words, they are constantly tweaking the system, thinking of ways to do it better, faster, cheaper, more competitively, or differently. They seem to have a burr under their saddle.

Activists stand out. They can be charismatic or they can be quiet, but they are constantly nudging and pushing for new ways to grow the business or make it more effective. They actively fight impediments. They point out rules that get in the way of value creation and try to remove, circumvent, or modify those rules. They tend to be stubborn and persistent, and they generally know how to persuade or irritate the organization into supporting their ideas without irritating it so much that they become "deselection" candidates.

Activists can focus their entrepreneurial energy either externally or internally. Corporate entrepreneurship research has typically looked at activists with an external focus because they are most similar to start-up entrepreneurs, but we have seen equally important value creation coming from activists with an internal focus. External focus is most often seen in managers who have direct access to and impact on the market. These folks are most often found, although not exclusively, in sales and marketing positions, new product development, corporate venturing, and business development functions. Because they are close to the market and work closely with customers, they are often the first to see new business opportunities. They see problems with customer relationships in an up-close and personal way. They know those strengths and weaknesses of competitors that could be exploited, and they see where gaps exist in their own company's promises and ability to deliver on these promises.

Externally focused entrepreneurial leaders are different from their non-entrepreneurial counterparts. Their counterparts hear customer complaints, apologize to the customer, and then move on to the next. Activists apologize to the customer, and then they return to the company with a determination to stop the complaints at the source. In short, they take personally their company's failure to deliver and are annoyed enough to do something about it.

Activists also can focus their energy internally on processes, procedures, operations, and asset management. Often, internally focused activists are not in direct contact with the customer or market, but can affect customers indirectly by influencing how the business is run. They see opportunities for value creation in making the company more streamlined or rearranging assets for increased competitiveness. Their focus is on making internal changes that create external differentiation. Internally focused activists are often found (although, again, not exclusively) in operational jobs like manufacturing, engineering, operations, human resources, and finance. Their nature is to take an aggressive stance in actively changing the way the business runs, but in ways that impact the customer and growth, not just the bottom line.

Of course, the external or internal orientations are not mutually exclusive. Market-derived new business opportunities frequently require internal changes before they can be implemented. Operationally focused changes that make the organization more competitive must be packaged and marketed to the external market as a differentiation feature. But, in our work, we find that activists usually start from one focus or the other. Some of this choice is based on where they are in the organization, but not always. I refer to activists who are externally focused as "explorers," because they are often out where the action is and they pay attention to the latest trends, competitor moves, and customer opportunities. They often generate industry or market changing new business ventures.

Internally focused activists are best thought of as "miners," because they see from inside the business those opportunities that can affect markets and customers. They actively attack the bureaucracy from within and try to bring about changes that make the company faster, friendlier, more focused, more profitable, more competitive, and more effective. As an example, John Kelley of VeriTrust, an insurance and financial services company[1], completely reorganized the company's annuity services center from 13 different functional areas to four cross-trained self-managing teams. Not only did this rearrangement of resources and assets have a significant impact on VeriTrust's cost structure, it also affected the speed of their processing so much that agents now refer more business to VeriTrust. You will read much more about John Kelley later, in Chapter 6. VeriTrust is a perfect example of how rearranging current organizational assets in new and innovative ways can both leverage these assets more effectively and efficiently and also positively affect business growth. Miners do not qualify as entrepreneurial leaders simply by rearranging resources or cutting costs. This rearrangement must also create economic value through organic growth.

Procter & Gamble has recently recognized that mining can be a good strategy for top-line growth. Craig Wynett and his team of entrepreneurial leaders in P&G's Corporate New

Ventures (CNV) group were tasked with literally "mining for gold" at P&G by focusing on lost opportunities that fell between the P&G brands. Before the CNV group's advent at the company, it literally took 10 years for P&G to migrate the technology from their fabric softeners over to Kleenex tissues and other paper products. Here was a great opportunity to expand the Kleenex brand, which languished for years because no one was really responsible for seeking out and managing these cross-brand opportunities. Finally, in frustration, P&G put this group together to try and realize much of P&G's lost potential.[2]

Catalyst Orientation

"Catalysts" are not ordinarily the direct drivers of opportunity. Rather, they help set up, or induce, conditions within the organization that allow innovation and entrepreneurial opportunities to be consistently and persistently pursued. Catalysts are often cultural value setters. They believe strongly in innovation, trying things, taking risks, allowing mistakes, and learning continuously, all of which helps support a climate in which people are motivated and simultaneously permitted to pursue business growth in unusual and unique ways.

In many respects, catalysts are more like "entrepreneurial pot stirrers and architects" than specific opportunity drivers. While the activist's attention is directed toward pursuing specific opportunities, the catalyst's attention is directed toward building a structure or climate in which others may identify, develop, and pursue value-creating activities. Catalysts worry about things that get in the way of organizational innovation and value creation, and they try to structure the organization, or their part of it, to empower creative effort, rather than inhibit it. They are both cheerleaders and challengers. They push managers and employees to think differently about how they might do their jobs, and they try to encourage and stimulate a climate of entrepreneurial thinking and acting.

In Chapter 2, I mentioned the *Journal of Business Venturing* study that looked at entrepreneurial leadership behaviors. In many respects, the journal's leadership questionnaire really focused on catalyst behaviors. For example, the behaviors examined included:

· Efficiently gets proposed actions through bureaucratic red tape and into practice
· Displays an enthusiasm for acquiring skills
· Devotes time to helping others find ways to improve products and services
· Goes to bat for the good ideas of others

As you can see, these behaviors are not opportunity-specific but are clearly aimed at creating an environment in which innovation, new approaches, and entrepreneurial thinking are encouraged.

Catalysts can be either internally or externally focused. Most often, internally focused entrepreneurial leaders take an entrepreneurial leadership approach within their own unit or department. I call internally focused catalysts "accelerators," because they try to increase or accelerate the pace of innovation in their units by evoking entrepreneurial vision and values. They try to evoke a "can-do," "can-try" attitude; they encourage risk taking; and they are constantly pushing their employees to think about how to work smarter, not harder. In some cases, they will actually do things to provoke or spur people's creative brain cells. One division manager in an optical products company would not allow employees to use company meeting rooms unless these meetings involved at least one customer. He did not want his people bogged down in endless internal meetings, discussing problems. He wanted them talking to customers, because he knew that customers were the key to this division's resurrection. Catalysts are pot stirrers, knowing that something good will eventually come out of the stew.

Alfred Weschlesbaum at Siemens was dogged in his attempts to build and implement a meaningful suggestion box system within Siemens Medical in California. He believed strongly that some of the most important innovations come from the minds of the employees, and that most suggestion box schemes fail because they do not follow up, measure, or reward the gains realized from implementing a good employee suggestion. Alfred likes to tell people that he happily paid a line employee a $78,000 bonus based on the value created by that employee's suggestions. Alfred is typical of many accelerators, and he is profiled in Chapter 7. While not the implementer of the value suggestions, he is the CEO ("chief encouragement officer").

Catalysts also can be externally focused. Most of the externally focused catalysts whom I have encountered have a wide breadth and scope of responsibilities in their organization. They are most frequently found in executive positions and are what I refer to as "integrators," because they focus more on the enterprise as a whole rather than on specific units or specific opportunities. Their focus is generally to make the whole organization more entrepreneurial. In many respects, Jack Welch of GE and Pat McGovern of IDG were integrators. Welch, in his early years with GE, was appalled at how slow, bureaucratic, political, and archaic GE had become. His tactics for making GE "lean and agile" are now legendary. McGovern continually subdivided IDG into smaller, more-entrepreneurial units to eliminate the entrepreneurial antibodies that largeness so often engenders. If a unit got too large, he would split it into smaller, faster, more-competitive subunits. Integrators also are very good at pulling people and resources from around the organization to create an opportunity-supportive, informal organization within the larger organization.

I refer to integrators as organizational, or enterprise, architects because they try to create a more entrepreneurial organization as a total entity. First, they create an entrepreneurial strategy, and then they try to align the organization's assets, finances, structure, processes, and human resources in ways that keep the entrepreneurial spirit alive.

Permission and Commitment

Often, at the end of one of my public speaking engagements or executive education classes concerning entrepreneurial leadership, some participant will say something like, "This all sounds good, but my company would never let me play an entrepreneurial leader role. They shoot mistake makers, so this entrepreneurial leadership stuff could never happen here." Some of these people suffer from what I described in Chapter 3 as an external locus of control. They believe that fate controls them, not the other way around. But, apart from this attitude of control, the different foci of entrepreneurial leadership do, in fact, raise the question of gaining permission from the organization in terms of organizational commitment. Figure 4.2 shows the relationship between organizational commitment and permission required for the four different entrepreneurial leadership roles.

In this figure, the vertical axis refers to how much personal control or authority the individual has to aggressively pursue an opportunity, either directly as an activist or indirectly as a catalyst. The horizontal axis refers to how much organizational commitment the entrepreneurial leader must pursue in order to capture their opportunity or make the organizational changes necessary to capture an opportunity. Thus, the less personal control and the more organizational commitment the individual has, the more selling, persuading, cajoling, arm twisting, and the like is required before the opportunity can be pursued.

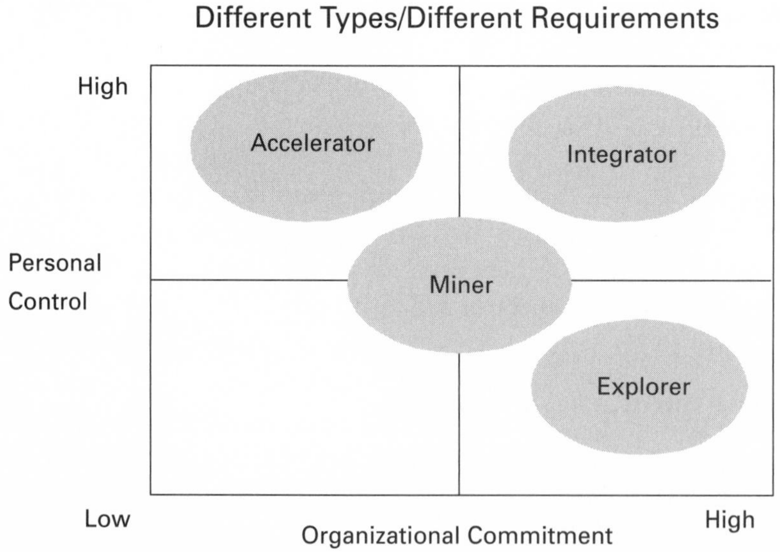

Different Types/Different Requirements

FIGURE 4.2   Entrepreneurial leadership and influencing requirements.

Accelerators need very little permission, since they run their own units, and encouraging more innovation is generally under their control at least in terms of their own unit. Practicing those 11 Entrepreneurial Behaviors Scale (EBS) behaviors I mentioned in Chapter 2 does not really require anyone else's permission. An accelerator can do things in her own unit without having to broadcast it or get a greater degree of permission and commitment from the organization. This changes, of course, if one of her employees comes up with a world-beating opportunity that could affect many others inside the business.

Miners generally need more organizational permission and have somewhat less personal control, because they often embark on internal opportunities that require organizational lines to be crossed. If, for example, a miner wishes to rearrange the value chain in some way, this usually impacts myriad other individuals in the organization who control various links in the chain and over whom he has limited or no control. Thus, the miner's ability to influence others outside his unit becomes increasingly important to capturing the opportunity.

One miner within one of our client companies needed the cooperation and technical expertise of a sister division over whom he and his project team had no control. He tried several times to attract this division to his opportunity, but to no avail. They said, in essence, "Sorry, we have enough work to do." Instead of giving up, he and his team went to a competitor of the sister division, who had the same technical expertise. They outlined the opportunity to this competitor, offered them a potential partnership agreement, and came away with an initial letter of intent. The team then took this letter back to the sister division that had originally brushed them off and gave them one more chance to sign on or lose this new opportunity to the competitor. This division immediately agreed to help. Pretty clever.

Explorers, especially if they identify new business opportunities that involve new products or services or modifications to existing ones, have to marshal people and resources from the organization. To do this, they must enlist the help of senior management. If the opportunity is so significant that it could change the current business focus or strategy of the company, then extensive buy-in and investment may be required. Explorers can only take their ideas so far without the commitment of many others in the organization. In many ways, explorers have to act like start-up entrepreneurs. They may have to do extensive market research and write a comprehensive business plan in order to convince others of the merits of their idea.

In a large auto parts supplier, one entrepreneurial leader who was the manager of product development grew frustrated with his attempts to convince senior management of the dangers of not moving quickly enough to bring an exciting home-related product to market. He knew that the opportunity could be huge but, as in many large companies, the decision was taking forever; senior management did not feel the same urgency he felt the opportunity needed if the company was to beat the competition to the punch. So, he decided to help motivate management by printing up a very good mock-up of a trade journal related to this product. The front page had an article showing that a competitor had just launched this new product to rave reviews. He then made sure that all the senior managers had a copy of what they thought was a real article from the magazine. They reacted immediately, believing the article to be real, asking, "How could they have beat us to it?" He let them stew for a few hours, and then let the cat out of the bag. Needless to say, he had their attention—and funding. It was a little risky, to be sure, but that is what entrepreneurial leaders do.

Integrators realize that, to create and sustain an entrepreneurial spirit within their company, they must start with entrepreneurship as part of the overall strategy. Then, they need to support it with structures, systems, and the right people (skills) with the right style, in the right place (staff) to keep the entrepreneurial candle lit. To bring it all together, they create and support a shared value system that supports risk taking, empowerment, and an entrepreneurial mindset. IDG not only has an entrepreneurial strategy, its ratio of headquarters staff to employees was 19:14,000 under Pat McGovern's stewardship. Pat proactively fused all of this together, and he allowed high levels of equity in new businesses that those entrepreneurial leaders below him created. He sustained this entrepreneurial spirit through an atmosphere of competition and cooperation, the selection of highly entrepreneurial people (despite their resumes), and he oversaw the multitude of small businesses that make up IDG. In Chapter 5, I profile IDG because it is so successful at weaving a durable entrepreneurial fabric and boasts a stellar track record for value creation through the development of a multitude of new businesses. Integrators like McGovern have a lot of personal control—after all, it is his company. But, he also needs a lot of underlying commitment from everyone in the organization to help him pull this off.

In the remaining chapters of this book, we'll look at each of these entrepreneurial leadership types—explorer, miner, accelerator, and integrator—in more detail through some real-life profiles.

Summary

When the Pinchots first created the term *intrapreneur*, they did not really differentiate between different types of internal entrepreneurs. But, in working with corporate entrepreneurs over the last decade, it became clear to me that different kinds of entrepreneurial leadership exist. Entrepreneurial leaders can be activists or catalysts, and they focus their energy either internally or externally. Companies must be very clear about what they want, because each type carries with it different requirements and generates different outcomes. If a company wants new ventures to be birthed from within, then "explorer" type leaders are needed. If, on the other hand, a company wants to creatively organize for a better customer impact, then "miners" would be preferred. If a company wants more widespread focus on innovation throughout its ranks, then it should focus on developing more "accelerators." And, if the company wants to be more opportunistic as a total enterprise, then the development of "integrator" entrepreneurial leaders would be the preferred strategy.

Often, when companies come to us for help in rekindling their entrepreneurial spirit, we have to spend a great deal of time just getting them to think through what kind of entrepreneurship they are after. I often like to use the Cheshire Cat from the Alice in Wonderland fairy tale as a kind of coach for these folks. When Alice is lost, she runs into Mr. Cheshire and asks for help. I tell them to pay special attention to the following dialogue:

> "Would you tell me, please, which way I ought to go from here?" asked Alice.
>
> "That depends a good deal on where you want to get to," said the Cat.
>
> "I don't much care where…," said Alice.
>
> "Then it doesn't matter which way you go," said the Cat.
>
> "…so long as I get SOMEWHERE," Alice added as an explanation.
>
> "Oh, you're sure to do that," said the Cat, "if you only walk long enough."

So it is with many companies, who have a generalized desire for more entrepreneurship. Unlike Alice, they care, but are not really clear about where they are headed, so they just start walking. Understanding the different entrepreneurial leadership typologies can help provide the road map.

Chapter Five

Explorers: Market-Focused Entrepreneurial Leaders

In this and the next few chapters, we are going to take a close look at some actual entrepreneurial leaders. Their stories, some of them ongoing, are all interesting, memorable, and provocative. I have purposely chosen not to profile top leaders like Jack Welch, Bill Gates, or Richard Branson. All these people are interesting and colorful, but they also have a lot of control over their organizations. Nor do they lack for press coverage. I prefer, instead, to focus on people below the top level. These people make things run on a day-to-day basis in an organization. We can relate to them. They are the implementers, and they have the very tough job of trying to be both innovative and entrepreneurial in organizations that are not necessarily user-friendly in these areas. Yet, they are proof that you can be an entrepreneurial leader in an established corporation, despite the fact that you may not get a lot of organizational support at the beginning of your quest. In some cases, the entrepreneurial leader had to outwit, outsmart, and outmaneuver his own company's bureaucracy to accomplish his goals.

We also look at several examples of company-enabled entrepreneurial leadership. IDG, IBM, Siemens, 3M, and Geisinger, for example, have tried to develop strategies, processes, and procedures to at least partially help these entrepreneurial leaders get a start. Despite this help, however, you will see that entrepreneurial leadership still requires a great deal of grit, determination, and maze-running savvy.

You will find these stories instructive, because they are about people who are often ordinary in many respects and who were not necessarily born entrepreneurs. Some came to their organizations with the "right stuff," while others evolved the needed capabilities through self-development or educational intervention. The bottom line is that these people's inherent or learned entrepreneurial capabilities created a great deal of economic value for their respective organizations, and they had a lot of fun in the process. They made good things happen.

As you read about these leaders, look at their character, their persistence, and their courage. They often hire and rely on others whom they believe to be smarter than themselves—not something very many large-company managers are prone to do. Senior executives who read these profiles should realize that entrepreneurial leaders like these may help you identify the barriers to innovation and value creation that exist in your organization and, if you can identify and develop enough of these people, they can bring about a sea change in your organization's culture.

You will find that I have included more "explorer" profiles in this book than profiles of the other types of entrepreneurial leaders (Fig. 5.1). I have done so because many organizations are looking for this kind of entrepreneurial leadership. But, I will also cover the other types, since they represent great avenues for value creation as well.

Explorers: Market-Focused Leadership

Explorers are involved in value-creating events and activities that are aimed primarily at the development of new markets, new products and services, or both. They also can be involved in creating a new business model for delivering current products and services that is so unique that it results in significant

Focusing Entrepreneurial Energy

	Internal	External
Activist	**Miners** (Value Chain)	**Explorers** **(Market)**
Catalyst	**Accelerators** (Unit)	**Integrators** (Enterprise)

FIGURE 5.1   Explorers are often the most sought-after type of entrepreneurial leader.

growth and profitability for their company. As mentioned earlier, we call them explorers because they often are working in uncharted territory, which has an inherently higher risk profile than the base business. Since the risk of failure is higher, the organization expects either higher returns or tries to manage risks appropriately by using a staged, rather than capital, investment approach.

Explorers are also activists, who either give birth to the opportunity or are significant contributors to its birthing. Sometimes, as in the case of Intel, they have to adopt someone else's baby, but they learn to love it nonetheless. They see themselves as the main drivers in the opportunity process. They also hold themselves personally accountable for its success or failure. Explorers are lucky. Earlier, I said that luck was the intersection between experience and opportunity. Explorers are obsessed with finding new and different ways to grow the business, and they have a tendency to question the status quo and conventional wisdom. They enjoy flexing their creative brain cells, and they love to outsmart the competition by being cleverer. Explorers are usually very close to the customer or to market trends and cutting-edge activities. This closeness gives them both a logical and an intuitive feel for business-growth ideas. They see customer complaints as windows of opportunity, and they have a good eye for unexploited or undiscovered markets.

Business Plan Orientation

Explorers are also different from dreamers and promoters because they are willing to spend the time and energy to determine whether a good idea is a good opportunity. We often hear managers complain that their organizations never listen to their ideas. Sometimes this is true, but we often find that these managers present their idea only in idea form, not in business plan form. Explorers are inherently business plan–oriented. They know that very few people will be interested in their idea unless they can back it up with research. And, the research is usually hands-on.

In my travels, I often see managers make presentations on new business opportunities, but they are marketing presentations, not business opportunity presentations. The presenter looks at IDC or Gartner Group market data, assumes that their company will get some of that market share, and then makes some pretty astounding "hockey stick" financial assumptions and projections. Explorers do not make these kinds of presentations. They tend to underpromise and overdeliver. They are generally conservative in their projections, and they prefer firsthand customer information to secondhand market trend research. They are realists, in that they know that no real opportunity exists without at least one customer who is willing to write a check for their new business idea.

Rebels with a Cause

When I facilitate a case study on an explorer example, I like to ask the class two questions about the subject: first, Would you like to work for him? and second, Would you like to have him working for you? The majority of my executive participants would love to work for an explorer but are hesitant about having an explorer work for them. I love these two questions, because they bring out the issue of trying to manage rebels. Explorers can irritate their bosses, because they sometimes have better ideas than their bosses and are not afraid to make suggestions. And, explorers are often right. They often know their customers, markets, and technology better than the higher-ups, including their own boss. They are not afraid to speak their minds and back up their opinions with data. Thus, they are not usually the quiet subordinate that large-company managers either like to have or have grown used to. They will argue, they will drag their boss to an irate customer, they will challenge internal processes and stupid rules, and they are passionate about their ideas. And it aggravates the hell out of them when they see their own organization pass on a great opportunity.

On the other hand, they also are politically savvy. They know when to stop pushing, and they know who to approach in the organization when extra juice or leverage is needed. But, they are not afraid to go to the wall and "bet their jobs" on a really great opportunity. They work within the system, but put pressure on it as well. They are not rebellious complainers, but rather rebellious constructionists. They really can lead the building of a better mousetrap. Unlike typical leaders and managers, they focus on the opportunity and try to get the organization to go after it. They also tend to identify and develop relationships with people both inside and outside the organization who can help them get it done. They try to get a small group of like-minded people to help them, and they typically try to induce or seduce a higher-level manager into serving as their mentor, obstacle remover, blockade runner, and buffer.

I tell managers in my classes to not only look for some of these people but, more important, "don't be afraid of them." They are value creators who should be embraced for their assertiveness, their ideas, and their brain power. It is easy to find examples of constructive rebels who have either been thrown out or have opted out of an organization only to move to a competitor that then cashes in big on the entrepreneurial leader's idea simply because it chose to listen.

The Explorers' Playground

New business opportunities can be analyzed according to their risk–return profiles. As the risk of an opportunity goes up, investors expect higher returns to cover their increased risk. Figure 5.2 illustrates the relationship between risk and return in terms of opportunity sets or categories. The three categories are Derivative, Platform, and Breakthrough.

Opportunities that are close to home and don't require much more than the tweaking of current products or services are often referred to as *derivative opportunities*. They are natural extensions or progressions of what a company already does. Therefore, the company not only possesses current competencies that enable it to readily make these improvements, but the risk is also low since it is not going into uncharted and thus unfamiliar and risky waters. Mott's, the applesauce maker, decided to start coloring its apple sauce. Great derivative. Simply adding coloring to their current product got kids to get their parents to buy tons of purple applesauce. This derivative improvement helped Mott's put a new face on an old horse.

Companies wishing to create economic value and organic growth need to pursue some of these derivative opportunities. Mike Crosby, former chief knowledge officer of Mott's, knew that colored applesauce would not double Mott's shareholder value in 2 years. Thus, Mike prodded Mott's to explore both platform opportunities and breakthroughs because he knew that, even though the risks were high, the potential financial returns were also higher.

Platform opportunities are a notch or two up from derivatives on both their risk profile and their potential financial return profile. Platform opportunities leverage a company's core competencies in producing either innovative new products or going into nontraditional new markets with current products. *Breakthrough opportunities* push the risk profile up even further, but if they succeed, the financial returns and competitive

A Portfolio of Opportunities

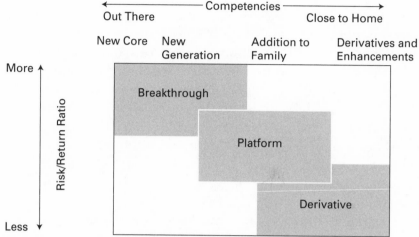

FIGURE 5.2　The opportunity map. (Adapted with permission from S. C. Wheelwright and K. Clark, *Creating Project Plans to Focus Product Development.* Boston: Harvard Business School Press, 1992.)

advantages can be enormous. Breakthroughs generally involve the introduction of both new products or services into new markets at the same time. Often, they involve the creation of markets that don't currently exist by the creation of products that nobody knows they need until they see it. I didn't know I needed a combined cell phone, global positioning system (GPS), and personal digital assistant (PDA) until I saw one.

Companies seeking to rekindle their entrepreneurial spirit must assess their current portfolio of opportunities in terms of these three categories, making sure the portfolio is balanced and not bottom heavy with derivatives. Too many derivatives can result in a company very focused on lots of small innovations that keep them very busy but don't get the kind of growth and financial returns expected from their shareholders. Too much focus on breakthroughs, although exciting, can quickly weaken a company's financial standing due to the heavy investments involved in these types of innovations. People often complain about the price of drugs, but look at the investment and risk in bringing a new drug to market. Not only are we talking about a new product, we are also talking about creating the market for it and getting it through the extensive FDA process. I do not begrudge these companies high profits, because they must plow a lot of this money back into high-risk drug development, where many false trails are pursued. Too many breakthroughs, without a few enormous wins (Viagra for example), and a company's risk profile would be so high that investors would have to be "high" themselves to give them money.

Platform opportunities, on the other hand, give a company the best chances of long-term entrepreneurial value creation with moderated risk. Since the organization already has core competencies, like technologies, manufacturing facilities, proprietary intellectual capital, distribution channels, and customers, it can moderate the risk of creating new products or new markets. Toyota's foray into hybrid cars is more platform than breakthrough. While clearly a high investment exists in the development of some of the technology, Toyota already has a brand, the manufacturing technologies, and the dealer network to mitigate against some of their risk. If you and I were to try to build a hybrid car, we would be in very scary territory. For Toyota, this car is clearly a platform opportunity, because it already has a lot of competencies to make this car a potential success and lessen the risk. For us, this same car would be a breakthrough opportunity, because we do not have any core competencies to leverage. But, Toyota does experience a higher risk than it does in simply creating a new derivative model. The risk is customer acceptance at a much higher price point than the nonhybrid model. So, a lot of people must buy into this technology to justify the investment.

In the figure, on the vertical axis you see the "Risk/Return" dimension. All opportunities carry a certain amount of risk, for which investors require a certain return. When little risk is present, like putting your money in a bank's savings account, you receive very little interest. Most accounts are insured against loss, so little risk and little return exists for this kind of investment. Some people are happy with this kind of risk–return profile. Others want higher returns and are willing to take the risk to get it. Thus, many folks play the stock market. The risk is greater but, over the long term, the rewards are much greater than putting money into a savings account. In the short term, however, the risk exists that you will lose your money, so you want higher returns for taking this risk. Those who are real risk takers might decide to give $100,000 to Uncle Mike to start his pizza business. A risk taker would certainly want a lot more return for this investment, because no one knows if Uncle Mike can make it, and the odds are clearly against inexperienced pizza start-ups. In fact, you would probably want Uncle Mike to turn over a percentage of his ownership in this business to help you mitigate the risk. You would probably encourage Uncle Mike to expand his business and eventually sell it, which would give you the possibility of cashing in big.

On the horizontal axis is the company's core competencies and capabilities. If the company sticks close to home, creating nuances of current products and services, this can be a good revenue-enhancing strategy that carries very little risk, since it has the capabilities in place to make these changes. Nokia changing a phone model by putting in a different keypad or offering faceplates that come in different colors is no high-risk venture, and these new features might help sell more phones. But, put in a camera and a PDA, and the risk profile goes up. Nokia is in the phone business, not the camera business, but it already has the phone platform to make this happen. Now, add a global positioning system, and make it a wristwatch with a heads-up display in your glasses, and you are talking about a breakthrough. The phone and camera are old competencies that play a very small part in the new wristwatch–heads-up display phone. Very new and different competencies are required to make this happen, and we have no idea if a market really exists for such an item. This means the risk profile goes way up, since the company must develop new products and new markets simultaneously. Now, if we are the first to market and we find that people really needed this product but never knew it, we sell tons, hit it big, and make tremendous returns. This makes the higher risk more than worth it.

Thus it is with internal business investments in opportunities. Upper management and shareholders want returns that are commensurate with the risks the company is taking with new initiatives. The higher the risk, the higher the expected returns. Too many derivatives, which are close-to-home and low-risk, will give low returns but are relatively safe. Too many breakthroughs, and the risk profile becomes so substantial that it could scare away potential investors or shareholders. Platform opportunities provide higher risk but better returns and represent where most new economic value is created by entrepreneurial projects. As you look at our explorer profile, note that most of the big new economic value creation comes from platform opportunities.

But, companies need a portfolio of opportunities just like most stock owners prefer to have a portfolio of investments. Companies wishing to be innovative must work in all three of these areas: platform, breakthrough, and derivative. They can't afford too many breakthrough opportunities because of the risk, but they need some breakthroughs if they are going to leapfrog the competition. Companies also need a lot of derivatives. Derivatives typically involve the continuous tweaking and improvement of existing products and services. Mott's apple-sauce is one example; changing the display or gauges on an automobile dashboard is an iterative example as well.

Research shows that platform opportunities are the most fertile ground for new value creation. While breakthroughs are exciting and can promise big dividends, they can also fail miserably, because the organization is working on pretty far-out things and markets for these products may not even exist. Platform opportunities usually are based on a company's current knowledge, skills, abilities, and capabilities. These attributes are leveraged into either new produces or new markets, but not usually both at the same time. Some companies that don't have the necessary attributes to enter an attractive market will acquire a company that does to lower their risk profile.

Explorers are good at developing platform opportunities. They know their organization's capabilities and look for opportunities to leverage these capabilities into new products and services or new markets that push the organization beyond what it can do now—but not so far as to take the organization too far out of its comfort zone.

Let's now turn to three explorers and examine how they brought entrepreneurial value to their organizations.

Explorer Profile 1: John Kilcullen, IDG Books

Perhaps one of the best examples of an explorer, or market-focused entrepreneurial leader, is John Kilcullen. He is best known for founding the now famous "Dummies" book series, despite a strong and vocal attempt to block the series from within IDG, the parent company. John was probably a latent entrepreneurial leader, never really hitting his stride or realizing his potential until coming across IDG. IDG is particularly good at spotting and encouraging entrepreneurial leadership talent. Fortunately for both John and IDG, their paths crossed. Here is John's story. As you read his story, pay particular attention not only to John's personal characteristics, but also to IDG's characteristics as a company. IDG has a history of developing entrepreneurial leaders and a great track record regarding value creation through the identification, development, and capturing of new business opportunities.

Entrepreneurial Leadership for Dummies

IDG Books was founded in 1990, with funding from International Data Group (IDG), a publisher of research and trade magazines for the information technology industry. John hit the division's first home run with the 1991 publication of *DOS for Dummies*, an unconventional, nontechnical guide to Microsoft's non–user friendly operating system. The title and its associated graphics and characters launched a brand that eventually took IDG Books out of the computer domain and into the business of teaching just about anything to everyone.

IDG Books went public in 1998, and sales hit $180 million for fiscal year 1999, as the company expanded beyond books into other forms of media and games related to its mission of providing education. The series has provided us with not only Dummies guides for DOS, but finance, wine, and even sex. *Sex for*

Dummies is, ironically, a best seller in France. The brains behind this venture belonged to John Kilcullen.

A Respectful Rebel

John was the sixth of eight children, born February 16, 1959, to lower-middle-class Irish immigrants. The tight-knit family was staunchly Catholic, raising its children with respect for authority and strict adherence to rules of conduct and propriety. John was an altar boy, literally and figuratively, and described himself as "very subservient, very respectful, a good kid, a good son." In school he was a straight "A" student, winning the altar boy prize one year and professing a desire to become a priest.

"There was always a sense of following a path," he says. "That I would be the pride of the family and would make my mom especially proud. There was some sort of obligation or conduct that was appropriate that I was supposed to obey."

John credited his large family, his "rigid upbringing," and the admonishments of older sisters with instilling core values in him, such as strong respect for people and an orientation toward team-work that served him well in later years. He also paid homage to the fundamental Jesuit principle of service, learned in Catholic schools and church, which deeply influenced his personal orien-tation and career goals. His parents made most decisions for him about schools and activities. Although he wanted to follow his one brother to Cardinal Hayes High School, his mother selected Cardinal Spellman, a co-ed school with more rigorous academic requirements. When college decision time came, however, John left his mother out of the loop and opted for Fordham, giving up a half scholarship at Iona College. It was a manifestation of the rebelliousness he always felt but could rarely express.

"I definitely know that I was born with a sense of marching to the beat of a different drummer," he says, "that I wanted to take the road less traveled."

The work ethic ran deep in the Kilcullen household. When he was younger, he earned money doing numerous jobs for the parish: paper route for Catholic Charities, cleaning the church and bingo hall, odd jobs in the rectory. Several summers during high school and college, he worked a midnight to 8 a.m. shift as an elevator operator in an elegant Fifth Avenue apartment house, and then went to a 9-to-5 day job as a camp counselor. The work ethic and the "sense of overachieving" remained through college, where he majored in communications, played competitive sports, and interned at a Madison Avenue advertising company. He graduated magna cum laude in 1981, and immediately took a job with Prentice Hall's Vocational Technical Division as a traveling salesman, serving northern New England, and forsaking a job offer in New York City.

John notes that "I chose publishing because I just felt it would validate my degree. My mother wanted me to work for the phone company: 'Take a job, and get a pension and security.' I love my mother, but if she said 'security,' I said 'no security.'"

The Budding Entrepreneur

Shortly after moving to Massachusetts, John followed an impulse to start his own business. Inspired by a fellow sales rep, he set up a company called JK Enterprises and planned to sell Amway products at night after his full-time day job. (Amway [American Way] sold household products through a pyramid distributorship system, with each distributor functioning as an independent business, receiving commissions on sales or products and a portion of commissions from the distributors they recruited.) The enticement of controlling his own destiny was quickly overshadowed by the heavy-handedness of the Amway motivational meetings and the demands of the two-job workload. After several meetings, John ended the venture, but he maintained the conviction that someday he would work for himself.

As a Prentice Hall salesman, he traveled throughout New England, making cold calls on vocational school faculties to sell textbooks. Gaining access to faculty was a daunting challenge, but he learned to "live in the customer's head," changing his dress, tone of voice, and body language to fit the style of his customers. John began to excel at sales, but his most significant reward was acquiring and publishing a new technical mathematics book. Scouting for fresh content was part of the sales rep's job description, but one that few paid much attention to. The words of his sales manager, however, made a profound and long-lasting impression on him. He said, "Don't sell what we acquire; acquire what sells." It expressed the concept of publishing as part of, rather than distinct from, the sales function, with those closest to the customer involved in anticipating and identifying customer needs. John signed Paul Coulter as the author of a mathematics textbook and developed the launch campaign, for which he received a national marketing award.

In spite of that success, John quickly discovered the walls that existed between the editorial and the sales sides of the business, and he felt the disdain that the editorial side held for sales. "I looked at myself as someone who had a high capacity to contribute, and I was outraged at the elitism and control of the home office editorial staff," he says. "There was always the philosophy that if the book sells, editorial did a great job, and if it didn't, sales did a poor job."

The Frustrated Entrepreneur

In February 1983, after 18 months in New England, John was promoted to the position of marketing and sales manager for computer books in the general publishing division. The unit sold computer books, but Prentice Hall decided to enter the emerging software industry, enticed by the high margins. In mid-1983, it launched an $800 accounting package, competing directly against IBM's Peach Tree brand and similar offerings from other software developers. The task of transforming a business built to sell $20 books into one selling $800 software was an "abysmal failure, a complete disaster," according to John. It was extremely frustrating to be responsible for the market success of the initiative but not to have control of launch decisions and sales projections. John did, however, gain a rapid-fire education in the activities of launching a product: hiring an ad agency and package design firm, conducting focus groups, and retraining the book sales force to sell software.

Despite his reservations and resentment, he fought to prove that he could make the software venture a success. For a while, he even handled a sales territory, flying out to Chicago at 7:00 on Monday mornings and returning Friday night for the weekend. The motivation to prove something in the face of difficult odds or to make a point in the face of superiors became a quality he looked for later when hiring staff.

In early 1985, he decided to leave Prentice Hall. He had grown increasingly disenchanted with the bureaucracy of the home office and the lack of respect that the editorial and publishing side paid to the business side. From New York, he moved to Indianapolis, trading his post at a stable company with a structured environment to be the national accounts manager at Que Publishing, an entrepreneurial start-up.

Although a compensation dispute marred the start of his new job, he enjoyed the work, which soon expanded beyond sales into corporate training and the development of training materials. He assumed responsibility for the editorial process and reveled in the sense of ownership, involvement, and control. Yet, in spite of the opportunities that accompanied the firm's explosive growth, he decided to leave Que after less than 2 years. A former colleague recruited him back to New York as national accounts manager at Bantam Doubleday Dell's newly created electronic publishing division. John handled a line of spoken-word audio products and was responsible for training and managing the entire sales force. He was then promoted to director of sales, a position that included editorial aspects such as package and cover design, titling, and idea generation.

Venturing Out on His Own

At the end of 1989, after 9 years of working for other people, with experience in both larger, older companies and smaller, new ventures, John was ready to strike out on his own. He was tired of bureaucracy, office politics, and cultures incompatible with his values. While still handling his job at Bantam, he developed a business plan to launch a virtual technology publishing enterprise to manage a brand on an outsourced basis. Eager to secure funding from an established publishing company, John approached Random House, which expressed interest in the proposal but decided to hire someone with an academic background to head up its new technology publishing division. After a second publishing house, Addison-Wesley, also turned down the proposal, he read that International Data Group (IDG) was starting a book publishing company.

Separately, Jonathan Sachs, the executive at IDG charged with launching the new venture, had been given Kilcullen's name when he pursued recommendations on the "best sales guy in the indus-try." Sachs offered him the job of vice president of sales and mar-keting, presenting the opportunity as akin to an entrepreneurial venture in which John would play a founding role and have a sub-stantial stake. As John recalled, "The words that resonated with me were, 'OK, Kilcullen, why don't you start your company on our nickel?'"

IDG Books

As declining prices and increasing ease of use swelled the sales of personal computers, Pat McGovern, the founder of IDG, saw a growing role for books to help educate millions of new users. Several corporate associates, however, fought against his idea of forming a book publishing unit, arguing that the book trade was "old-fashioned media," especially in the emerging online world, with slow growth and low profitability. The CFO somewhat begrudgingly agreed to commit $1.5 million to support the ven-ture, and McGovern tapped Jonathan Sachs, then senior editor at *InfoWorld*, an IDG publication, to head up the initiative. In decid-ing to hire John Kilcullen as VP of sales and marketing, Sachs and McGovern not only liked Kilcullen's energy, enthusiasm, and opti-mism, but they also appreciated his perspective on the book pub-lishing industry. As Sachs recalled, "Kilcullen saw the opportunity to create a book business that would be driven by marketing savvy and brand management rather than by the traditional skills of publishing: negotiating with authors to secure and edit manu-scripts. John saw a chance to create a brand that people would buy regardless of the author."

In late March 1990, John moved out to San Francisco to start work, taking a 35 percent pay cut, but thrilled by the risk and potential reward. Three weeks after the launch, Sachs announced that he was returning to *InfoWorld* to be CEO and that John was to be promoted immediately to publisher of IDG Books. With $1.5 million in funding, but no other guidance or assistance, John was off and running his own venture. McGovern recounted his typical approach: "We said, 'Here is the opportunity; here is how much money we are going to commit to you; you are the expert; go out there and make it happen. If you need us, if you want advice from us, call us. Otherwise we are out of your way. Go ahead and do it any way you want to.'"

Following intuition rather than research, John initially attempted to leverage the portfolio of IDG's corporate magazine brands—*GamePro*, *Omigaworld*, *PC World*, and *MacWorld*—by creating associated book brands. The magazines provided authors in return for cash advances and a royalty stream. By the end of its first full year, the operation had published nine titles, primarily special-interest computer books for niche markets, and revenues were about $1.5 million. By his own reckoning, two of the nine were moderately successful and the rest were "disasters," leaving the unit burdened with costly excess inventory. Although the books used the IDG brands, John recognized that they didn't have any internal coherence as a group. Sales force problems compounded the editing issues. A team of manufacturer's sales reps that John had hired to push IDG books resigned after a few days, citing pressure from a competing publisher.

At a conference in March 1991, where all the authors got together, discussion veered toward the idea of shutting down IDG Books. No one was satisfied with the products or market results. John was growing increasingly disillusioned with the people on his staff, including the editor-in-chief, who came from the magazine side of IDG and had no book publishing experience. In pursuit of their own ideas, his staff tended to pay little heed to his proposals. The failure of most of the books was hurting the credibility of the young company. Lack of performance on the inventory terms threatened the ability to keep shelf space that John's reputation had initially secured. With only $200,000 remaining, and no hope of additional financing from IDG, John knew that he had to take a risk with something new and dramatic. Convinced that his ideas were worth exploiting, he decided to take over control of the content program.

In trying to identify the "next big hit," John and his team focused on the upcoming release of Microsoft's MS-DOS 4.0, scheduled for June 1991. IDG had already tried two DOS books, one borrowing from the Nike tag line, *You Can Do It with DOS*, which did poorly, and a moderate success branded as the *PC*

World DOS Handbook. John's editor-in-chief had no DOS book for the upcoming release planned in the 6- to 12-month publishing program. As John remembered, "I turned to my editor-in-chief and I said, 'DOS for Dummies.' The title embodied everything I was about: contrarian, contentiousness, completely different. We would go in a different direction."

Entrepreneurial Leadership for Dummies

According to John, the phrase "DOS for Dummies" came out of a dinner conversation he'd had 4 years earlier with a good friend who was relating an incident the friend had overheard in a New York City bookstore: "We were having dinner, talking about new ideas, and Chris told me about being in a store where a guy walked up to the counter and said, 'I need a book on DOS, something really low-level, just for me. Really basic, you know, DOS, DOS for dummies, do you have something like that?' It stuck in my head in my idea file."

The concept got shuffled together with numerous other ideas over the 4 years, but came to the fore when John put it together with an author, Dan Gookin, whom he had heard speak at a publisher's conference. Gookin derided the dull, formulaic approach of the computer publishing industry and its propensity to suck all creativity out of his manuscripts. The author's humorous irreverence and contrarian point of view meshed with John's own perspective and offered the tone he was looking for in his *DOS for Dummies* book. The concept met with strong reaction from John's peers, who asserted that the *Dummies* book would degrade the esteemed IDG name and its authoritative reputation, as well as ruin John's career in the process. He remembered the editor-in-chief of *PC World* warning him. "He said, 'Don't do it. You're going to insult your customers. You've been draining our ESOP (employee stock ownership plan), and now you're going to destroy our brand.' I said, 'Screw you.' Every time someone said don't do it, it was just fuel to do it. I wanted to prove them wrong."

McGovern, who sat on the board of IDG Books, and who had remained supportive and encouraging during the difficult first year, recalled the situation: "Everyone's immediate reaction was that it would be a disaster: people would be embarrassed to take it to the checkout counter; the gift market wouldn't be available because no one would buy such a book and give it to a friend. But ultimately we said, 'John, it is your call—you're the boss.' They were down to their last $200,000. If it didn't work, that would have been the end."

DOS for Dummies was launched in November 1991, 6 months after the release of DOS 4.0, with an initial printing of 7,500 copies. John understood the psychographic connotations of the term "dummies" from his stint in advertising. The title conveyed an appreciation and sensitivity for the feelings of anxiety, frustration, and disenfranchisement that came from a lack of knowledge and confidence. The book promised to remedy these feelings by demystifying arcane subjects and making them accessible to everyone. In short, the book was everything all the other computer books were not—nontechnical, funny, and self-deprecating. It featured an eye-catching, glaring yellow cover with black print, and introduced a comic book–type character who personified the "everyman" who wanted to learn in a way that was easy but effective. The public responded. In its first year, the book outsold every competing title, the character became an icon, and the Dummies brand was born.

"It was entrepreneurial success born out of failure," recounts John. "*DOS for Dummies* was a big risk, but it was a big home run. It was alliterative; it was provocative; it was controversial; it was unconventional; it was contrarian. It resonated with the masses. I had a sense that this was something that was going to get attention that could be built into a brand."

Building and Extending the Brand: Books and Beyond

Competitor critiques doubted the sustainability of this "one-book wonder." Many peers at IDG shared that view and were concerned that John would build the infrastructure to support a series of best sellers that would never materialize. The naysayers only spurred him on to prove them wrong and validate his sense of brand potential in the title, tone, writing style, and appearance. He followed up the first effort with *Macs for Dummies*, fighting his own staff, which wanted to found an alliterative tradition and name it *Macs for Morons*. "I said, 'You guys don't get it. This is a brand. This is a franchise. You have your point product, *DOS for Dummies*, and you have to extend that brand.'"

Even internal associates questioned whether the formula could work for topics other than operating systems, which everyone acknowledged were confusing and required simplified explanation. They reasoned that customers would be unlikely to denigrate themselves as dummies by purchasing a guide to applications programs such as word processing. But the Dummies books for WordPerfect and Lotus 123 sold equally well. The basic software books were followed by *Quicken for Dummies*, which created demand for a Dummies book on finance. Soon, people were coming into bookstores asking for Dummies books on a variety of topics. Inevitably, a hot seller was *Sex for Dummies*, written by noted sexologist Dr. Ruth Westheimer. That book created some tension within the company and drove some insiders to question the direction of the brand, which was increasingly moving away from computers and a connection to IDG's information technology core. But as John explained, "Our whole thing was literacy: computer literacy, finance literacy, mutual funds, and taxes. It was about revolutionizing learning, leading the knowledge revolution."

To extend the concept of the "branded knowledge franchise," he wanted to purchase complementary publishing franchises, a strategy that ran contrary to Pat McGovern's approach and experience. IDG's own history had been one of organic growth, in which acquisitions played a small and unsatisfactory role. However, although McGovern did not fully support the strategy, he let the corporate dictum rule: "It all comes down to what the CEO wants to do." John made a series of acquisitions—CliffsNotes, Frommer's travel guides, Betty Crocker cookbooks, Webster's New World Dictionary—to enter underserved demographic markets and specific subject areas. He also moved the company into other media and forms of education and entertainment, such as board games, spoken audio, and TV projects.

In the late 1990s, IDG Books was growing by 10 to 13 percent a year, continually adding new titles and entering foreign markets. Though initially considered to be a U.S. cultural phenomenon, the Dummies concept proved equally valid around the globe—provided an appropriate translation of the word *dummies* existed. By the end of 1999, IDG Books had 400 Dummies titles, with cumulative sales of $1 billion over 10 years and a contribution of $180 million in pretax profits. John Kilcullen credited a large measure of that success to a corporate environment that fostered entrepreneurial thinking and activity, despite considerable tension in his relationship with his IDG peers, who resented his unconventional approach and independence. Fortunately, IDG Books was located in Silicon Valley, far from the IDG's Boston headquarters and its corporate bureaucracy. John did, however, enjoy an excellent relationship with Pat McGovern, based on mutual respect for each other's abilities. McGovern gave him wide latitude to set his own course for the book business, and John was deeply appreciative of the way McGovern encouraged and supported his actions, while giving him free rein to run the operation. As he explains it, "The key thing is freedom. No one is looking over my shoulder, second-guessing me. Pat is a very inspiring guy. He'd come in for the board meetings, but other than that you'd never see him. And frankly I never talked to Pat unless it was the eleventh hour. My feeling was, the less I talk to Pat in corporate, the better. Pat historically always took big bets on people. I mean big bets, on people who didn't really have a huge track record."

John Kilcullen's story is inspirational. Before he went to IDG, he would probably not have been described as an entrepreneurial leader. He was a great salesman, a rebel with a cause, and passionate about helping others, but not really a bona fide corporate entrepreneur. He tried being a start-up entrepreneur with Amway, but left this endeavor and went back to industry. IDG was smart enough to spot John's talents and his itchiness to run something of his own, and they were willing to place a small wager on his ability to come through. They won in a big way.

Explorer Profile 2: Dr. Bill Isaacson, 3M

At first, I was hesitant to put Dr. Bill Isaacson's story in this book. Not because his story is uninteresting, but because 3M and its vaunted culture of innovation are so well known that they are victims of overexposure. But, most of what is written about 3M deals with the corporate culture, not with actual people like Bill, who are in the trenches, tirelessly working to invent new things and whose only reward is to get a chance to do it again.

The Survival Instinct of the Entrepreneurial Leader

Like most entrepreneurial leaders, Bill Isaacson is a survivor. Throughout his career—most of which he spent at 3M Corporation—this chemical engineer and inventor has weathered all kinds of corporate storms while planting and nurturing the seeds of innovation. His early years helped foster that survival instinct, along with a strong sense of self-reliance—another trait shared by many entrepreneurs. As he puts it, "I was born in North Dakota before World War II. We weren't really very well to do. My father sold farm equipment and my mother was a teacher. As a kid, I was very shy and worked hard at school. I was always trying to prove myself. I developed a strong sense of self-reliance during my childhood. And, growing up in North Dakota, you really do develop a survival instinct. You do, quite literally, have to survive the North Dakota winters."

Like many entrepreneurial leaders, Bill was lucky enough to have a mentor, his uncle, a living example of where that survival instinct could lead those with the courage to follow. With just an eighth-grade education, his uncle became a successful entrepreneur and manufacturer. By applying principles he gleaned from work in the aircraft tooling business, he designed a diving board—the aluminum springboard—that has revolutionized the sport of competitive diving. The company he started, Duraflex International, Inc., has supplied all of the diving boards used in the Olympics since 1960, as well as those for all competitive diving venues around the world. Dr. Bill (as most people call him) remembered, "I went out to work for him when I was a junior in high school and that really changed my life. I got a lot of my philosophy of life from him."

After gaining his Ph.D. in chemical engineering at Montana State University, Bill joined 3M in 1963, where—just like back home in North Dakota—he felt he had to constantly prove himself: "I was one of just a few Ph.D. chemical engineers in the company at the time, so I always felt I had to prove myself. In fact, the very first week I was there, my boss said to me, 'Tell me what you're going to do to justify your salary.'"

Before long, Bill was proving himself to be worth every penny of his paycheck. He was one of the first people at 3M to use computers to solve scientific problems and do research and one of the pioneers in doing designed experiments—now a standard in scientific research. He recalls that his drive to innovate was nurtured by the climate in the country at the time. The country was in the midst of the Space Race. The sprint to put a man on the moon was, according to Bill, "the perfect way of promoting innovation across the country. At the start of the space program, we only had about 10 percent of the technology to reach that goal, hence the program challenged the minds of scientists and engineers and created a demand for many more."

3M was one company that Bill felt had always been more interested in discovering new technologies and innovations than tearing down and rebuilding brick walls. Since its early days, in the beginning years of the twentieth century, 3M has been built on an entrepreneurial ethic and has stimulated and supported innovation and entrepreneurial behavior. William McKnight, who served as 3M's first chairman of the board from 1949 to 1966, actually began his career with the company in 1907. He is credited with setting the entrepreneurial tone at the company. At one point, McKnight directed his managers to "delegate responsibility and encourage men and women to exercise their initiative." As Bill Isaacson pointed out, "It is just this kind of leadership that fosters the creation of a culture of innovation and real growth. McKnight operated on the premise that creativity should be supported and promoted in every possible way. That kind of encouragement—coming right from the top—proliferates through a whole organization."

In fact, 3M is famous for its "15 percent rule," which states that at least 15 percent of each employee's time and energy should be dedicated to work on independent, innovative projects. Bill said that, over the years, this very concrete support of entrepreneurship has held the company in good stead. "I would say that every single major innovation at 3M has grown out of the 15 percent rule. But, the effect goes further than that. The rule actually institutionalizes support for creativity and innovation. It's not just 15 percent of a person's time dedicated to creativity; it's the creation of a whole mindset built on the support of innovation. In my mind, the 15 percent rule was a statement of commitment from management that we respect you for your ideas and we encourage you and support you to be creative and innovative."

Expecting the Unexpected

During his years at 3M, Bill helped steer the company toward some of its most groundbreaking innovations. Of course, the innovation now practically synonymous with 3M is Post-it Notes. Those now-ubiquitous little stick-ons grew out of an unsuccessful batch of adhesive and some apparently very successful prayers. When it all started in the early 1970s, Bill was serving as supervisor of chemical process development. As was often the case, he and his research-and-development team were asked to produce pilot plant quantities (larger than laboratory test tube) of new materials to promote thorough testing. "At the time, we were trying to develop stronger adhesives than what we already were selling on many of our products. We were asked to produce a large quantity of a new adhesive formulation, only to discover it was an adhesive that didn't stick. That's really an oxymoron—an adhesive that doesn't stick. It's like the sun coming up in the west. So, we had this big vat of the stuff. Art Fry was one of the chemists involved in the project, and he was a member of the choir at the Presbyterian Church. He liked to mark his place in his hymnal during services, so he tried some of the new adhesive on pieces of paper. He found that he could mark the place and then reuse the paper. It was an adhesive that didn't stick. The researchers then sent samples of the nonsticky paper to several 3M executive secretaries, who immediately found a myriad of uses for it. Then the CEO and chairman of the board, Lewis Lehr, sent Post-it prototypes to some fellow executives in other companies. The rest, as they say, is history."

Bill notes that another incentive to growth and innovation at 3M was the corporate dictate that 25 percent of the annual sales in each business unit should come from new products introduced to the marketplace within the past 5 years. Since Bill's retirement from the company, that figure has now been raised to 30 percent within 4 years. Thus, each unit and each department is required to constantly build new growth through innovative, internal projects.

The company also took a unique step toward stimulating entrepreneurship by creating a dual engineering–venture development career path. In 1986, Bill became one of just three people in the company's history chosen for the venture position. "That was the best job in the world. My boss used to say, 'Do whatever you want.' But, there was catch. Within 3 years, I had to come up with a business plan that would fit the strategic direction for what 3M wanted to be when it grew up. And, it had to be so good that it could stand on its own. My reward for doing all that was to go back and do it all over again."

If At First You Don't Succeed…

Bill was charged with developing business plans for ventures that could be $50 million to $150 million "hits" for the company at maturity, he said. Two of his entrepreneurial ventures involved what he calls "revolutionary vision correction technologies … breakthroughs in the industry."

The first venture grew out of a job interview Bill had with Bausch and Lomb, at that time the clear leader in the vision care field. "I understood that my experience with fluoropolymer materials could be translated to optics. I realized that 3M had the technology to enter the vision care market. The fastest growing segments of that market at the time were in contact lenses and contact lens solutions," he explained. "I saw a $500 million market opportunity using old technology when I knew 3M had materials on the shelf that were technologically superior and addressed many of the unmet needs of consumers."

The entrepreneurial leader remembers that 3M gave him a "grub stake" of a few hundred thousand dollars and two full-time employees to prove his concept. In the best entrepreneurial tradition, Bill made the most of those resources by involving people all over the 3M system in the enterprise. As a result, he and his team developed a material and technology for producing extended-wear contact lenses. The first patient to be fitted with new lenses was able to wear them for more than 1 year. "And when the doctor took the lenses off the patient's eyes, he said his corneas looked as if he'd never worn contacts," Bill said.

Unfortunately, Bill was unable to convince 3M management to hire the independent sales staff necessary to give the venture a life of its own. The program was merged with the company's intraocular lens department and saw limited market use before 3M decided to exit the vision care business. He later was asked to license all the technology to a major vision care company, and did so.

Bill's second vision care venture was even more ambitious and revolutionary: an intraocular multifocal lens based on diffractive optics, rather than the usual refractive optics technology. "I realized initially there was another $500 million market opportunity for bifocal contact lenses without a technical solution," he related. Bill knew from his previous experience in 3M's Traffic Control Materials Division, which makes reflective signing materials, that 3M had the technology to solve the problems that had kept other companies from making bifocal contacts. "We could do this, and we did," he said. "I also realized that there was another $200 million opportunity for a multifocal intraocular lens implanted in the human eye after cataract surgery. This was the first time since the beginning of mankind that this technology was used for a commercial vision care product. Until then, everything being implanted was basically a 'Brownie Box Camera,' when we needed a 35mm, wide angle, autofocus."

Initial clinical trial results were "fantastic," Bill recalled, with patients experiencing dramatic vision correction. The new lens changed depth of field by a factor of three to five times and added five to seven lines of near vision, without corrective glasses. Thousands of lenses were implanted in Europe and Canada, while the lens remained an investigational device under the control of the Food and Drug Administration (FDA) in the States. But, the entrepreneur's survival skills were to be tested once again, as he and his team tried in vain to convince the FDA that the technology was safe for use in humans. The agency, Bill said, "just never really understood the technology. They just kept asking more and more questions and never gave us approval," he explained. One of their conclusions basically was that old people shouldn't drive cars at night.

Although neither of Bill's vision care ventures made it to market as independent ventures, the innovations he spawned and the inventive passion they embodied transformed the shape of research in the industry. And several lives—including Bill's mother's—were changed along the way. "My mother was one of the first people to have a bifocal lens implanted. The procedure changed her life. For the last 5 years of her life, her vision was so improved that she was able to paint beautiful pictures with watercolors. That, in itself, made me feel I'd been a success. When I first arrived at 3M, my supervisor asked what I wanted to do there. I answered that I wanted to impact people's lives."

Explorer Profile 3: Shahrom Kiani, Siemens Dematic

I first met Shahrom in one of my corporate entrepreneurship classes that I taught for Siemens. The course was part of Siemens S3 General Managers program, and its intended mission was to immerse the participants in the principles of entrepreneurship and general management. The program utilized both classroom education and action learning projects. Shahrom was one of those participants who immediately stood out. He was quick-witted, funny, charismatic, a little irreverent, and liked to spar with the faculty.

Shahrom, like the other participants, was expected to come to this program (which lasted over 9 months in total) with a real new business opportunity. They then shopped these opportunities to the other participants in sort of an "open market," in which 35 projects had to be eventually culled down to five or six. Participants got to sign up for another person's project if their own did not fly or they found the project more interesting. Participants voted for projects by putting their name next to the project that they most wanted to be on. With some wheeling and dealing, cajoling and selling, all participants wound up on one of these five or six projects.

Out of the gate, Shahrom's new business opportunity was one of the most popular. His was one of the projects that was elected to go forward, and he was able to convince a diverse group of people to work on his particular project over the year.

I wanted to profile Shahrom for this book, because he demonstrates so many of the characteristics of a good entrepreneurial leader plying his trade in a large, complex, often process-driven organization. But, more important, his profile gives you an excellent look at how an entrepreneurial leader goes about the three phases of the opportunity process (Identification, Shaping, Capturing) that I described in Chapter 3. And, his story also illustrates how large companies like Siemens can create a learning environment that not only develops better managers for life, but can simultaneously result in the creation of economic value through real-life project work.

Experienced managers in large companies often are in the best position to spot new business opportunities if they have the mind to do so and if they get a little encouragement. Shahrom created good luck. He had enough industry experience, marketing knowledge, and technical background to spot (actually create) an opportunity when he saw it. And, he was entrepreneurial enough to be able to capture it. Remember our definition of luck: Luck happens when experience meets opportunity in the presence of an open mind. Shahrom could be the poster child for how entrepreneurial leaders can "get lucky." In some respects, Shahrom's story is a capstone for all the previous chapters. You will see the leader, his entrepreneurial bent, the nature of the opportunity process, and the challenge a large company faces in trying to rekindle its entrepreneurial spirit. His story represents the best of entrepreneurial leadership, as evidenced by managers caught in the middle.

As you read his story, pay particular attention to how Shahrom and his team were able to identify a great business idea and then use cleverness and persistence to get this idea through their own company's maze.

The Opportunity

Shahrom Kiani, General Manager of the Commercial Mail division of Siemens Dematic group, slowly signed the $225,000 contract with Siemens U.S. Corporate R&D unit. After more than 6 months of negotiation, Kiani and Siemens R&D had agreed on a scope of work that Shahrom hoped would provide key technology to enable his unit to go to market with its first version of a license plate reading system. The target market was police vehicles, where such systems would allow officers to read license plates that were out of range of human vision and then be able to check them against state and national databases to identify outstanding traffic warrants or other citations. Later versions would incorporate optical character recognition (OCR), the core technology of Siemens mail sorting systems, and would electronically interface with databases. For the present, however, Shahrom felt it was critical to get a product to market and generate some revenue.

The concept of a license plate reading system was one of many ideas that Shahrom and a few associates at the Siemens mail division had batted around in their quest to find other applications for their mail reading and sorting systems. Siemens was the major supplier to the U.S. Postal Service (USPS) and also sold machinery to private commercial mailing companies. Although the markets had not been impacted by the Internet as much as predicted during the late 1990s, the growth forecast was not robust. Moreover, the USPS was eager to encourage competition in the mail sorting business to reduce its reliance on Siemens, further dampening prospects for growth. Shahrom proposed the license plate reading idea as a project for a corporate entrepreneurship executive education program, during which he headed up a team that developed a business case for the endeavor. A year later, during which the demands of other business priorities limited the time he could devote to the new venture, Shahrom was determined to renew his efforts to turn the idea into a viable business. He decided to pare down his R&D spending on other projects to pursue the license plate reading application. "This would be the first phase of a total solution, but we needed to do something fast. If I don't do something this year, then I might as well forget it and close it down. Part of the entrepreneurship that I have learned—your first idea is never the one—it evolves; you have to be able to adapt to the changing conditions and constraints. We need to bring in some revenues soon. If you start to have revenues, then a lot of things become easier. If you don't make money, you are under a microscope."

Entrepreneurial Lessons Learned Early

Shahrom Kiani was born and raised in Iran. His seminal child-hood memory is of engaging a bully, who delighted in tormenting Shahrom's friends, in a bloody round of fisticuffs. This incident hinted at Shahrom's entrepreneurial tendencies: willingness to challenge an incumbent and a preference for direct action. Shahrom also recalled his mother rebuffing his attempts to sneak out of the house to play soccer with friends, and later boasted that he succeeded not only in getting out of the house, but also getting out of the country and off the continent.

Shortly before the Shah of Iran was deposed, Shahrom's parents brought him and his younger brother, aged 16 and 15 respectively, to Texas, and enrolled them in a high school. After several months, his parents returned to Iran, leaving their sons on their own in an apartment. Shahrom gained an early sense of independence and self-reliance, especially when having to endure the discomfort of being an Iranian in the United States during the Iran hostage crisis in 1980. He concentrated on his studies, certain that he would ultimately return to Iran to live and help his country. As his high school and college years passed, he became settled in the States and his parents immigrated permanently in 1983. He attended the University of Texas at Arlington, and then went on for a master's in engineering, specializing in software development.

During his final semester, Shahrom had an opportunity to do contract work for a private company called Electrocom Automation. He was offered a full-time job after graduation in 1986, and was at the same company nearly 20 years later, even as it endured a series of changing corporate identities and eventual acquisition by Siemens Dematic.

In spite of his consistent employment, for many years Shahrom held the idea of starting his own business. He held a strong conviction that "to really make money, you had to have your own business; you had to be your own boss." He enjoyed thinking up ideas for new ventures, though few got past the pure concept stage. Finally, in the late 1990s, Shahrom struck out to commercialize a software program he had developed to keep track of golf scores and statistics for the country club where he was president. "It was difficult to do with an Excel spreadsheet, so I wrote a program to do this, and little by little it got better and better, and I thought I could market it. So, I got a kiosk at a local mall and got a bunch of golf stuff, shirts and caps, and spent my whole Christmas vacation doing this. I didn't lose much, but didn't make much either, so eventually I gave up this dream and decided to focus on my job and be a corporate-type entrepreneur. I realized I could have a lot more impact here. Everybody has to go through that once, I guess."

A Prisoner of Its Success

Siemens Dematic Postal Automation (SPDA) had a near monopoly on the global postal automation industry, holding 89 percent of the worldwide market share. The USPS was by far the largest postal system in the world, and the industry's biggest customer. SDPA had 15,000 systems installed in 300 regional USPS processing and distribution centers across the country, representing more than 80 percent of all automation equipment. Siemens machines, which combined electromechanical handling systems with sophisticated OCR software, could handle up to 40,000 letters per hour and perform a complex sets of activities: cancel stamps, face mail in the same direction, read addresses and check them against a national database, spray 11-digit bar codes on each item, and then sort them into racks of up to 300 compartments according to the delivery sequence of the mail carriers.

Survive, Divide, Thrive

To move beyond its single customer market, in the early 1990s, SDPA launched a series of diversification efforts. At that time, the volume of direct mail expanded substantially, and SDPA began selling its postal automation systems to large businesses and commercial mail houses, to handle presorted bulk mail. Shahrom oversaw the software development for the unit, known as Commercial Mail Solutions (CMS), for 5 to 6 years in its start-up phase and then, following a 5-year stint in Reading & Coding, he returned to run the commercial operation, in 2001. Initially, CMS sold its top-line systems at good margins to commercial buyers, but competitors emerged with "good enough" equipment and lower prices and captured a share of the market while reducing overall profitability. Shahrom described the situation: "The market was really good at the beginning, but then competitors came in, prices declined, and the market is saturated right now. We were the innovators, we had the solution but, over the past 10 years, people caught up and surpassed us in some cases. We have taken back the technology lead, but the market is struggling. We are struggling to sell machines."

The core business of postal automation consumed nearly all of SDPA's R&D budget, effectively blocking out other potential research and development. As Shahrom explained it, "I am lucky to have a small business so I can do a lot of things, as long as I make money. By the nature of the business they put me in, you have to be entrepreneurial. We don't have one big customer like the post office. We have to come up with ideas."

An Idea a Day and Other Entrepreneurship Enablers

The source of many ideas for diversification that Shahrom and others pursued came out of a group of senior managers that met on a regular basis to brainstorm possible business concepts. In addition to Shahrom, the group included Ben Bruce and John Mampe, whom Shahrom called "a true ideas man." The group had two signature maxims, "an idea a day" and "a poor man's solution," which governed the frequency and the preferred design-to-cost approach to his thinking. Ben Bruce described the way the group worked: "We continually try to keep an eye on what is out there and think about how we could adapt our technology to meet new requirements. We sit around the room and talk and someone comes up with one idea and, in the course of talking and thinking, you come up with 20 other ideas that are wrapped around that first idea. That is where the entrepreneurship really starts cooking."

According to Bruce, the group and the respective businesses they managed, extracted from those brainstorming sessions the more feasible ideas that could be implemented. As Bruce described, "We try to keep three or four or five balls in the air all the time. When looking at sales—5-year forecast—it is not necessary to have all balls come through. If one or two come through, then we are in good shape."

Shahrom had an approach and a perspective that facilitated the implementation of viable ideas. Having worked for the company since 1986, he had helped develop and knew intimately most of the technology that SDPA had, and he viewed all of it both in terms of the big picture and as part of a continuum. "I always have in the back of my mind the idea of using the building blocks of technology we have here, and I also have an idea of a migration path for our products. So, every time an opportunity comes up, I look where we could go and I push for having a part of the technology built. I can't start out saying 'I need $4 million to do this next version.' I could not get the money for that, but I can do building blocks of technology under different projects."

The Million Dollar Idea

One of the balls that Shahrom had in the air in early 2002 was an idea for a license plate reader (LPR) system. LPR systems had been in use in the United States for more than 20 years, primarily to monitor traffic and in parking lots. In its most basic form, the system captured an image of a motor vehicle license plate using a video camera. Advances in digital technology and software enabled significant advances in how that image could be used. It could be converted to digital form and automatically compiled into or checked against a database. Depending on the specific application, the results could be transmitted to police or traffic officers to signal them to action (for example, in the case of an outstanding warrant), a fee could be billed to an account (for parking or traffic violations), or the data could be logged into the database as part of a study (traffic flow or trip surveys). Current LPR systems generally required a camera, an illumination source, a vehicle-sensing device, an image processor, and a computer. Although LPR systems have been in existence for a long time, the "ideas group" at Siemens Dematic believed that their extensive experience and expertise in optical character recognition could provide technology advantages for LPR. In addition, their idea was to focus on an application that current industry participants were not actively pursuing—mobile units mounted in police cruisers.

Ben Bruce worked a second part-time job as a sergeant with the police department of Dalworthington Gardens, Texas, a small enclave within the Dallas–Fort Worth greater metropolitan area.

The job gave him an insider's perspective on the value of an LPR system that could be mounted in a police car and used to read and recognize license plates. A key issue many police departments faced was that of determining appropriate pursuit policy—when to pursue a motor vehicle that refused to stop or that appeared intent on avoiding police confrontation. While law enforcement argued for trying to apprehend people who were breaking the law, instances of innocent bystanders killed in the course of police chases led some communities to prescribe certain circumstances under which cars should not be pursued. As Bruce described, "We are under tremendous pressure not to pursue. But, people don't tend to flee just to avoid a traffic ticket. They usually have a good reason for not wanting to be caught. The thing that you want the most is to be able to get close enough to get a good, accurate read of the license plate."

When police officers chase a car, they have to be attentive to numerous tasks simultaneously: maintaining radio contact with the dispatcher to record the progress of the chase; observing street signs and other location identifiers; watching out for other cars and pedestrians—all while also trying to read a license plate that may be darting in and out of sight. A system that included a roof-mounted video camera that could read the license plate image at 200 yards and transmit it to a central police database could help determine the appropriateness of a pursuit, while reducing the level of danger to the officer engaged in the chase.

Although the ideas group thought the concept was technically feasible and would be welcomed by law enforcement officials, other more pressing priorities prevented them from actively moving forward on it. In mid-2002, it hadn't yet "percolated to the top," according to Bruce. But in June of that year, Shahrom Kiani started the first week of a three-module Siemens executive education program called S3, which included group work on a "business impact project (BIP)" between the modules. He asked Bruce about using the LPR idea, and Bruce agreed.

A Little Knowledge and a Great Team

According to Shahrom, the S3 program enabled him to push along the license plate reader idea much faster than would otherwise have been possible, due to lack of time and resources available in his commercial mail division.

Refining and Pushing the LPR Market Concept

A key aspect of the course project was an analysis of the competitive landscape—which companies were active in which areas of the market. The work uncovered many players in the license plate reader field, some of whom had been around for more than 20 years. Shahrom recalls the value of his business colleague's analysis: "Initially, my approach was 'I have an OCR (optical character reader), I can read a license plate'—but there are a lot of products out there that can do that. That was not really unique. So, you have to adapt as you go. Having the competitive analysis helped us see what was out there and what niches were not covered."

All the established competitors offered LPR systems that were used in stationary applications, such as traffic flow surveys, parking lot management, or traffic speed monitoring. At one point, Shahrom made a presentation to security managers at the Dallas–Fort Worth airport, describing the potential applications of an advanced LPR system with OCR capabilities. Although police officials were excited about the technology, competition in that type of market was already intense. Encouraged by Ben Bruce's enthusiasm for using LPR to assist police in deciding when to engage in pursuits of autos, Shahrom recruited a colleague in Arlington to help research the potential of that opportunity. She created a survey targeted at police officers to understand what they would want in a LPR system, and she conducted a series of one-on-one interviews with police departments.

The use of mobile LPR in police vehicles appeared to be a largely virgin market, which at the high end included the approximately 200,000 marked and unmarked police cruisers in the United States. Shahrom decided to concentrate on the seven or eight major cities in Texas as the initial target market, representing about 28 percent of the entire state and accounting for 5,000 to 8,000 vehicles. Research indicated that the LPR units had to be priced under $10,000 per car, forcing Shahrom to focus on cost reduction and think about using commodity components wherever possible: "It is really a mass market, so the key is reduction of the costs. We needed to look at consumer-like electronics to come up with a solution that met their price point."

Shahrom involved several of the team members to make a presentation to the CEO of SDPA, Heribert Stumpf, who praised the quality of the work and showed his enthusiastic support by pledging to commit $250,000 for further R&D. As Shahrom related, "That was a big success—to get the funding. He said that he wished a lot of other projects would be run like this. Heribert was very impressed. He could have easily said this is not a core competency of mail processing and asked us what the hell we thought we were doing. But he didn't."

Keeping the Idea Alive

In spite of the progress that Shahrom and the team made, the LPR project ran out of steam in mid-2003. With the conclusion of the S3 program and the formal presentation of the LPR project, the team disbanded. Shahrom himself was soon overtaken by the demands of running his commercial mail business, where sales of new equipment had stalled. As the fiscal year crunch approached, he focused his group's resources on developing and selling upgrades to the installed base.

But, even though his own time and his unit's resources were tied up in the grind of daily work, Shahrom refused to let the LPR concept die. "I didn't have any resources to dedicate to this, but it was too big an opportunity to let go. So with one of my key engineers, we started to reevaluate what we could do. One of our patent searches found that Siemens corporate R&D in New Jersey had some patents on solutions for tracking vehicles, specifically systems to check tunnels and monitor congestion in Europe. So, we decided to see what they had. The key for me was not to have the genius here develop this product but to have a product wherever we could get the technology in Siemens and bring it to the market."

Shahrom negotiated with the R&D center for almost 6 months, eventually signing a contract in March 2004. During the negotiation period, he reshaped and simplified the project to bring the R&D price down from $1 million to $225,000 and to focus on a workable product that he could bring to market as quickly as possible.

Rather than attempt to develop the entire LPR system, he decided to focus first on the digital photo capture of the license plate. The most difficult aspect of the system was the viability of mounting on cars cameras that could work accurately under all lighting and weather conditions. Siemens R&D proposed mounting two cameras on a car connected to a touch screen viewer on the dashboard. One camera provided a wide area scan, which an operator could survey and touch to indicate the part that required enlargement, signaling the second camera to zoom in on the indicated area. In the initial phase, police officers would obtain a visual image of the license plate and radio the information in to headquarters. Optical character recognition could be incorporated into later phases of the system.

Market reaction to a prototype model was "extremely positive" according to Shahrom. "They loved it. They said, 'Wow, when can we have it?'"

Confident about the market demand for his product, Shahrom eagerly awaited the results of corporate R&D's work. He reflected on the challenges and opportunities in trying to bring the LPR project to fruition: "Our company, over the past 20 years, has tried and failed to move beyond the USPS as our sole customer. I am confident we will change that trend. I am lucky that I am responsible for P&L in commercial mail, because it is up to me how I do that. I am not micromanaged. But, once I start growing and become bigger, then I will have more constraints. That is why I think you need to keep entrepreneurs out of the limelight—under the threshold. In order to succeed, you have to have small innovative groups and be under the radar. If it becomes big, then you have to go through all these processes of approval, and it becomes overburdening. So, one of the things that you learn is the thresholds, and you try to be under those thresholds, and that way you can get a lot done—building little blocks one at a time.

"You also have to have support—people who believe in you and trust you to do things. Expertise and the right skill set by itself is not enough. An opportunity has to present itself, and you have to be able to respond to that challenge. I have been lucky to have people to give me the opportunity and to foster my independent streak. Also, I go around the rules whenever I can."

Summary

Shahrom's case is particularly insightful because of the size and complexity of Siemens. It is a very complex company and, although they are trying to train many of their managers to be more entrepreneurial, the company is still not always a fertile garden for this type of leadership. 3M and IDG both had reasonably good gardens so, while John Kilcullen's and Bill Isaacson's jobs there were not necessarily cakewalks, these companies already had an entrepreneurial bent and some history of supporting entrepreneurship over the years. Siemens was trying to build these things, and for Shahrom Kiani to have gotten as far as he did is a compliment to his perseverance, passion, and cleverness at growing things in a garden that still has some weeds.

Explorers are as close to start-up entrepreneurs as you will find among corporate entrepreneurs. They identify, shape, and capture new business opportunities, but within an existing organization. They have many constraints not faced by their start-up counterparts, but they have many assets as well: good people, an infrastructure, capital, a brand, support systems and processes. Their biggest challenges are to get the organization interested in their idea and then to marshal the resources necessary to turn their idea into an opportunity. Often, they must successfully run their own organization's bureaucratic gauntlet in order to succeed. Therefore, they must not only have the political savvy necessary to succeed, they must have some entrepreneurial DNA. The three explorers profiled in this chapter have clearly demonstrated these qualities and give us hope that the words *corporate* and *entrepreneurship* are not always oxymoronic.

Chapter Six

Miners: Operationally Focused Entrepreneurial Leaders

Some entrepreneurial leaders are less close to the marketplace than explorers. They demonstrate the same kind of leadership, but they typically focus their entrepreneurial energy on internal operations. They reconfigure current assets in ways that create new value propositions for the company's customers, thus resulting in growth of the business. Operationally focused entrepreneurship, or "mining," as I call it (Fig. 6.1), can result in cost cutting as well, since the operationally focused entrepreneurial leader often looks for less expensive ways to run the business while creating better value for the customer. But cost cutting is only entrepreneurial if it creates organic growth and economic value.

Miners face inward. They look for ways to identify and excavate the unearthed gold that often lies in the company's own operations and processes. I would describe Craig Wynett, the former head of Corporate New Ventures at P&G (whom I mentioned in Chapter 4), as a good example of a miner. He believed that P&G could find within the company a great deal

Focusing Entrepreneurial Energy

	Internal	External
Activist	**Miners** **(Value Chain)**	Explorers (Market)
Catalyst	Accelerators (Unit)	Integrators (Enterprise)

FIGURE 6.1   Miners—Operationally focused entrepreneurial leaders.

of the "gold" that often falls between or outside the purview of P&G's brands. The mission of his team was to find and unearth this gold, connect it to emerging market trends, and create new businesses for the company.

Another miner I know worked for a large oil producer. He led an internally focused team through an assessment of the company's value chain from the pumping of raw crude through to its resting place in the tanks of motorized machinery. He was also mining for gold: looking for something in his company's processes that could be leveraged into new value creation. He and his team discovered that one of the waste products of oil had properties that, when slightly modified, could actually help clean up oil spills. After this discovery, they created a successful new business using this throw-away product.

This very same approach led a large paper and pulp manufacturer to look at their value chain and realize that one of their throw-away products could be reused and resold, thus creating a brand-new business for the organization. This company looked at their value chain from start to finish and discovered that contractors using their wood often paid waste companies good money to come and haul away the wood scraps left after the house was built. In stepped this company, which offered to pick up the scrap wood for free if the builder simply separated it from the other debris. They then brought the wood back to their plants, turned it into particle board, and resold it to builders and home-supply companies. This possibility had existed for a long time, but someone needed to take the time and entrepreneurial energy to focus in on the opportunity, which was quite literally at their feet.

Operationally focused miners enjoy the shell game. They like to creatively move assets around or out of the organization. They do not see the ownership or increase of assets necessarily as a good thing. They actually like doing more with less to prove their cleverness. Most managers complain about edicts from above to "do more with less," but miners enjoy the creative challenge. They like to prove that they can outsmart even the most draconian cost-cutting mandates.

In many ways, miners think like owners, even though the business is not theirs. In Chapter 3, I told you about the German word *Unternehmer*, which means both "entrepreneur" and "undertaker." But, most Germans would probably associate the word with "shopkeeper." Shopkeepers were traditionally start-up entrepreneurs responsible for running their own little shops, and shop owners do not last long if they don't understand how to squeeze a penny. Pennies add up and allow for future investment. People who think like owners are always thinking about how to grow their business without becoming overburdened with unnecessary assets, overhead, or people, because they know that, if bad times hit and cash flow dwindles, that's the end of the game. Miners think like shopkeepers. They worry about leveraging assets and often find new business opportunities by creatively rearranging what they already have.

Many good examples exist of entrepreneurial leaders rearranging their organization's value chain to create significant new value—while along the way also changing the rules of competitive engagement in ways that give the innovative company significant competitive advantage. IKEA's founder, Ingvar Kampsraad, is one such example.

IKEA: Mining for Gold by Rearranging the Value Chain

Many industries can be described as having an "industry code," or rules by which most of the players abide. New entrants look at old entrants and tend to follow the industry code, differentiating themselves primarily by product, placement, service, or location. But they generally accept the industry code. Figure 6.2 represents a common code in the furniture industry.

Most new entrants to the furniture industry would probably see the industry value chain or code as well represented by the diagram in Figure 6.2. First, designers design the furniture, and then the parts are made and assembled in the company's factories. Finished furniture is then sent to warehouses, where it is stored. Sample items are displayed in the retail shops, where customers come to the store to pick out furniture. When they find something they like, either on the showroom floor or through the store catalog, they order it. The furniture is then shipped to the customer and placed in their home or office. This is the typical furniture industry code.

Or, at least it was until Ingvar Kampsraad came along and started a business called IKEA. Most of us are now familiar with the Scandinavian furniture company (even if we can never quite get the pronunciation right). IKEA was founded by actually disaggregating and rearranging this value chain to create a new pattern, or code, that resulted in a strategic and defensible competitive advantage. Figure 6.3 shows IKEA's value chain and how it differs significantly from the norm in the industry.

The Furniture Industry Business System

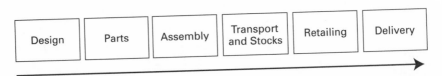

FIGURE 6.2   The common code of the furniture industry. Source: Phil Dover, Marketing Professor, Babson College.

IKEA Redefined the External Value Chain

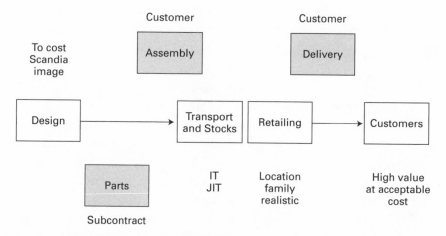

FIGURE 6.3   The IKEA system breaks the industry code. Source: Phil Dover, Marketing Professor, Babson College.

IKEA still owns the furniture design, but it has outsourced the manufacture of parts. The "parts" (the disassembled pieces of the furniture) are then shipped in boxes to IKEA's retail stores, which are also warehouses, where they await the customer. Customers visit the store, make their selections, and then, basically, deliver the furniture to themselves. IKEA will even rent them a truck to do so (or will deliver, for a fee). IKEA stores are usually found along large highways or freeways, so that customers have easy access with their vehicles.

This rearrangement of the value chain gives IKEA several advantages. First, by outsourcing the manufacturing of the parts, it does not have to carry the multiple fixed costs of having manufacturing facilities. It also "outsources" the assembly and delivery to the customer. This creates tremendous cost savings for IKEA, which in turn allows it to offer good furniture at a great value. It also allows it to appeal to a different segment of the market, one that wants good value for the money and enjoys putting the furniture together. It especially appeals to men. They like to snap the furniture together, then call the family into the room and brag, "Look what I just built!" "Built" might be an exaggeration, but it works for IKEA and appeals to the male ego.

Cheaper and Better

Miners like to play with value chains, both internal and external. Their talent seems to be in the ability to find innovative ways to rearrange and use assets. They aren't afraid to spend money to make money but, if they can make money by using other people's money, they prefer it. If they can pass on overhead to others and throw out unnecessary and costly steps to an operational process, they will do it in a heartbeat. Over the years, many large companies accrue unnecessary processes and assets. Very few people challenge their existence or the need for the people who shepherd these processes. Miners always have their antennae up to see ways of running the business in a more clever, less asset-intensive way.

The end game for the entrepreneurial leader is always the creation of value—for the customer, the owners, and ultimately for society. As I said earlier, luck happens when opportunity and experience collide in the presence of an open mind. This is particularly true for miners. Organizations are complex entities. Even mapping a company's value chain can take several days and can be fraught with debate as to how things actually work. Miners must know the details of internal processes so that they can see opportunities to make things work differently. Meddling with a company's value chain or rearranging its assets into new patterns can be risky, especially for the uninitiated. It requires a great deal of cross-organizational hand-holding and soothing, since a change in one part of the chain can affect everybody else up and down the line.

This intimate knowledge of how the business actually runs is invaluable for miners. They know, because they are there. (We will see an example of this in a later story.) Not only do miners know how the business works, they are compelled to make it work better. This is why miners are considered to be activists and why their focus is generally inside the organization.

The remainder of this chapter will be devoted to an in-depth examination of the experience of John Kelley,[1] a middle manager at a large insurance and financial services organization who clearly fits the miner category. Not only was he able to reduce costs by reorganizing in a very innovative way, he reduced the company's asset base while simultaneously affecting customers in a way that grew the business. His focus was internal, but the overall effect had a significant external impact on the marketplace as well. His story will not only enlighten you about how this sort of magic can be done, it will also point out the dangers of being entrepreneurial too quickly, thereby causing peer jealousy and political backstabbing. It is a story with many dimensions and many lessons.

John's story also demonstrates that rearranging assets never happens in a vacuum. Almost always, this rearrangement affects others and often results in unpredictable organizational change. Sometimes, these changes are minor; sometimes, they are profound. As you will see from John's story, he set into motion a much larger organizational change than either he or his senior managers had foreseen. John's story perfectly illustrates the following statement from Machiavelli's *The Prince (1513)*: "The innovator makes enemies of all those who prospered under the old order, and only lukewarm support is forthcoming from those who would prosper under the new."

John's story is a compelling one. He was asked to do the impossible and succeeded. I have included a fair bit of information about Kelley's organization and the nature of the industry, because miners are usually not very good at spotting opportunities until they have significant experience in both the industry and their organization. So, to really understand John's entrepreneurial leadership talents, you also must understand the milieu in which he operated. The story then moves on to show how John grappled with senior management's edicts and his employees' wariness and distrust. This story has a surprise ending…it is a story of change, but the change was a consequence of entrepreneurial action, not an antecedent. When you rearrange existing assets, and in so doing discover an innovative new service model, this discovery can cause a ripple effect through the rest of the organization.

Miner Profile: John Kelley, VariTrust

John Kelley is a fun, aggressive, driven guy who is not afraid to share the limelight with others. This often is a trait of the entrepreneurial leaders with whom we have worked. He challenged, cajoled, and confronted his people to think out of the box and try some pretty daring things inside a conservative financial services company. John was a good manager and leader, but his entrepreneurial skills did not blossom fully until he was put under intensive cost-cutting pressure. Then, his ability to think and act entrepreneurially came to the fore. He focused his entrepreneurial energy inside, on the operational aspects of the business, and he put himself in the position to be the activist driver of a very innovative strategy. Over and over, I have seen the application of the right amount of pressure and the absence of obvious solutions bring out the entrepreneurial genetics of an individual and lead them to do some very creative things.

The VariTrust Annuity Service Center

It was a hot August day in 1995 and, as the heat started to rise off the pavement of downtown Boston, John Kelley gazed out the window of his corner office on the 12th floor of 64 Water Street and pondered the challenge before him. The gauntlet had been thrown, and he picked it up.

He had eagerly accepted the new post as director of the VariTrust Annuity Service Center (VTASC), a dramatic shift from his tenure as a product manager in the VariTrust marketing department. His predecessor, Roger Edgarton, had resigned unexpectedly on August 1st and, a week later, John took charge of the troubled operation. Years of management by Cambridge Financial Services Center, Inc. (CFS), a wholly owned but independently operated VariTrust subsidiary, had left the Annuity Center with a bloated organizational structure, severe cost issues, and performance problems. Moreover, when VariTrust assumed direct control of the center in 1993, its efforts to align compensation with that of other VariTrust units had negatively affected staff morale. Although that transition had started 2 years before, in 1993, the loss of benefits and self-esteem still bothered many employees.

Cost Reduction Mandate

Senior management at corporate headquarters in Montreal had seen enough and, 2 months before John Kelley took charge, they handed his predecessor a mandate to cut costs 9 percent per year for 3 consecutive years—effectively a 25 percent cost reduction. In spite of the strategic necessity of maintaining the servicing of annuity contracts under its direct control, VariTrust executives were very concerned about the high cost of operating the Service Center.

The best indicator of the cost problem was the cost per contract (CPC), a key measure of efficiency in the industry, which was calculated by dividing the total number of annuity contracts by the total expenses incurred in operating the center. Currently, the CPC was about $90, nearly twice the price to outsource the work and up to three times the cost factor built into the pricing structure of many of the annuity products. In addition, this cost structure was about double that of VariTrust's closest competitors.

John's challenges were immense. He was to address the cost issue while maintaining and improving high-quality customer service, in an environment of low employee morale and dissension. Achieving these goals would require innovation and a dedicated and energized workforce. Cutting costs in the face of a workforce already demoralized by the transition 2 years earlier would require, in John's own words, "either suicide, homicide, or something very creative."

Structure, Processes, and Work Flow

The Annuity Center was a complex, process-driven operation that had a direct impact on both its intermediary sales force and the end customer seeking diversified retirement products. The "customers" of VTASC included the clients (annuity contract holders), retail broker/dealers, the CFS Wholesale department, the VariTrust Product Development and Marketing departments, and pension trustees. The Center had 13 functional areas some of which, such as Licensing, operated fairly independently, while others, such as Accounting Control, performed functions closely interrelated with other departments. Although some functions shared managers, each area had at least one and sometimes several separate management hierarchies. To allow for promotions, VariTrust had often allowed reporting relationships in which a boss only had one or two direct reports, thus adding more hierarchy to the already hierarchical structure.

Servicing variable annuity products, by phone and written communications, included the following processes:

- Establishing new client accounts
- Receiving and depositing investment funds
- Handling requests for account maintenance (e.g., address changes), exchanges (moving money from one type of investment fund to another), and liquidations (disbursement of funds to clients)
- Licensing brokers to sell products

Employees were involved directly in performing tasks to accomplish these processes or indirectly in support functions. Other than licensing, the completion of these processes required the input of many different functional areas. Figure 6.4, for example, illustrates that the process of establishing a new client account (new business) involved eight different functions, each with its own separate management hierarchy: (1) In consultation with a broker, a client filled out an application and sent it along with a check to the Service Center. (2) The Mail Room distributed the materials to (3) Underwriting, which reviewed the information on the application and checked with (4) Licensing to make sure the broker was properly licensed. If there were any questions or problems on the application, it was sent to (5) Administration for research. Fully completed application forms were then sent on to (6) Data Processing for inputting into the computer system, and (7) Underwriting deposited the funds. (8) Accounting Control reconciled all financial transactions to make sure that funds were properly invested and that an agreement existed between bank and internal accounts.

Management Change

It was no accident that John was on the short list of successors to Edgarton at VTASC. Ron Gillen, Kelley's boss, had noted some of Kelley's talents: "I'd seen a tremendous growth in John's self-confidence and abilities. He had a real grasp of the marketplace and

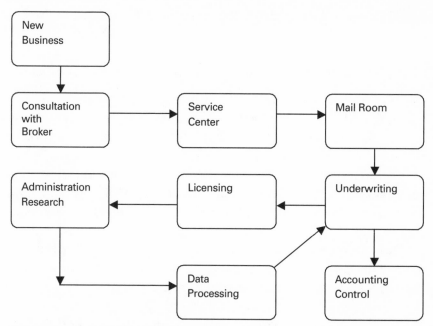

FIGURE 6.4   VTASC work flow diagram.

an ability to deal with the big hitters in the variable annuity business. He was a green eyeshades guy in the early '80s—but he went through an incredible transformation in his role as a product manager. When I offered him the job, he was so pumped up about being the head of VTASC, it was unbelievable."

Gillen also elaborated on John's personality: "He was a dynamo, a very forceful driver for change, with an incredibly quick sense of humor. Kelley is very up-front."

A Canadian by birth, John Kelley graduated from McGill University in 1986, and started his career as an accountant at VariTrust in the Montreal corporate headquarters that year. Early in his career, he was selected to be part of the team to open the U.S. headquarters in Woburn, Massachusetts. After completing an MBA program in 1990, John assumed the newly created position of product manager, a function that historically had received little attention in the insurance industry. With the successful introduction and management of new products, he elevated the importance of the job. John had garnered some notice by designing and bringing to market several innovative new variable annuity products, but no one anticipated that he would be able to utilize his entrepreneurial talent in resurrecting a sick organization.

Kelley's First Moves (Engaging the Entrepreneurial Mindset)

Many managers in John Kelley's situation would have taken out the knife and immediately slashed away at costs, starting with the easiest target, the work force. But, VTASC was already working overtime with fewer people than before and, in some cases, it had a year-long backlog of licensing agreements that had not been completed. Simply cutting people would not be the solution. John had to take a holistic approach and completely redesign his organization from the ground up if he was going to be successful. John and his team would have to be entrepreneurial. They would do more with less, and do it better. But, this would require a major rearrangement of available resources and some pretty big risk taking within a very conservative, risk-averse environment. John and his newly constituted design team (his direct reports and a cadre of VTASC employees) set themselves the following goals to guide them on their challenging and previously uncharted journey:

- **Service**—Maintain or improve the delivery of superior customer service to help grow the business.
- **People**—Develop people's skills and abilities and reward them for performance.
- **Market**—Respond flexibly to new products and bring them and related services to the market quickly.
- **Costs**—Drive down cost per contract and improve the profitability of each product.

The clock had started ticking, and the design team was itching to get started on transforming VTASC. John believed that this cross-functional and cross-level design team would be the best vehicle for promoting change within the organization.

An Entrepreneurial Flair

John took charge of the design team with a style that contrasted sharply to that of his predecessor, who had been a passive listener and a hoarder of information. John became an active participant who kept few secrets. While he pushed the committee hard, he did so more in the role of Socratic questioner than autocratic chief, always prodding the group to think creatively about how they might rearrange their current assets in a new, less-costly, and more-efficient organization. Starting in mid-August, shortly after his arrival, the pace of activity accelerated sharply: According to Patty Healey, one of John's direct reports, "Things really started to roll when John came in." Working with some outside consultants, John and his team spent long hours exploring various organizational designs and evaluating them against the key objectives. From analyzing the value chain and its associated assets and processes, the group really began to see the organization at a granular level. They drew numerous diagrams of the work flow and began to examine ways of rearranging what was there. The goal was to improve service while at the same time reducing costs. But, unhappy employees do not deliver good service, so the group had to figure out a way to do all this while maintaining and improving department morale—not an easy task.

Design committee members were mixed in their assessment of their work. One design team member considered the workings of the committee to be merely a smoke screen to give the new structure an "in-house" flavor, to lessen resistance to its adoption. "He should have saved time and just given an edict."

Another team member described the development process as something of a voyage of mutual discovery, although with John clearly at the helm, handling the rudder and trimming the sails: "He'd slowly feed you what he wanted you to discover. He'd refer you to articles and build support. 'Let me tell you about this team' kind of thing."

Gillen had yet another perspective: "John took a giant step in terms of working with current assets, and moving towards a self-directed team concept. Although the concept had been around a while, John took it to a new level due to his focus on creatively managing and rearranging assets as well. It was big-time change, but ...we wanted to have big-time change, so I was happy to support it. I thought it was due. My boss was also supportive, even though it meant committing ourselves to this course far in advance of where the rest of the organization was."

John was confident about the potential benefits that reorganizing into teams and the creative rearrangement of current assets could offer to both the Service Center and the employees themselves, and he had invested substantial energy and personal commitment in the change process. He knew that the directors' enthusiasm for his entrepreneurial ideas ranged from wholehearted endorsement to skeptical acceptance to grudging participation. He would need their full support to gain the momentum necessary to get the transition back on course.

Creative Destruction

The design team's plan was revolutionary. The 13 functional areas would be dismantled and replaced by four self-directed work teams. An immediate consequence of adopting the team approach would be the outright abolition of three layers of middle management, along with their titles: assistant supervisor, supervisor, and assistant manager. All positions below that of manager essentially were collapsed into the team units. The managers of the 13 functional areas would be absorbed into the teams, and new team leaders would be chosen based on team leadership skills, not tenure or title. None would be fired or have their current salaries reduced. In addition, team members would be cross-trained in each other's jobs so that each self-directed team would have all the skills and knowledge necessary to serve their assigned block of customers. John and his team also planned to divert some of their budget to buy a relatively inexpensive IT system that would allow team members to keep track of each other's actions and contacts with customers, so that there could be seamless customer service. Theoretically, a customer might talk to one team member in the morning and another in the afternoon and find that their issue had been moved along as though the same person had handled the issue throughout the entire day.

The introduction of the team concept was combined with a partial realignment of processes and a reorganization of departments. While some of the existing functional areas, such as Licensing and Systems, remained virtually unchanged, others were disbanded and new departments formed to combine

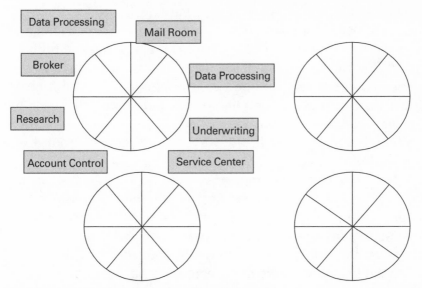

FIGURE 6.5   Example of one team structure redesign.

process-related functions. Figure 6.5 shows a proposed VTASC redesign into four self-directed work teams cross-trained in each other's functions. Each team would be responsible for a specific customer group.

The Announcement

In April, 1996, 8 months after the design team had started its work, the plan was finished. At a company-wide meeting at the Sheraton Plaza Hotel in Boston, John Kelley outlined the sea changes to come. He had selected a nice location away from the Service Center offices to ensure everyone's full attention, to lend weight to the import of his message, and to add a touch of fanfare to what he was convinced could be a tremendously positive change for the center. The committee met with 15 VTASC managers just before the general meeting to give them a preview of the announcement. John then addressed the assembled employees: "Good morning! I know that these last few months have been anxious ones for all of you. The rumor mills and grapevines have really been working overtime. That's understandable and probably unavoidable. After this morning, however, that will all be behind us, and we can get started on what I know is going to be an exciting, challenging, and rewarding future for all of us. I would like you to sit back, relax, and open your minds to the message I am going to give you. It may seem confusing and probably even a bit frightening, but it is a message that is absolutely full of hope and opportunity. When I say 'frightening,' I mean frightening in the sense of change: change in our structure, change in our values, change in the way we manage our work and our people, and, above all, change in the way we deliver our product and service."

The Annuity Center employees were quiet as John expanded on the "New Annuity Service Center." His direct, upbeat speech addressed the need for change and described the elements of a team-oriented organization and the magnitude of the change on the structure, management, and values of the center. John emphasized the benefits both to the center, in its ability to provide cost-efficient service, and to the employees, in the increased responsibilities and opportunities that team empowerment could offer. In place of creating narrow functional specialists, the team approach would encourage, and demand, knowledgeable generalists. He presented several scenarios of empowered teams: better trained, more responsive, and ready to serve customers and each other. Sensitive to the general anxiety wrought by change and to the specific fear of job loss, especially in the recession-wracked New England economy, John declared that the change would not translate into layoffs. "There is a place for each of you in the new Annuity Service Center that we are going to build together, starting now." Emphasizing the collective nature of the enterprise (*we, us, together*)—and the immediacy of the change—(*starting today, now*) John promoted the idea that the team spirit of the concept had already begun.

As part of the announcement, slides detailed the new organizational structure, identified the team managers and personnel, laid out changes in asset control, and outlined the basic workflow modifications. Absent from the charts was any reference to the three middle layers of management that had been eliminated. As of that moment, the titles ceased to exist, and a quarter of the people in the room were stripped of something in a matter of minutes that they'd worked hard for many years to earn.

Initial Reaction

The initial reaction to the announcement was one of uncertainty: What would the change to teams mean specifically for individual jobs and people? Secondary reactions ranged from optimism about the potential opportunities to belittlement of the latest management fad, to fears about job security and disappointment over the loss of titles and positions. Although employees knew instinctively that some kind of change was necessary to deal with the overabundance of managers "stepping on each other's toes," no general perception existed of the need for such a total reorganization of the facility. The comparative cost data were not widely published, and few employees were aware that expenses were very far out of line with the pricing structure of the annuity contracts or with the external market. What was most intriguing was John's challenge to them to think creatively about doing what they had done before in revolutionary ways that could translate into both reduced costs and increased growth.

Under Roger Edgarton, the goal had always been "service at any cost," and the idea of competitive cost control while improving performance had never been introduced, much less internalized into the thinking and actions of the employees.

Creative Reconstruction

In September of 1998, over 2 years after the Sheraton meeting, John Kelley was feeling both satisfied and a little arrogant. He and members of his organization were now being benchmarked by other organizations, not only for their excellence in customer service but also for their creativity in asset management. John was frequently courted by other organizations and associations as a keynote speaker at industry conventions and trade shows. But, true to form, he told his suitors to call one of the self-directed team members to speak in his stead. He would often say, "You should talk to so and so, one of my team members. They know a lot more about what works than I do. They would be your best bet for a keynote speaker. I was just a catalyst for what happened. They are the experts."

John also walked the talk. By virtue of his position at VariTrust, he had a very nice mahogany-appointed office. He was feted at the executive dining room, where managers were served from an extensive menu, and he had a special reserved parking spot in front of the VTASC building. But, because John believed so strongly in the power of teamwork and flat organizational structures as essential elements for developing and sustaining an environment of innovation and joint problems solving, he gave up his mahogany office as a team meeting room and moved his office into the cubicles where the teams worked. He started eating in the employee cafeteria, and he gave up his parking spot for the employee of the month, as voted by the teams.

Getting from There to Here

While many small efforts helped the transition, all parties agreed that the principal ingredient for success was simply innovative thinking, detailed analysis, perseverance, and persistence. Most in the organization credited John's tenacity with keeping it going. As one of the team member says, "Without his determination and obsession with possibilities for improvements, enabled by both the team concept and some better IT, the difficulties would have overwhelmed us, the effort would have lost momentum, and we would have gone back to some version of where we'd been."

John himself described his role in keeping the process moving forward:

"We just kept plugging away, addressing the problems, talking to people. I have enormous persistence. I am an extremely stubborn person and I am, perhaps to many people's chagrin, the ultimate optimist. Even in very bad situations, I don't look at them as bad situations; I look at them positively and say it could be worse and, if we use our collective brain power, we can come out of this better off than before. That can be very frustrating to people who are really feeling that this is the pits, because they can't see how it can possibly get any worse and yet here is this smiling idiot saying, 'Isn't this wonderful; aren't we doing great and headed in the right direction?'... It was absolutely mandatory that I say to my people, 'Hey, we are going to do this.' We could all see through it, but I think I could see a lot farther ahead than they could, because they were much more into the nuts-and-bolts of the day-to-day operations."

That environment and the entire culture of the Annuity Service Center changed dramatically from the days when Roger Edgarton had ruled. He had depended on a few people ("Roger's boys") to accomplish his mission and had extended his trust only to that small group. According to Gillen, John relied on everyone at every level. His office door was left wide open, and he spent most of his 2 days a week at VTASC walking around and talking to people. Employees did not cringe when John came into sight. Open communication replaced the "need to know" basis on which information had been divulged in the past.

Watch Your Back!

In spite of the demonstrable success of the Annuity Service Center in reducing costs, improving customer service, and enhancing employee morale, the larger VariTrust organization had been slow to jump on the innovation bandwagon. According to Kelley, front-line staff in other divisions had shown tremendous interest in the concept, but management had resisted its implementation. The traditional hierarchies, pervasive through the corporation, formed a massive inertial block. Although several areas in the company talked about the progress they were making with teams, their approach had focused principally on superficial changes below the management level. Line employees had been arranged into teams, but unlike VTASC, the hierarchical structure—assistant supervisors through managers—and the corresponding allocation of responsibility and authority had been left largely intact.

John described the problem:

> "Unfortunately, the whole thing is stuck with the label of 'reengineering,' which is equated with layoffs and downsizing. That is one by-product, but the real product is delighted customers, excellent operating performance (CPC now $54), and people in the organization who are committed to the company, to what they're doing, and will walk through walls to get things done. In fact, our increased speed of performance has significantly grown the annuity business despite the fact that the products are basically unchanged."

And John was looking for further improvements in performance down the road:

> "We don't look at it in terms of the number of people. What matters is unit cost and handling increasing amounts of business with the same size staff. In fact, there is no reason why eventually we couldn't do annuity administration for external customers. If we can get our costs down to $30 per contract, we can charge $40 or $50 and still save other firms probably half what they pay to do the work themselves. In fact, maybe it's wrong to think about reducing the amount of space we lease. Maybe in a few years, we will have to expand our offices to handle all the outside work flowing in."

The "Rewards" for Shaking Up the Organization

Still, some wondered whether VTASC and VariTrust had taken on more changes than the company could assimilate effectively. On a late Thursday afternoon, July 13, 1999, 4 years after Kelley had made his daunting journey into the realm of entrepreneurial leadership, he walked into the plush office of his new boss, Jacob Peters, concerned about the reason for the impromptu summons. Due to John's success at VTASC, he was given In-Force Services, a new area of responsibility in which the company thought his skills in innovation could play a critical role. His recent meetings with Peters had become increasingly contentious, with the senior VariTrust executive seeming to question John's judgment and motives. Although the Annuity Service Center was operating smoothly—its team-based approach was delivering on both cost cutting and new business growth due to improved service—the situation at John's other area of responsibility, In-Force Services, in Needham, Massachusetts, was unsettled. Delays in implementing new technology had placed considerable strain on some of the teams and coaches, and John's peers in other departments were increasingly critical of the changes he had wrought, concerned about the potential implications of John's new organizing principles on them personally.

Well aware of the problems and the discomfort he was causing, John was shocked but not entirely surprised by Peters' pronouncement. According to John, Peters said, "John, you are relieved of your duties at Needham. You can remain as head of the Annuity Service Center, or we can look at other opportunities elsewhere in the company. Or, you can leave. Effective immediately you are no longer in charge of Needham, and don't tell anyone, because I want to tell them myself first thing in the morning. So, take 2 weeks off and come back and tell me what you want to do."

At the end of 2 weeks Kelley returned to the office, where he handed in his letter of resignation.

Summary

Now, before you reach for your Kleenex, the story does have a happy ending. John left VariTrust to become the CEO of a small software company, where he did quite well for several years before he was offered a senior VP job at a very large and successful international insurance company. They sought John out because of his entrepreneurial leadership capabilities, and wanted him to shake things up a little bit in their rather staid and conservative culture. He was quite successful there, living and working overseas. I spoke with him recently, and he had just quit the company after several years to become part owner in a private consulting firm helping other organizations become more innovative. John gets bored easily, so once he has brought about some significant value creation, he likes to move on to the next challenge, either inside or outside of his current business.

John Kelley also embodies a lot of what we say about miners. I know him personally, and I can vouch for his obsession to run things better, always with the customer in mind. Even under the pressure of cost cutting, he consistently asks himself, "How can I still improve the customer experience despite this internal challenge?" Even though John's job was internally focused on operations, he had significant opportunities to create value for the company as a whole, beyond the bottom line. John also was the quintessential activist, in that he saw the process through from start to end and was seen as the program's official and emotional driver. He also had to manage a number of cross-organizational relationships to make his novel reorganization scheme come true. His only real flaw was not realizing how frightening his entrepreneurial leadership approach could be to his peers. They could see their nicely structured, coddled world rocked to the core by John's proof that the organization might actually run better and make more money without them, if it were seen through a different, more innovative lens.

John Kelley's story illustrates the systemic impact that the implementation of a mining-type opportunity focus often can bring. In John's case, his reorganization not only helped grow the business, it also put pressure on other areas of the business to change and follow in his footsteps. And, as you may know, change is not always welcome. It sometimes involves the sacrifice of some sacred cows. And sometimes the cows fight back.

Chapter Seven

Accelerators: Unit-Focused Entrepreneurial Leaders

"Accelerators" are generally internally focused and catalytic, and they usually manage a unit, division, or branch of the business (Fig. 7.1). While they themselves are not the lead entrepreneurs on a specific opportunity, they prod, poke, challenge, push, cajole, and sometimes irritate their employees into getting *them* to act in more innovative and entrepreneurial ways. Accelerators want their employees to argue with them and to challenge current ways of doing business. Their goal is to literally accelerate innovation in their particular area or department. They like to "stir the pot" in hopes of stimulating new and different ways to run their part of the organization. They look to their employees for the development of novel ideas, and try to create a culture in which people are rewarded for trying new and different things, not punished for making mistakes in the learning process.

Accelerators are focused on two types of value creation, so they try hard to engage their employees in the process. They focus on *economic* value creation, as do all our entrepreneurial leaders but, more important, they focus on the creation of the *human* values and behaviors that lead to economic value. They

Focusing Entrepreneurial Energy

	Internal	External
Activist	Miners (Value Chain)	Explorers (Market)
Catalyst	**Accelerators** **(Unit)**	Integrators (Enterprise)

FIGURE 7.1   Accelerators are internally focused catalysts for change.

often encourage employees to bend or break the rules if it will grow the business. They encourage their people to learn new skills and try different things—knowing that mistakes always happen in the learning process. Accelerators often shield their people from the bureaucracy, knowing that they themselves are taking a personal risk in the process.

Accelerators view their roles as coaches and catalysts in freeing the creative potential of their employees. They are not afraid to hire people who are smarter than themselves and even perhaps somewhat rebellious, thus allowing for the possibility of quantum leaps in their department or area. Although they are good coaches, they are also very good at getting their employees to accept both responsibility and accountability. They know that getting their people to act in more entrepreneurial ways requires both support and personal accountability.

Because accelerators are often unit heads, they can be found in line or staff positions. They don't focus on specific opportunities, as explorers and miners do. Rather, they focus on a long-term approach to fostering a climate of innovation and entrepreneurial thinking that they believe will provide the seedbed for identifying, developing, and capturing serial opportunities. Accelerators plant the seeds and then add "fertilizer" to hasten the pace of innovation. Accelerators, because they head up their own units, rarely need a great deal of permission to encourage a more entrepreneurial environment, and thus they can do a lot without arousing the suspicion or interference of others.

Accelerators are usually quite adept at outmaneuvering their own organization's cumbersome rules and regulations, and they encourage their people to do the same. They have excellent political connections and are well-versed in knowing what buttons to push or people to schmooze in order to navigate their own organization's maze. They are very aware of their company's financial metrics and how to tie these to their initiatives. Accelerators create a climate within their own units that encourages innovation and entrepreneurial thinking. They expect and demand that their employees see innovation as a job requirement, whether or not it exists as a line item on the performance appraisal form.

Accelerators also insist that work be fun, and recognize that all work and no play not only makes Jack dull but saps his creative juices as well. They tend to encourage a life outside of work and are big fans of education and training, both formal and informal. Employees who work for an accelerator often are asked a thousand questions: "What if ...?" "How about ...?" "Suppose you ...?" and "What would you recommend?"

Accelerators push and prod employees to think of doing things differently even when they themselves don't have the answers. Nor do they hold themselves responsible for having the answers. They are satisfied with stirring the pot, knowing that this type of behavior will eventually lead to the answers. They want suggestions from their people, no matter where in the hierarchy they live. They often do not see themselves nor describe themselves as "entrepreneurial," because they are not actually pursuing a specific opportunity. But entrepreneurial leaders they are, by leading others to act in entrepreneurial ways.

Back in Chapter 2, I introduced you to the entrepreneurial leadership behaviors that Pearce et al. wrote about in their article in the *Journal of Business Venturing*.[1] As you look at these behaviors, you will see that they are really the behaviors of accelerators. At the time the article was written, I had not yet

Corporate Entrepreneurship Behaviors

• Efficiently gets proposed actions through bureaucratic red tape and into practice	• Devotes time to helping others find ways to improve products and services
• Displays an enthusiasm for acquiring skills	• Goes to bat for the good ideas of others
• Quickly changes course of action when results aren't being achieved	• Boldly moves ahead with a promising new approach when others might be more cautious
• Encourages others to take the initiative for their own ideas	• Vividly describes how things could be in the future and what is needed to get there
• Inspires others to think about their work in new and stimulating ways	• Gets people to rally together to meet a challenge
	• Creates an environment where people get excited about making improvements

FIGURE 7.2   Entrepreneurial leadership behaviors match those of accelerators.

developed the entrepreneurial leadership typologies. But, as you can see from the list of behaviors in Figure 7.2, these are closely related to how we see accelerators practice their entrepreneurial orientation.

Work Smart, Not Hard

Accelerators are not "floggers of the troops." In difficult times, the mantra of many organizations is to worker harder, not smarter. Managers expect, and often demand, that their people stay longer in the office, call on more customers, lay off more people, or cut more costs. They believe that sheer effort and force of will can somehow overcome the obstacles in front of them. One of my colleagues likes to quote that the definition of insanity is doing the same thing two or three more times when it didn't work the first time. This approach reminds me of Einstein's definition of insanity. "Insanity is repeating the same behavior and expecting a different outcome."

Accelerators don't like to be called insane, so they try to figure out how to do it differently the next time. They rely on their people for the best ideas on how to work smarter rather than harder. Alfred Weichselbaum of Siemens Medical in California is a good example of an accelerator. As you will remember, I profiled another manager from Siemens earlier, Shahrom Kiani. They were both inspired to act in more entrepreneurial ways through the S3 General Managers program. While both men clearly had some "entrepreneurial genes," the course activated these genes through the entrepreneurial projects that were a large part of the coursework.

I described Shahrom Kiani as an explorer, because he focused his entrepreneurial energy externally, and he was the main driver of the opportunity. Alfred Weichselbaum, on the other hand, chose an internally focused project and was an "accelerator" of innovative thinking within his unit. In his profile, you will also see that he did not create the system that led to innovation, but he is the catalyst who ensures its implementation. His innovativeness does not come from the development of the system but through the political savvy and drive with which he stirs the pot, leading to the innovation's adoption and successful implementation.

Accelerator Profile: Alfred Weichselbaum, Siemens Medical Systems

In March 2004, Alfred Weichselbaum and Alan Kirby met to discuss the status of the 3i initiative at Siemens Ultrasound Division (USD) in Mountain View, California. They had launched 3i, an employee suggestion program, almost 2 years earlier, borrowing heavily from the corporate model that was pervasive in Siemens' European plants. Siemens had acquired the ultrasound business through its purchase of Acuson, a leading U.S. manufacturer of ultrasound systems, in late 2000. Alfred, a 15-year Siemens veteran, was installed as head of manufacturing for the new division. His initial mission was to consolidate and rationalize the Acuson manufacturing and assembly operations, which were then located at three U.S. sites: the Mountain View headquarters; Issaquah, Washington; and Ann Arbor, Michigan. In Mountain View, production was spread out over five buildings.

Alfred wanted to radically change the manufacturing system and layout, and he knew that such change could be difficult to accomplish, especially if employees felt it was contrary to their interests and was being forced on them by management—and foreign management to boot. He needed a way to get them involved in the process. The 3i program, which Alfred was familiar with from his years in Germany, offered the vehicle. It paid employees hard cash for well-developed ideas that were able to be implemented and saved the company money. Alfred appointed Alan Kirby, a former Acuson production manager, to head the 3i program. Along with a 3i team composed of eight midlevel manufacturing managers, the two leaders launched 3i on April 1, 2002. In 2003, its first full calendar year, USD paid out $254,000 for ideas that were projected to save the unit $3.4 million over the following 3 years.

Nearly a quarter of the way into 2004, however, the number of ideas submitted and approved, and the amount of savings and rewards, was trending significantly below 2003. The initial excitement for the program had dissipated, and the "low-hanging fruit" had been plucked. Weichselbaum and Kirby were struggling to transform the program from a one-time success into an inherent part of the culture of continuous improvement—to get every employee to adopt it as part of their daily working life, something they were attuned to all the time, as Alan described: "We are in a bit of a lull right now. We need to keep at it and figure out new things to do and try things until we get something that works. It is partly a function of priorities and the business climate. When we have a number of super-high priorities, it is tough to focus on something lower down the totem pole and get people to keep going. Everyone is very busy and has lots of other priorities."

Siemens Ultrasound Division Background

In 2004, Siemens AG was Europe's largest electronics and electrical engineering giant, with sales of more than $85 billion and a global workforce exceeding 400,000. It had operations worldwide in sectors as varied as industrial automation and control, information and communications, lighting, medical equipment, power transmission, and transportation. The medical business, Siemens Medical Solutions, was led by the U.S.-based subsidiary Siemens Medical Systems, a group of businesses that made and marketed a wide range of medical equipment, including magnetic resonance imaging (MRI) systems, radiation therapy equipment, ultrasound, and patient monitoring systems. In late 2000, Siemens significantly expanded its presence in the ultrasound market by acquiring Acuson, then one of the leading makers of ultrasound systems that included GE and Philips. Siemens combined Acuson with its existing ultrasound business, based in Issaquah, Washington, the core of which Siemens had acquired in 1990 with the purchase of Quantum Medical Systems. Shortly after the 2000 purchase, the ultrasound headquarters was transferred from Issaquah to Acuson's home base in Mountain View.

As in many acquisitions, employee reaction was mixed. Acuson was an independent company with an entrepreneurial environment, and Siemens was perceived from a distance as bringing Germanic order and process. Yet, while such attributes may have been somewhat disparaged, they were also widely regarded as being absolutely necessary. Acuson had a reputation for excellent technology but poor management. According to one long-term employee, the founder and CEO continued to spend most of his time in the engineering lab rather than in running the business.

In March 2001, Siemens transferred Alfred Weichselbaum to Acuson to head up manufacturing for the new unit. Alfred had joined Siemens directly after graduating from college in 1986, and he spent 6 years in the MRI service department installing and repairing 15-cabinet MRI systems. He became one of 20 experts sent out to repair Siemens MRIs anywhere in the world. In the early 1990s, Alfred spent a few years in systems integration R&D, then moved into MRI testing, and eventually was promoted to head of the MRI factory in Erlangen, Germany, where numerous Siemens production facilities were located. In the late 1990s, Alfred managed the successful design of a new factory and, when Siemens needed someone to rationalize the newly acquired Acuson plants, they turned to Alfred: "They asked me to come over here because I designed a new factory that was very successful. There was a need to consolidate the plants and to bring

Acuson into compliance with Siemens processes, because it was seen as a big waste to have different plants with different approaches. The company had three trucks just to move material around. The main stockroom and the main manufacturing facility were in buildings on opposite corners of the campus."

3i Program

Alfred's mission was to consolidate and rationalize the Acuson manufacturing and assembly operations, which were then located at the three U.S. sites and spread out all over the Mountain View campus. He knew that the change would be significant and that it would be much more difficult to accomplish without the enthusiastic support of the employees: "There was the urgency— a huge logistics project to consolidate from six buildings to one and change the entire environment, and we needed to get buy-in from people or we would never get it done. We also needed people's ideas. They know much better the work that they are doing, and there are so many opportunities to improve processes. So, we needed a good program to make that happen. What could we do to get the complete buy-in of everybody and to encourage people to come with more and better ideas? If they come up with good ideas, and they see we do something with them, that is good for the company and for the employees. And then we would have motivated people, excited people, who like to be in this environment and who want to support this project."

Alfred believed that the Siemens Idea Management program, known as 3i (for ideas, innovation, and initiatives), could provide the means he sought to bring employees into the consolidation project. The basic concept of 3i was to pay employees to think creatively about changes to operations and processes that could save money, which could then be reinvested elsewhere in the company. Based on how well the idea was developed into an implementable solution, employees were paid a share of the savings, ranging from 2 to 16 percent.

The 3i program had originated in Germany in the early 1980s, and was firmly in place when Alfred began work for Siemens in 1986. By 2001, it had become deeply embedded in the culture of many Siemens units and in the mindset of employees. In 3i facilities, ubiquitous posters and other forms of advertisement wall-papered the corridors and meeting rooms. Employees were motivated by more than simply receiving cash—competitions were held between divisions and even across units to see who could develop the most ideas and generate the highest level of savings. The number of facilities at Erlangen created a critical mass that enabled extremely large incentives. A new automobile, to be awarded via a drawing for those employees who had been rewarded for multiple 3i suggestions, sat in the middle of the campus for all to walk by and covet.

Siemens did not usually mandate that units adopt the 3i program. The corporate office did publish a generic template that businesses could use and adapt to their particular needs, and it managed an intranet site with information to support 3i implementations. The guiding principle of the program was "the rapid, nonbureaucratic, and responsible implementation of an improvement process." In addition, employees were called on "to act on their own initiative and develop *and implement* suggestions for improvements" (author's emphasis) and managers to "encourage and support employees."[2] Key precepts of the program were that it be employee-focused and action-oriented. The goal was to unleash the creative power of frontline employees to think up and propose changes, and the emphasis was on "fully developed solutions" that could be implemented quickly, not general ideas that required substantial additional work. A useful suggestion had to show what, specifically, should be improved and how it was to be improved. Core elements of the template included a well-articulated structure and process to manage and operate the program.

3i Program at USD

In exploring the feasibility of some type of employee suggestion program, Alfred Weichselbaum consulted with Mountain View plant managers and especially enlisted the advice and support of Alan Kirby, a long-time Acuson employee with extensive experience in the manufacturing process and company culture. Alan had started his career in computer manufacturing at Hewlett-Packard and, after several stops, had joined Acuson in 1991, as a production supervisor. Since 1993, he had been one of two production managers. Alan was enthusiastic about Weichselbaum's idea, and the two agreed that it made sense to closely follow the corporate 3i program template, rather than create a new program. They wanted the initiative to produce real results, not be seen merely as a suggestion box for collecting ideas of little value. As Alfred stated, "We don't want ideas like 'Donuts on Wednesday, not Friday.'" 3i was thoroughly proven and well-documented and could be implemented quickly—a critical necessity, given the urgency to move forward with the plant consolidation. Moreover, having the same program as other Siemens units would enable meaningful comparison of results and cross-fertilization of program ideas, tools, and support mechanisms.

Alfred hoped to deploy 3i throughout all of Siemens Ultrasound, but he met unanticipated resistance from various executives, especially some who had been part of the former ultrasound unit based in Issaquah. An employee suggestion program, apparently mandated there by Siemens in the mid-1990s, had been "a disaster," and the memory of that effort biased current thinking: "We shouldn't do it; it doesn't work here." In Alfred's view, the principal reason for the failure of the earlier program was the lack of commitment and support by senior management. The lack of attention, combined with insufficiently defined processes and systems and inadequate marketing, all doomed the program and made executives skeptical of further iterations.

Alan Kirby noted that another Siemens division in New Jersey also had been unsuccessful in its attempt to promote employee suggestions because its program lacked structure and rigor. As Alan described the situation, "If you just have a box on the wall where people can put their ideas, then someone else has to do something with the piece of paper to turn the idea into a visible, tangible result. If you don't follow up quickly, then people aren't going to turn in more ideas. But whose job is it to follow up?"

In spite of the initial resistance, Alfred persisted, contacting a friend in Germany to send him detailed information about the corporate 3i program. He and Alan labored over a presentation and eventually persuaded senior ultrasound management to allow them to deploy 3i as a pilot program in the manufacturing area. Alan Kirby officially was appointed as the 3i coordinator ("officer"

Siemens Corporate 3i Program Template Structure

Structure

The 3i program had defined roles for up to seven groups and individuals:

- **Employees**—The focal point of the 3i program.
- **Managers**—They function as "partners" and supporters of employees.
- **Decision Makers**—A manager or "technically competent employee at the lowest possible decision-making level" who is responsible for a 3i suggestion.
- **3i Officers**—A senior-level manager responsible for overseeing the 3i program in a business unit, encouraging participation, chairing the 3i team meetings, and reporting to management.
- **3i Team**—A cross-functional team of midlevel managers, each of whom was responsible for a group of 3i projects. The team approved submitted suggestions and decided on cash awards.
- **3i Advisors**—If necessary, 3i advisors could be appointed to support employees and managers.
- **3i Group Officer**—An executive-level manager overseeing the 3i officers in a group of businesses.

Process

The program specified the existence of clear processes for submitting and approving suggestions, calculating awards, objecting to rejections, handling copyrights and potential patent opportunities, and protecting data and confidentiality. A strong bias existed for actionable solutions rather than just ideas.

Calculation of Savings

The 3i suggestion had to include an estimate of how much money the unit could save over a 2-year period by implementing the idea.

in the template) and assembled a small group of managers to help refine the program details and develop an implementation strategy, with appropriate training and communication tactics.

One element of the program that posed a common challenge in all facilities was the determination of whether a given suggestion fell within an employee's job description, and therefore whether it did or did not merit an award. For example, it was the job of design engineers to improve products, thus a suggested improvement in a product design would not qualify as a 3i suggestion. However, a design engineer could submit a suggestion for an improvement in a manufacturing process. This challenge arose in the context of the management hierarchy as well as with frontline jobs. How should a supervisor, manager, or director be rewarded for an improvement suggestion? To address this second area of subjectivity, the 3i team used the existing 3i matrix to determine the appropriate percentage based on management level and improvement impact.

Launch of 3i

In early 2002, even before all the planning was complete, Alfred and Alan introduced the 3i program to all 250 manufacturing employees at a semiannual all-hands meeting, with staff at Issaquah and Ann Arbor connected by videoconference. This initial overture was a brief pitch, with promise of more to come and, over the next months, the two traveled to the different sites and presented the details of the program using a 24-slide PowerPoint presentation that had been meticulously refined to keep it "easy and simple and straightforward." The presentation described the program, its purpose, goals, and mechanics. In addition to attending the presentation, every employee received training on such technical details as how to fill out forms, solicit assistance, and calculate savings and awards. Alan headed the 3i team, which included managers from a range of cross-organizational functions. The team was responsible for evaluating suggestions, offering guidance for those proposals that needed more information or clarity, identifying the appropriate "decision maker" for suggestions that could not be implemented by the submitter, and determining the award amount.

On April 1, 2002, the 3i program officially launched. Reaction to the announcement of the program ranged from enthusiastic to skeptical. Some employees who worked outside the manufacturing group, and were therefore not technically part of the program, were so eager to participate that they started exploring improvement opportunities on their own time. Other workers simply did not believe that the company was going to pay them hard cash for their ideas. As Alfred recalled, "They didn't believe us; they didn't trust us in the beginning that we were actually going to pay them money." The pervasive perception of the old "suggestion box," with tickets or small gifts handed out in return for trivial ideas, remained an obstacle to accepting the program. Even for some employees who supported the concept, the process for developing an idea and completing the paperwork seemed like a daunting prospect.

In spite of the skepticism, two factors helped lay the groundwork for the acceptance of the 3i program. The underlying culture of the manufacturing unit was positive. Acuson had always been an "employee-friendly" place to work, where people generally felt respected and relatively empowered. Weichselbaum and Kirby were not trying to implement something into an antagonistic environment, where the need for drastic culture change existed. Additionally, according to Kirby, Weichselbaum's persona and approach helped to foster a measure of trust that had been lacking with the previous director of manufacturing. "Alfred has credibility, and he is forthright. He does what he says and says what he does, and tells you the good and the bad stuff, so people trust him to start with."

A key initial objective was rapid implementation—processing a submitted proposal within 4 weeks. As ideas started to trickle in, the 3i team turned them around fast and, in mid-May it paid out the first awards. Of the first eight suggestions, five were awarded a total of slightly over $5,000 for 3i savings of $236,000. At first, the identities of the winners were kept confidential. Because this practice deprived the program of a significant marketing opportunity, it was quickly changed, but only with the approval of the recipients. When employees began to hear that awards were being paid, they started to believe in the program. When they actually started to witness fellow line workers being handed checks, the level of interest escalated significantly. On one occasion, a few months into the program, Alan handed out a check for $16,000 in a group setting, and "the next week the group started to turn in a lot of ideas." Kirby soon passed on the enjoyment of handing out the award checks to the supervisors, and then to the managers to give to the supervisor to hand to the frontline workers, multiplying the satisfaction threefold.

The emphasis of the program was on "fully baked" solutions that could be implemented quickly. Future plans would allow employees to develop these by themselves or with a selected group of associates, who could share in the award under any arrangement the group negotiated. For a large award, the group submitted the implemented change to the 3i team. Suggestions that were outside the area or capability of a manager, or that required several departments to implement, could also be submitted to the 3i team.

Several issues affected the implementation of individual projects and the operation of the program. Many suggestions were submitted to the 3i team with incomplete data. At the outset, this was usually due to a lack of familiarity with the program and its submission requirements. Employees also often came up with ideas that needed engineering detail or costs that were beyond their knowledge or competence to assemble. If the right people were not included in the submitter's team, such proposals could lag for months, waiting for someone to give them attention. Convincing employees to include the appropriate people on a team was a major goal, as Alan Kirby stated: "What we struggle with is getting enough resources to help people on the production floor with 3i ideas. When a needed expert, such as a manufacturing engineer, isn't on the 3i team and isn't going to get any money, it's just another thing for that person to do. As time goes on, people will get smarter about whom they include on the 3i to make sure they have buy-in from all the people needed to make the project work."

In the first 6 months, during the pilot phase in the 250-person manufacturing unit, employees submitted 39 suggestions, of which 21 were accepted and 13 refused; 3 were withdrawn, and 2 remained pending. Projected savings amounted to $705,000, and almost $31,500 was paid out in awards. Starting in January 2003, the program was expanded to all of USD, which had approximately 1,100 employees. For the 12 months from October 2002 to September 2003, the suggestion total rose to 204, with 80 accepted, 70 refused, 22 withdrawn, and 32 in process. The projects were estimated to save $3.4 million, and the 3i team paid out more than $254,000 in awards. Although the number of employees eligible to participate quadrupled, most of the suggestions continued to come from the manufacturing area, where money-saving ideas were most often not part of an employee's job description.

Reaping the Benefits

The consolidation of the six Mountain View facilities was largely completed by mid 2002. Component manufacturing was outsourced, and the remaining assembly operations were moved into one building. In total, square footage devoted to building machines was cut by 80 percent, the material flow was condensed from 2,000 to 200 feet, and cycle time was reduced from 10 days to 1. Although only a handful of 3i suggestions related directly to the consolidation, the existence of the program facilitated the significant overhaul by convincing employees that management was eager to pay attention to their ideas.

Common 3i suggestions included changes to the specifications of purchased components used in assembly, efficiencies in purchasing, reduction in the generation of waste, and changes in the accessories shipped with products. For example, USD had formerly purchased electric extension cables, which it cut and combined with a second cable, added a connector to, and kitted up. By changing the cable specification to the appropriate length and connectors, USD was able to remove a time-consuming step in the manufacturing process by making the supplier do the work. Similarly, by asking a workstation vendor to take responsibility for kitting together various accessories (such as cables and drives), USD was able to eliminate those tasks and their associated inventory and reduce its supplier base. In several cases, accessories that were automatically included in product shipments, such as bar code readers and large buckets of gel, were switched from standard to optional gear, with a price adjustment that allowed USD to save money and enhance its margins.

Some purchasing efficiencies were realized through more rigorous shopping and analysis of competing vendors, others by substituting used products for new ones. One employee found a high-end scanner that was comparable to one specified but cost $20,000 less and was available within days rather than months—saving on both the purchase price and the interim cost of using an outside vendor at $100 a day for several months. Although most projects, by far, involved savings, a few created incremental revenue, usually by selling something that would otherwise have been considered waste.

Rewarding Innovation

One of the principal roles of the 3i Team, as well as one of its ongoing challenges, was the calculation of the 3i award. The corporate template defined four types of awards, of which USD focused on two in its program:

- **Lump sum award**—An award of between $20 and $8,000 for a suggestion whose economic value could not be calculated.
- **Economic value award**—An EVA-based award calculated by multiplying the projected savings over 3 years. Guidelines for submitting a 3i proposal for an award utilized the following three factors. The maximum 3i award was $150,000.
  - The submitter's 'scope of task'; that is, the extent to which the suggestion was outside a submitter's normal scope of work
  - The originality of the suggestion
  - The implementation maturity factor, ranging from 25 percent for ideas that could be implemented within 4 weeks to 10 percent for average time to maturity and down to 5 percent for a project requiring long-term maturity.

The Siemens template also had categories for "ideas" and for "best practices." Neither Alfred nor Alan was eager, however, to pay for just an idea. Their concept was to make people think through and participate in the implementation of the suggestion, not simply come up with an idea and drop it in a box for someone else to manage.

Although the calculation of the award was based on only a few pieces of "data," those numbers could involve a degree of subjective judgment. This meant that sometimes submitters who received less than they thought appropriate became somewhat disgruntled. In most cases, these issues were part of the start-up and shake-down process as USD fine-tuned the program. Determination of the estimated savings required a clear understanding of what the "as-is" costs would be if the project were not implemented. As-is costs, however, were subject to change under pressure from factors other than the project, making an estimate of the baseline difficult. Internal labor costs were another potentially difficult area. Although "saved" time could, in theory, be redirected to value-adding work, it did not necessarily result in a recognizable cash savings.

Determining whether a person's idea fit within or outside their normal job responsibilities also presented frequent challenges. In one example, an employee in purchasing suggested an improvement to a purchasing process for a certain part. The 3i award submittal was initially turned down because it was judged to be within her job duties. Upon review, the decision was reversed because she was in "logistics" not "strategic" purchasing, although management also clarified that henceforth anyone in either purchasing group should consider similar improvements to be within their work scope. Alan explained the approach: "The acid test is that we ask the manager or supervisor, 'Do you expect this employee to do this as part of their normal job?' If 'no,' we make the award; if 'yes,' we turn it down."

Sustaining the Program

For the first 5 months of fiscal year 2004 (October 2003 through February 2004), activity in the 3i program appeared to be slipping. A total of 60 submissions came in and, combined with those already in the system, produced 21 accepted projects with 31 refusals, 12 withdrawals, and 33 in process. Savings (additional business value) amounted to $355,341, and awards totaled $53,809. Alan knew that, with the easy pickings gone, the program needed to become "more baked into the culture" if it were to continue to be a meaningful contribution to the business. One of Alan's objectives was to secure a higher level of commitment and buy-in from managers, to galvanize them to encourage their staff to submit ideas. In contrast to the benchmark Siemens plant in Germany, where 3i suggestions flooded in at the rate of 30 per employee per year, Alan's modest goal was to get to one per person per year. "We have to start to talk more about it and do more marketing and advertising within the company. In part, it is a function of time. Germany has been at it for decades. We need to keep it in front of people and talk about it over and over again. Our employees have to get used to it—have to adopt it as part of their daily working life. We need to get it in front of managers to get it in front of troops. Until we have all managers talking about it in their groups, supporting it and participating actively, it won't be part of the culture. The seed is there. Now we just need to water and weed it."

Apparently, the gardeners did their job. Just before going to press, I got an e-mail from Alan Kirby with some of the most recent 3i statistics:

- 3i savings from awarded suggestions in fiscal year 2005 totaled $2,871,321.
- Total submissions were 205.
- Awarded suggestions numbered 43.
- Awards totalled $343,736.

This program is not only an innovation factory—much of the money which is saved is reinvested in value-creating activities. I hope you are as impressed as I am.

Summary

Alfred Weichselbaum and his 3i story is a great example of the importance of the accelerator's role in developing and nurturing a climate of serial innovation. As we saw from the profile, it is not always easy to do this. It requires persistence on the entrepreneurial leader's part, and it also helps to have a few like-minded individuals around to help in the process. Alfred was also fortunate to have a system that could systematize innovation, if accepted by employees. To his credit, Alfred's entrepreneurial leadership capabilities caused this to happen.

I often ask participants in my executive education seminars on entrepreneurial leadership for a show of hands on which type of entrepreneurial leader they would be if they have the opportunity. I expect everyone to raise their hand when it comes to being an accelerator. As we saw in Chapter 4, in the entrepreneurial leadership typologies, accelerators need very little permission to play this kind of role, and it is totally under their control whether they want to push their units, as Alfred Weichselbaum did, toward a sustained culture of innovation.

Chapter Eight

Integrators:
Enterprise-Focused
Entrepreneurial
Leadership

Integrators are entrepreneurial leaders at the enterprise level who focus on the total organization or a major part of it. Their goal is to not only create an entrepreneurial strategy for the business but to develop the people, structures, processes, and culture that support this strategy. They are highly focused on the marketplace, yet also create the organizational architecture for opportunism. Sometimes the architecture is formal, but often it is informal. These structures can stay informal or, over time, can become formalized. Creating this type of architecture typically helps the integrator bypass the unnecessary rules, regulations, and bureaucratic nonsense that inhibit creative thinking and acting from an enterprise-wide perspective. They understand the importance of procuring funds and other resources outside the normal channels. Figure 8.1 shows that integrators, like explorers, are externally focused but, unlike their counterpart, they are more interested in creating an entrepreneurial organization than in pursuing a particular opportunity. They want to create the conditions that will lead to serial opportunity identification.

Integrators also look for individuals like themselves, who have either latent or obvious entrepreneurial characteristics.

Focusing Entrepreneurial Energy

	Internal	External
Activist	Miners (Value Chain)	Explorers (Market)
Catalyst	Accelerators (Unit)	**Integrators** **(Enterprise)**

FIGURE 8.1   Integrators are externally focused catalysts for change within the enterprise.

They tend to hire or connect to key players as much on personality as on credentials or resumes. They know that all opportunities require learning and that mistakes always happen during the learning process. They also know that it is often necessary to destroy current business models or approaches to let in the new. Integrators like to put many boats in turbulent waters, knowing that only a few will make it to the other shore. Thus, they make a lot of small bets on interesting opportunities and then decide which of these are worth supporting and pursuing.

Most integrators I have encountered are at the executive or senior levels of management or are in high-visibility jobs. They typically hold positions in which they have direct access to or actually control the power and resources that make the vision of a more-entrepreneurial company a reality. Their goal is to make the company a "surpriser" and leader of innovation, rather than a "surprised" organization or follower. They are often attracted to organizations that need an innovative "kick in the butt," and they enjoy unleashing an organization's potential. While the other entrepreneurial leaders I have profiled focus on either specific opportunities or the culture of their particular area, integrators know that, for an organization to sustain entrepreneurial thinking and acting over the long term, it must have an entrepreneurial strategy. A. G. Lafley at Procter & Gamble, Jack Welch at GE, Andy Grove at Intel, and Pat McGovern at IDG all evolved entrepreneurial strategies in one form or another. But they have also been successful in implementing these strategies by creating supportive structures, processes, procedures, and systems to create an environment for discovery, opportunity focus, learning, risk taking, and serial new business development. In cases where the integrator is not the top leader but in a high-visibility position, he often develops an entrepreneurial path so that others can follow. Once the integrator blazes the entrepreneurial trail, he tries to keep it open and gives the road map to others.

Building the Entrepreneurial Organization

Integrators are not "wild and crazy" entrepreneurs; they tend to be systematic in what they do and how they do it. They view organizations from a systemic perspective and realize that all organizations are holistic. Simply having an entrepreneurial or innovation strategy is not enough. Unless the other elements of the organization align with and support that strategy, then nothing meaningful will come about. As you remember from Chapter 5, Pat McGovern put together a number of elements that led to the successful spawning of businesses over several decades. This type of success does not just happen from strategy alone. IDG had to align its selection and recruiting processes behind this strategy, reward people differently, and keep corporate staff at a minimum so that it did not encumber creativity and entrepreneurial efforts.

Unlike start-up entrepreneurs, entrepreneurial leaders in large companies don't always get the luxury of picking their own team or having the resources they need under their own control. They often have to pull out and then knit together talent and resources from different parts of the organization to pursue an opportunity. Integrators are particularly talented in this arena. Because they are focused on the enterprise, integrators realize that they frequently have to be the catalyst for cross-organizational cooperation and teamwork, especially as it relates to greater entrepreneurial action. They also tend to have great influencing skills that allow them to create very strong bonds between themselves and others both inside and outside the organization. These bonds allow the integrator to literally *integrate* people's efforts in creating a more entrepreneurial enterprise. As you will see in the two profiles that follow, integrators are adept at finding throughout their organizations people who are willing to help them. But they don't necessarily "own" these people from an organizational-structure or reporting perspective.

Integrators do not promote going after extreme or risky ideas. Instead, they seek ways to link and balance new opportunity focus while keeping existing business strategies in mind. They don't mind leading their organizations down interesting new roadways, but they are wary of going too far astray from current strategy. They like to enhance and extend their organization's brand and reach.

They believe that the best way to protect a company and its employees from bad luck is to create good luck. They like to create and focus on growth strategies and to encourage entrepreneurial thinking across the organization. And they know that ongoing opportunity identification, capture, and development can occur only if the organization systematically induces this kind of behavior. Thus, they are interested in being the designers and architects of organization-wide systems that support and sustain serial entrepreneurial activities. It is not just a specific opportunity they seek, but the underlying sets of processes, procedures, structures, and values that are the antecedents. They believe that if they build the conditions for opportunity development, then the opportunities will come.

Integrators are very familiar with their own organization's vision, strategy, and core competencies, and they are highly attuned to marketplace conditions, including trends, emerging technologies, the competition, and regulatory decisions. They then try to identify the intersections between what their company has to offer and what the marketplace needs or will need. In this position, they try to push their products and services into underserved "white spaces," and they try to use market knowledge to push their organizations into new products and services. They constantly help their companies calibrate themselves against the market realities and start yelling vigorously when the gaps between what the market wants and what their company can deliver become too large.

Like transformational leaders, they still must convince a lot of people to come along for the ride, but unlike transformational leaders—who tend to focus on honing the organization's strategy and vision—the integrator's focus is on opportunism and creating the kind of enterprise that can take advantage of opportunities, in both creating them and finding them.

Compared with explorers, integrators tend to be less overtly rebellious. They respect and often use those tendencies in others to good ends, but they are where they are in the organization because they know how to play politics. They rock the boat without getting thrown out. They know who the important people are and what buttons to push to make things happen. They generally have a great deal of loyalty to the companies with which they work and do not typically hop from company to company. They do their best work when they have had a chance to build the solid network necessary to effect significant change. The integrators I have met usually have a great deal of respect from others in the organization, and they seem to have uniformly good relations across the company. They often work quietly behind the scenes, and I have found them to be relatively humble. Perhaps this characteristic helps them push people without ticking them off.

In the remainder of this chapter, you will read the profiles of two integrators: Denise Prince, at Geisinger Health System, and Don Cotey Jr., at IBM. Denise has a great story, and it is exciting to see a not-for-profit get creative in developing for-profit ventures to help deliver excellent health care at an affordable price. I've included her story here especially so that it could serve as an inspiration for many struggling health care organizations in this country and around the world. Geisinger did not wait for government largesse or fate to control its destiny. Instead, it aggressively took charge of its own destiny, despite the many difficulties in this industry today.

Denise Prince's story is also interesting because, in many ways, she was somewhat reluctant to step into the integrator's role. It was a big step for her and a risky one for her organization, but the bet is paying off.

Integrator Profile 1: Denise Prince, Geisinger Ventures

"It was late in October 2002, and I was just trying to get through the day when Glenn came up behind me and asked, 'So Denise, do you want the job?'" Denise Prince recalled. Glenn Steele was the newly appointed CEO of Geisinger Health System, and at the time, Denise was the senior vice president of Geisinger Diversified Services. Steele was offering her the newly created position of COO of Geisinger Ventures, and Denise was not sure how or when to give him an answer. The timing was bad. She was leaving the next day to pick up her newly adopted child from Guatemala, and the adoption agency had just called to say there could be travel problems. She was also in the middle of her group's annual strategic planning meeting. During the meeting, her group had identified some pressing problems that made it apparent it was not the best time to be taking time off. "Not a good day," as she was to say later.

Nonetheless, when she returned in November, Denise accepted the position.

Geisinger Health System

Danville, Pennsylvania, is an unusual place to find large-organization entrepreneurial leaders like Denise Prince. The town is about an hour and a half from Scranton, in the middle of rolling hills and farmland. The economy is declining, as industries shut down or move out and, unlike many other places in America, housing prices are falling.

Yet, in the middle of Danville (population around 5,000), sits the campus of Geisinger Medical Center, a sprawling complex of buildings, hospital facilities, specialty clinics, two research centers, and a health care company that is one of the biggest employers in the state. Geisinger is well known throughout the state of

Pennsylvania and is building a national reputation for its innovative focus, health service delivery, and increasingly entrepreneurial strategies. The center has been able to recruit internationally acclaimed researchers and clinicians to its facilities because of its reputation for patient focus balanced with fiscal responsibility. (For example, the organization recently recruited a nationally known physician and his wife to move from La Jolla, California, to this small, rural town, where winters can be long and cold.)

Founded in 1915, Geisinger Health System provides a complete continuum of quality health care to more than 2 million people in 38 counties in Pennsylvania. Medically necessary treatment is provided to anyone, regardless of race, creed, religious preference, or ability to pay. Figure 8.2 shows Geisinger's mission, vision, and values.

Founder Abigail Geisinger, born and raised in Danville, was a down-to-earth woman of average education and life experiences who often used her expensive Hupmobile auto to drive patients to the Bloomsburg hospital for emergency medical care. After the death of her iron-mining tycoon husband, George Geisinger, Abigail used her considerable fortune to build a hospital and clinic modeled on the Mayo Clinic. The George Geisinger Memorial Hospital was completed in 1915. Ultimately, the hospital became the Geisinger Health System.

"Make my hospital right; make it the best," she demanded of Harold L. Foss, the young physician she chose for her first surgeon-in-chief. Trained at the Mayo Clinic, Foss shared her vision and brought to it the professional expertise that would change the dream to reality. He was committed to the concept of group practice, where specialty-trained physicians worked together to benefit their patients.

Renewing the Discipline

By 2001, however, Geisinger had begun to feel the strain experienced by the health care industry as a whole, and the board of directors decided to bring in new leadership. Glenn Steele Jr., a noted surgeon and savvy businessman, was recruited from Chicago to head up the leadership team. He brought with him Joanne Wade, a trusted associate with whom he had worked in

Mission, Vision, and Values

Mission

Enhancing quality of life through an integrated health service organization based on a balanced program of patient care, education, research, and community service.

Vision

To be the health system of choice, advancing care through education and research.

Values

Excellence

We strive for the best, continuously improving quality in all our activities.

Service Orientation

Our physicians and staff use their skills, creativity, energy and loyalty as resources for effective and quality services in every community and each setting in which we serve.

Individual Dignity

We provide humane, compassionate and expert care, always emphasizing the dignity of the individual.

Teamwork

We take great pride in recognizing and empowering good people who demonstrate the importance and value of teamwork.

Physician Leadership

We are physician-led—both across our entire organization and within the many communities we serve.

Diversity

Diversity among physicians, staff, students, and volunteers promotes an environment of mutual support and respect.

Education

We believe in the intellectual and professional pursuit of new knowledge and its dissemination to colleagues, students, and the public at large, as an instrument of our health system that adds value to all of our customers.

Research

We believe that basic science, clinical, community health, and health-services research advances the overall health and well-being of our patients and their communities.

Fiscal Responsibility

We exercise prudent use of all resources as part of our stewardship responsibility for fiscal and organizational success.

Tradition

We take pride in our history, for it is the foundation of our future and our long-standing commitment to your health.

FIGURE 8.2   Geisinger mission, vision, and values.

both in Boston and Chicago. She became executive VP for Strategic Programs. Steele had served as a consultant to Geisinger when it went through a merger with—and then painful "de-merger" from—Penn State's Hershey Medical Center. He had a great deal of respect for Geisinger's values and patient orientation and knew it had tremendous untapped human and financial assets. But he was aware of its shortcomings as well. During the first 6 months in his new position, he met with people throughout the organization, taking its pulse and working with various constituencies in the organization to build a 5-year strategic plan.

It became clear early on that Geisinger could not remain the same organization that it had been in previous years. The leadership team would capitalize on the best of Geisinger's traditions and values, but they would also raise the bar on performance and accountability.

So, Steele's early days focused on cost cutting and fiscal responsibility, as well as on growth. While costs were cut in some areas, investment was increased in others. Steele was considered very astute at motivating his staff and deciding whether money, technology, or facilities was the hot button. He told the doctors that if they supported the 5-year plan and made necessary changes, they would have the money and other resources to get the things that turned them on. This strategy not only appealed to their love of state-of-the-art technology, it also supported the long-standing Geisinger value of excellence in patient care. It was hard to argue against this approach. However, not everyone was comfortable with the changes. One of Steele's rules was "If you miss your budget once, you get a free pass; the second time you're gone"—either out of your current job or out of the organization. However, many Geisinger employees appreciated Steele's direct (if sometimes confrontational) approach and his willingness to listen. Some silent applause could also be discerned when a few senior people left the organization.

It took 4 years of selling, listening, and pushing by Steele and his leadership team, but 2004 was a good year for Geisinger both in terms of financial results and human resource development. They had been able to recruit highly qualified medical and research talent and position themselves as both excellent health care providers and leaders in health care research.

Although Steele was happy with the results of his first 4 years, he knew that Geisinger's employees had to keep pushing to think of new and innovative ways to grow if they were to fulfill their mission. In March 2005, he began working on his next 5-year plan, again going around the organization asking people for their input. When asked about his leadership approach, he said it was fairly simple: "You emancipate people's energy and creativity by engaging them and challenging them to do their best. Then you give them a great deal of freedom in determining how they get their results. And then you hold them accountable. You also have to make sure that they have the authority and control necessary to influence the outcomes."

So, while he demanded accountability, he also changed some structural processes and reporting relationships so that responsibility and accountability would be commensurate.

Leveraging Assets

One of the first things Steele did when he came to Geisinger was to walk around the organization to meet his various constituencies. He was interested in getting to know Geisinger in greater detail, and he wanted to get a handle on the quality and capabilities of the people working in various areas. Steele was convinced that Geisinger had a lot of assets, especially several small "for-profit" businesses, that were not being leveraged to their greatest potential. He knew that these businesses, if managed properly, would help underpin Geisinger's primary mission, which was patient care. Due to his entrepreneurial orientation, he believed that Geisinger should be able to develop new businesses from its vast array of underutilized assets.

Geisinger became involved in corporate entrepreneurship in 1978, when its leaders created a for-profit company called Geisinger Medical Management Corporation (GMMC). In 1984, GMMC acquired International Shared Services (ISS), a small biomedical service company. In 1998, Geisinger Community Health Services (GCHS), a not-for-profit company, was formed and combined with GMMC to form a new division called Diversified Services. This portfolio of small companies formed the basis for Geisinger's foray into the entrepreneurial sector. These businesses were meant to add top-line revenues to the organization. Table 8.1 shows the financial performance of these ventures compared to all other Geisinger Health System (GHS) operations in fiscal year 2000.

TABLE 8.1   Fiscal Year 2000 Information for Geisinger's For-Profit
Portfolio

Entity	Return on sales	Return on assets	Return on equity
ISS	5.73%	15.46%	30.66%
GMMC/GCHS	3.59%	13.89%	17.05%
Total	4.36%	14.55%	21.60%
All other GHS	–0.04%	–0.4%	–0.8%

The Foundation of Geisinger Ventures

Denise Prince began her career at Geisinger in 1989, with Geisinger Medical Management Corporation (GMMC), a for-profit entity within Geisinger Health System. The last of four children, Denise had tried early in life to "just stay out of the way and not be a bother." Her parents had emigrated from Canada and built their first house with their own hands. They were self-educated, and her father had learned two trades while her mother worked as an Avon lady. So, Denise learned from them early in life the importance of hard work. But it was not until college that Denise came to understand the importance of initiative and having a take-charge attitude. Her teachers impressed upon her the importance of *not* "staying out of the way," and she decided to pursue a career in business.

Denise was promoted to acting (later permanent) head of GMMC in 1991. As mentioned, from 1992 to 2001 several other businesses were either developed or acquired by Geisinger. They continued to grow, and were eventually consolidated into the new Diversified Services division, which was headed by Denise. These businesses were seen as generally supportive to the organization as a whole, but not critical to its overall mission.

So, when Steele challenged her to draw up a proposal for the creation of a new unit within Geisinger, it was with some trepidation that she accepted. She was reminded of the saying "Be careful what you wish for—you might get it."

The job would be a big challenge. It would mean building the new unit, Geisinger Ventures (GV), from the ground up, instilling a venture capital orientation, and hiring new people from the investment and banking community, something Geisinger had never done before. It would also involve a great deal of interaction and involvement with the external venture capital market— again, something that neither Denise Prince nor Geisinger as a whole had much experience with. At the same time, Denise had a new child at home, and she was committed to her personal values of balancing work and family.

Denise completed her proposal for the formation of Geisinger Ventures and presented it on May 9, 2001. It was called the Incubator Proposal. Steele then presented the proposal to the board, and after a great deal of discussion it was accepted. Steele noted that, "We have an exceptional board. They are also successful in their own businesses and were very supportive of the incubator concept. They believed that, while there was risk, and we would have to spend a lot of money to hire some very experienced outside help, the potential to create some serious revenue-generating businesses was there. They also thought that we were taking a risk offering Denise the job. Should they go to an outsider with a lot of experience in venture capital, or with Denise? It would be a big step for her!"

When Denise was handed the reins to GV (Geisinger Ventures), not everyone was convinced she could do the job. According to Russ Showers, director of Human Resources, "It was considered a big risk, but she was the only natural inside runner. She had successfully built Diversified Services and had done a great job of learning about running for-profit businesses and how venture capital markets work." He also felt that Denise was savvy about hiring people who knew more than she did, and that she managed them well. "She doesn't try to do their jobs for them," he said. "And this has been a very effective strategy for her." Rich Merkle, VP of HR, agreed. "She had been successfully growing our 'entrepreneurial' companies. She has spent a lot of time with venture organizations and has learned a lot from them." Showers also said that, before taking the job, Denise wanted to know a lot more about the structure and workings of GV than either Joanne Wade or Frank Trembulak, the COO, were prepared to answer. They were hoping that Denise would step up to the job and answer these questions herself. Denise delivered many of these answers in her Incubator proposal.

Purpose, Mission, and Team

Prince's first job was to create a new organization. She developed a business plan, estimated a budget, and began recruiting a new team of experienced people from outside the organization. These new team members would have significantly different skill sets than most Geisinger employees. She sought people with proven track records as start-up entrepreneurs and venture capitalists. They would have to possess excellent skills in business planning, financial analysis, and market research and to have been intimately involved in the world of investment banking and venture capital. In addition, this team would be paid on the basis of value creation, instead of the normal Geisinger job-evaluation system.

GV's primary mission was to develop selected Geisinger assets into profitable businesses that are attractive to outside investors and generate significant returns. To accomplish this mission, GV would have to shepherd the development of new businesses from concept to launch. Their specific goals were:

- To aid in the advancement of life sciences and health delivery
- To enhance Geisinger's brand through leadership in health services and technology innovation
- To generate capital for investment in core programs
- To support economic development in northeast and central Pennsylvania

"Other people's money" (OPM) was a core tenet of the GV team. They were given limited resources aside from their significant recruitment and hiring budget. Thus, they would have to get funding and support from internal departments and clinics that were interested in commercializing their own intellectual property (IP) and from outside investment sources. Much of the work that Denise and her team did involved scanning Geisinger for ideas and technology that could be commercialized, as well as for people who, with the right coaching, could drive some of these opportunities to market.

Looking for the First Deal

When Glenn Steele arrived in 2000, he found that Geisinger's pharmaceutical business had grown steadily. The original strategy, prior to the formation of GV, was to place these pharmacies within Geisinger's hospitals and Geisinger-owned medical office buildings. The typical floor space allotted to these pharmacies was relatively small, between 500 and 1,000 square feet, and each carried prescription drugs, some over-the-counter medicines, and a relatively small assortment of other consumer items.

The value proposition was to provide personal, convenient, customized service to patients at a competitive price. Elderly patients, for example, could get much more personalized advice, because the pharmacists generally knew the physicians who had hospital privileges or offices in the building. The pharmacist might ask how or when the patient intended to take the medicine and could then provide advice on how to make the drug the most effective or safest. In addition, Geisinger's sophisticated health care IT system could link the doctor's office directly with the pharmacy electronically so that, as the patient was leaving the doctor's office, the prescription was being filled. Some competitors existed in this niche market, such as The Medicine Shoppe, but very few had the same brand recognition or technology advantage that Geisinger had in the state.

Although the pharmacy business was bringing in around $25 million a year (gross), it was reaping only a fraction of its potential value. Denise was often frustrated in her desires to grow the business as rapidly and as expansively as she would have liked, due to limited capital. She knew that her business would probably never get the proper funding, because it was not perceived as a core Geisinger activity providing direct medical care. Realistically, Diversified Services would always be a poor cousin, relegated to taking a back seat to computed tomography (CT) scanners, magnetic resonance imaging (MRI) equipment, and other medical devices. She knew that patient care was and would always be Geisinger's primary mission. But this did not dissuade her from thinking creatively about how to help grow her organization. She knew that real opportunities would always attract people and money, from outside the organization if not within it.

To get the capital to grow, Denise and her colleagues decided to involve outside investors. They took their seven Geisinger retail pharmacies, plus their long-term care pharmacy, wove them into an offering, and hired an investment banker to prepare "the book" and shop it to potential external investors. Denise, the pharmacy group, and the investment banker presented the book to more than a hundred prospective private equity groups, looking for the right investor-partner. They were looking for an investor who would be willing to operate the business. She was asked if she wanted the job of pharmacy CEO, but turned it down. She saw herself as more of an architect of new business development infrastructure than as the CEO or COO of any particular business in the portfolio. According to Denise, "We wanted investors for both money and management. We were particularly interested in seeing if the model would work in non-Geisinger sites. Our original business plan involved putting Geisinger pharmacies in other people's office buildings, and we needed to jumpstart the organization with an outside investor.

"Eventually, we settled on a deal with EDG Partners, and signed the deal on December 23, 2004. Mike Gaffney became CEO of the company we now call SureHealth LLC. He recently recruited a permanent CEO and, in 5 years, we plan to have 50 to 70 new pharmacy locations. We can now maximize the value of this asset in a way we never could have done had we left it in Geisinger. It would have been a real uphill battle to put capital in non-Geisinger sites."

Geisinger now has two-thirds ownership of SureHealth, and EDG owns the rest—although this balance is expected to change over time. Future plans could include entry into pharmacy benefits management and an expanded mail-order business. Denise believes that, because of the outside investment, they were able to recruit the kind of talent that they would never have been able to otherwise, given their limitation on capital expenditure. The first non-Geisinger SureHealth site opened on April 15, 2005, in Reading, Pennsylvania.

The Next Deal

The GV team identified many interesting opportunities. One involved using Geisinger's sophisticated IT system to increase the speed of clinical trials—something that would interest many large pharmaceutical companies. Another idea involved data services. Geisinger could offer sanitized data (patients' names removed) from their large patient database to outside organizations such as drug developers, payers, insurers, and patient advocate groups. Geisinger's urology clinic was one of the early adopters of advanced technology, and the GV group was thinking of helping this department sell consulting and teaching services to other medical groups that were or might be interested in deploying this technology.

Denise Prince was glad that she had accepted Steele's offer to run GV. Sometimes bad days turn out all right.

Integrator Profile 2: Don Cotey Jr., IBM Life Sciences

When you meet Don Cotey Jr., IBM's Global Business Development Executive, you know immediately that he says what he means and he means what he says. And you know he will get things done. He garners great respect among his various organizational constituencies, and he works hard to develop good working relationships. He is always looking for ways to grow the company's business and is good at knowing what buttons to push and what levers to pull to make things happen. Don seems to have an innate sense for spotting holes in the market that can be exploited and a knack for networking that allows him to bring organizational capabilities and market white spaces together. Don was a relative newcomer at IBM, thus his ability to get their Life Sciences business off the ground so quickly is a credit to his ability to wire into the IBM culture. This is no easy feat, given IBM's complex array of people, services, products, and structures.

I put Don's profile in the integrator category because of his incredible talent for pulling people and resources together both inside and outside of IBM in order help develop and grow IBM's fledgling Life Sciences business. And to capture this opportunity, Cotey had to take an enterprise-wide approach. So, while he was quite adept at identifying the market opportunity, he was equally adept at pulling together the organization's capabilities (many outside of his authority) to capture that opportunity.

His story also is interesting from another perspective—IBM's determination under Lou Gerstner to become more entrepreneurial as a company. As you will see, Gerstner and his executives created a new strategy for identifying and developing emerging business opportunities (EBOs) so, in many ways, these folks are enterprise-wide integrators for the whole organization, focusing not on opportunities but on IBM's ability to be entrepreneurial. I hope this will be an inspirational story to you. It shows that large companies can rekindle their entrepreneurial spirit, and do so with some pretty dramatic results, by looking for and developing the Don Coteys of the world to make it happen.

IBM Life Sciences

In 2005, 4 years after its founding, the Life Sciences business at IBM had become a multibillion-dollar venture. Launched in 2000, as one of IBM's emerging business opportunities, the unit confronted challenges common to start-ups within large organizations: battling their well-established, money-making brethren for resources, channel mindshare, and management attention. Although endowed with the many technology strengths of IBM, the Life Sciences business also had to enter a market where well-entrenched competitors had already staked out major claims. Don Cotey, a relatively recent hire at IBM, with considerable consulting experience, was given the task of overseeing the global services component of the Life Sciences business. In spite of the lack of a well-developed network within the organization, Don was able to influence and integrate players across a range of units and geographies to share his passion for the Life Sciences initiative and help drive its success.

Background

Don Cotey grew up in a small suburb outside of Milwaukee, Wisconsin. He was the youngest of seven children, a position that he credits with teaching him early on how to operate as a small unit in a large organization. "At the dinner table, if you didn't get in there and get your fair share, there might be nothing left. So, you had to learn pretty fast to be quick and nimble." Don's father ran his own dental practice, and many of his older brothers had their own businesses. Don believes that an entrepreneurial atti-tude is hard-wired into his system: "I've always looked for oppor-tunities to bring new ideas—products or business ideas—to market. It's part of my DNA." Early on, Don displayed an interest in finance. As a child, he watched *Wall Street Week* every Friday night with his father, and his strong suite in high school was math.

Don majored in accounting at the University of Wisconsin, Madison, but also pursued his entrepreneurial instincts. He and his roommate developed a glow-in-the-dark flying disc for night-time use, found a tool-and-die manufacturer to make the molds, put together a marketing plan, and started selling the products through retail outlets. During one summer vacation, he also start-ed a business building and selling storage sheds. After graduation, Don was hired by Arthur Andersen in Milwaukee and joined the start-up business consulting practice targeted at Wisconsin's mid-dle-market companies. He worked with dozens of small-business owners in his first few years, providing a wide range of services—strategic planning, business plan development, organizational design, operations, and technology consulting. As he explains, "My clients were entrepreneurs, and you start thinking like them to help them improve their business. I also got involved in some organizations like SCORE [Service Corps of Retired Executives], which function as a kind of incubator, helping small start-ups."

After several years, in which he worked on more than a hun-dred projects across a range of industries, Don became a practice leader, first for Wisconsin and then for the Midwest region. During this period, Don became a principal investor in a health care infomatics and medical billing start-up, and he was tangen-tially involved in several other ventures. Most of his entrepre-neurial tendencies, however, were devoted to starting new consulting ventures within Andersen. In addition to the Wisconsin consulting practice, which went from zero to $50 million with a hundred-person staff, Don was heavily involved in an initiative called the Financial Function of the Future, helping CFOs improve their finance and accounting organizations. Another new practice was in knowledge management, known as Knowledge Dynamics, for which he ran the Midwest region and sat on the U.S. leadership team. All three consulting ventures became fast-growing, profitable businesses.

Move to IBM

In 1998, at the age of 30, Cotey left Arthur Andersen Consulting and joined IBM to help start up a knowledge management consulting practice for North America. Although the "career promotion" was the primary reason for the move, Don later realized that he was also attracted to IBM because of the scope of services that it had to offer: "I always had great admiration for IBM, but I didn't fully appreciate the depth and breadth of its capabilities. As a professional consultant at Andersen, we always had to partner with hardware or software vendors to provide a complete set of solutions to clients. At IBM, we have the ability to offer a more complete set of capabilities. Also the culture—the DNA—at IBM is innovative: 'THINK.' People at IBM think and innovate. The research capabilities, the number of patents, are incredible. How far is entrepreneurship from that? Of course, we also have a lot of the challenges that other big companies deal with in terms of bureaucracy and process, so it can be tough to be truly entrepreneurial. But on the flip side is that you have very talented thinkers and a lot of resources at your disposal to create and build large businesses quickly: investment capital, business processes and systems, teams of people who can get new ideas in front of customers."

Don served as the Americas practice leader for knowledge management for 2 years. At the time, it was a very hot topic, incorporating business intelligence, data warehousing, decision support, document management, and collaboration—areas that companies were starting to invest in. In October 2000, after 2 years in that role, Don was asked to start up the worldwide consulting and IT service business within IBM Global Services for a new life sciences venture, one of the first to be designated as an emerging business opportunity under a new IBM program.

Frustrated by IBM's tendency to miss emerging new industries and markets, in late 1999, Lou Gerstner had formed a task force to diagnose IBM's failure to identify and adequately support new ventures. A team of senior executives traced the company's problems to six root causes, under all of which lay the fact that IBM's management systems were designed to support large, established businesses and lacked the flexibility to foster entrepreneurial ventures. Recognizing the difficulties of vesting responsibility for new businesses in either an overly centralized (corporate) or a distributed (line) approach, the team recommended the adoption of a hybrid model—corporate guidance and oversight combined with line authority and accountability. Using a Horizons-of-Growth model,[1] the Corporate Strategy group initially identified 17 initiatives to be emerging business opportunities (EBOs). EBOs had to have significant growth potential and cut across multiple industries and IBM brands, and unique IBM intellectual property assets or relationships had to exist that could be mined to pursue the large market opportunity and create a leadership position. One of those initial EBOs was life sciences, an area that had earlier been terminated for lack of funding and that had spurred Gerstner on to action. At the time, the mapping of the human genome was being completed, and the life sciences arena was becoming an increasingly active and attractive market. The EBO program officially launched in September 2000, and Don Cotey was in place for the start of the life sciences venture.

Life Sciences EBO

For IBM, the life sciences category included a broad range of market segments in the private and public domains that were involved in the research and development of pharmaceuticals for health care and agriculture as well as basic research in health care–related fields. Pharmaceutical companies, biotechnology firms, government research labs, health care organizations, hospitals, and research universities all collectively fit under the life sciences umbrella. IBM had existing business relationships with some of these organizations in commercial areas, but not in the research and drug-development fields. Entrenched competitors in this market included software companies such as Oracle; hardware vendors Hewlett-Packard (HP), Compaq, and Sun Microsystems; and numerous medium- and small-sized scientific equipment and software vendors for lab equipment and systems.

Although IBM was "coming from relative obscurity," according to Don, it had significant capabilities that it could bring to bear on the life sciences market: leadership in supercomputing, decision support, information mining, analytics, and complex computing. IBM also had a team of computational chemists in a research lab called the Computational Biology Center, which focused on developing technologies for computer-intensive activities such as gene sequencing and proteomics.

IBM organized a Life Sciences committee and core leadership team from across the various IBM organizations (hardware, software, services—known internally as the IBM "brands")—all were asked to provide funding or staff. Don Cotey headed up the Services area, a virtual team composed of geographic regions (United States, Canada, Europe, Asia) and functional areas (sales, solutions, business development, and marketing). The organization operated as a federation, with representation from the multiple brands forming a leadership council, not unlike a venture capital board, which met monthly to hash out issues and make decisions. Council members were at the vice president level and controlled resources and budgets. The life sciences EBO was housed under the Public Sector, which included all governmental, academic, and health care markets.[2]

Early activities of the EBO were very similar to developing a business plan for a new start-up, as Don described: "We started looking at the market, customers, products and offerings, financing, and how to organize the business—a lot of the elements of a business plan except within a much larger organization. We talked to customers to figure out their problems and needs, and then tried to understand what products, services, and solutions we had that could help them solve their problems. There was a lot of trial and error to get going. Our client list grew, we started developing business partner relationships and announcements, and we publicized wins with key marquee customers. Once you start to build momentum over time, you become a player and you grow."

To compete against well-established competitors, the life sciences EBO differentiated itself by taking existing components of IBM IP and technology and configuring them in new ways to develop new solutions to meet customer needs. It was a matter of taking capabilities and converting, extending, and expanding them into real new products and solutions. As the EBO grew, it also developed "net new" solutions, based on IBM's broad capabilities, that competitors could not match. IBM used trial balloons (known as first-of-a-kind projects) with early adopter clients to validate its solutions. It also brought customers together in "customer councils" to discuss their needs and challenges, and then used that insight to inform its solutions development. Don considered the solutions business to be inherently a trial-and-error effort that required a balance between being product driven and being market driven. As he explained, "You have to listen to the customers to understand what their needs are, but sometimes customers don't know what is possible, so you also have to push new technology to see if you can create some innovative solutions that will capture customers' attention."

Challenges

In spite of strong corporate leadership support for the EBO program, start-ups faced significant challenges gaining traction within IBM as they battled with mature businesses for resources and channel attention. For Don Cotey, who had started at IBM just 2 years before the launch of Life Sciences, there was the added challenge of having to work across multiple brands and geographies while lacking the kind of internal network that many senior leaders had built up during longer careers with the company. In his position as head of the (virtual) Services team, Don had to influence many people with whom he had no official reporting relationship, often not even a dotted line in the vast IBM matrix. To all of these challenges, he brought the kind of energy and passion that typically characterizes an entrepreneur trying to secure funding to launch a new business or attempting to sell a new product or service to the world. Don ascribed the basis for his energy largely to his personality, but also credited the fact that life sciences was a "feel-good" industry in which IBM was helping companies develop life-saving therapies, making it an easy cause to be passionate about.

One of the toughest challenges he faced was competing with other IBM businesses for the attention of the various IBM sales groups—the channels through which products and services went to market. Those channels had a large array of existing and well-proven IBM offerings that they were accustomed to selling, and they did not automatically jump at the chance to sell new services simply because they were made available. Don humorously likened the situation to trying to add McRibs to the McDonald's menu: "There are lots of tried-and-true products and brands, so that adding something to the menu is tough. And, when you are inventing a new business, whether it is product, or a solution or a service, you are basically adding another thing to the menu, and you struggle to get people's attention to sell it."

Cotey saw his role as that of an evangelist for IBM's Life Sciences business, and he spent considerable time traveling internationally to meet with sales teams, spreading the word about the opportunity. The Human Genome Project was generating considerable press in those years, and he attempted to leverage this to show salespeople that it was in their interest to get up to speed in this emerging market. To influence the channels, Don adopted what he termed a "franchising model" approach, building a success story in one place, and then replicating and refining it for other geographies and venues. He called it "build the network as you go"—identifying key decision makers and thought leaders and educating them about the opportunity. As he describes it, "You try to play to individuals' personal motives. You have to help them get up the learning curve to become a player in this business. You have to demonstrate that customers are spending money here and try to help them figure out how to start selling to those customers. Then, all of a sudden, they become a Life Sciences player. Providing market intelligence is important—helping incubate and sell and start to get a core nucleus of people on the ground. It is like spreading a religion."

In Don's view, several factors weighed against IBMers simply following leadership directives to support new ventures. The highly matrixed model, scale of the organization, and the culture all constrained the translation of top-down mandates. Competing initiatives and numerous other opportunities diluted the message. The IBM culture, however, often fostered an interest in the "next new thing—the next hot topic," and Cotey leveraged that cultural trait to bring people on board the Life Sciences train: "A big part of the IBM culture is enticing people to join up on the next new thing. The critical success factor for having something new become a successful business is leveraging the fact that people gravitate naturally toward the hot new stuff, not because their boss told them to, but because it *is* cool new stuff and clients are talking about it and need it and you want to be the best provider to your customers. So, if you understand that and operate under the belief that what you have to do is create a fervor and excitement, and educate and channel the energy that IBMers have to go after something new, then things can move quickly."

In addition to using his excitement and enthusiasm to influence the channels, Don was also successful in building an internal network of people interested in the Life Sciences EBO. By providing education through conference calls, web seminars, informational lunches, and other means, he built up a community of interest that shared his passion for the topic. A growing number took on Life Sciences as a part-time role in addition to their "day jobs." The community expanded through network marketing as people got fired up and spread the word; soon, a critical mass supported the cause. "It catches fire, and before you know it you have a huge amount of talent focused over the target quickly," Don recalled. That community, which grew from 300 to 400 within a year, then served as a natural source for recruitment when Don needed to add people to full-time positions in his organization. Although Don had the ability to build a network quickly, he also credited his success to the fact that he had strong executive sponsorship: "For the Consulting and Services team, I organized a lot of the effort globally, but there were strong leaders and teams in the individual countries and people I could call on up the food chain—other people that did have a network—so I had good sponsorship myself. That is important. In a global organization like IBM, nobody is going to know everybody."

Although the EBO program recognized that it was unproductive to manage new initiatives through IBM's standard management systems, start-ups such as Life Sciences still had to operate in a large organization with processes geared toward maintaining the legacy business units. The systems for such activities as budgeting, planning, resource management, hiring, deployment, and product development did not match the needs of a start-up that had to be nimble, move quickly, and make decisions fast. Don endured numerous battles to win his fair share of resources and to make decisions at the pace that Life Sciences required. He also was not averse to breaking rules when necessary to move the business forward, citing the at-times-conflicting mandates under which he operated. He described the attitude and behaviors necessary to survive and thrive in the ring with the 800-pound gorillas: "You've got to fight City Hall. You have to have a lot of scar tissue and thick skin. There are plenty of people who will tell you every reason why something can't be done, but if you are going to succeed, you have to take risks, be the corporate entrepreneur, and get something off the launch pad. You can't take no for an answer. You've got to ruffle a lot of feathers to blaze the trail and sometimes that is painful. Change is hard."

Cotey was particularly challenged by limitations on head count, which ran contrary to the expectations for how fast he could grow the business. Building a service business was directly related to capacity, which was a function of numbers and staff talent. Because IBM did not have sufficient domain expertise in life sciences, Don needed to hire, train, and develop subject matter experts. He also developed partnerships with other firms to augment his capabilities and, in 2002, IBM acquired PwC Consulting, which had a large number of talented people in the pharmaceutical industry vertical. Internally, Don fought numerous battles with country managers, who controlled resources and budgets, and he often had to challenge the status quo and persuade them to think beyond their monthly and quarterly financial targets to persuade them to devote resources to the Life Sciences effort. As he says, "This is the future of our company, and we have to grow—sometimes at the expense of other groups that have to shrink, and that will cause pain. It really is at the crux of the success or failure of rapid growth at a large organization. Head count and funding are oxygen for the start-up—just like with VCs and two guys in a garage. It is even more so in a large organization, because you have so many people competing for the same resources and the same budget. It is an ongoing competition every day."

According to Cotey, leading an EBO at IBM required the right entrepreneurial attitude from a career standpoint, because it did not fit a clear career path. The fact that IBM took a portfolio approach to EBOs, recognizing that some would succeed and others would fail, meant that some executives would be part of unsuccessful efforts. Many IBM executives were reluctant to risk becoming engaged in projects that appeared to have significant downside and uncertain results.

The people involved in EBOs are taking personal and political risks in their careers. They must believe in their EBO, just as an entrepreneur would, even though there are lots of chances to fail and very few to be successful. Some of these positions require bet-the-career type decisions, and not everybody wants to see an entrepreneurial manager succeed. It is important to stay positive, focused, motivated, and upbeat throughout the tough times, just as an entrepreneur would. This is ultimately a limiting factor in getting executives involved in EBOs. People say, "What is the upside? All I see is plenty downside." Not many executives are risk takers: A lot of people are content to stick with the bread-and-butter businesses.

Life after Life Sciences

In early 2003, with the Life Sciences EBO operating with significant momentum, Don Cotey moved on to a business development role with Global Services headquarters, joining a team that was responsible for launching multiple EBOs. In addition to his entrepreneurial aptitude for new businesses, Don brought to his new position a growing ability to identify and leverage emerging IBM ideas and technologies. He had made a point of developing relationships with IBM's research community, the source for new ideas and innovation. In addition to visiting five of the eight research laboratories himself, Cotey had frequently hosted client visits to the labs, which were attempting to become more customer-facing organizations. Don also had a personal goal of keeping abreast of new technology trends and state-of-the-art projects at IBM research, scanning the IBM intranet, and participating in communities of practice.

As he summarizes, "I try to take the initiative to reach out and find talented people in the organization and become a conduit to turn interesting ideas into new businesses. Sometimes, you go looking for one thing and you find something completely different, and you are amazed at the capabilities. Customers want to pay for the best ideas and best thinking, and you need to find the best stuff in your company and your business partners."

Don credited his work in the knowledge management field with expanding his corporate entrepreneurial capabilities: "The time I spent in KM strengthened my entrepreneurial thought processes. Entrepreneurship is very knowledge-based—it comes down to taking a propriety knowledge asset or idea, patenting it to make it IP, and then turning it into a viable business proposition. So, becoming adept at all those knowledge-capture and knowledge-based models played a big part in helping me to become more of a corporate entrepreneur."

Summary

Both Don Cotey and Denise Prince have a broad entrepreneurial perspective of their organizations. They are not just after one big hit or one big win—they want to create organizational structures, processes, procedures, and networks that allow for serial innovation and value creation. Geisinger Ventures will continue looking for deals to keep Geisinger at the top of the health care game, and Don Cotey is already using his network and experience within IBM to launch more EBOs. Integrators are interested in enterprise opportunism that is replicable and scalable, and they know that they have to knit both people and resources together to make this happen.

Chapter Nine

Buy or Build?

So far, we have talked about the characteristics of entrepreneurial leaders, and we've looked at a number of them plying their trade. But for large corporations wishing to be more entrepreneurial, a more fundamental issue arises: How do we get more of these people? Eventually, the answer to the question involves deciding whether to "buy or build." People who are already entrepreneurial leaders are easy to spot if one looks hard enough for them, either inside or outside the company. Unfortunately, companies that do not value entrepreneurial leaders often wear them out, wash them out, or fail to attract them at all.

Entrepreneurial leaders are not usually the typical direct reports in command and control structures. They often bend the rules and are not afraid to state their opinions about how the business could work better. Large bureaucratic organizations don't often reward these sometimes "rebel-like" or counterculture behaviors. This leads to a self-reinforcing policy that develops good soldier-managers. So, it is no wonder that so few entrepreneurial leaders exist in large, structured companies. The odds are decidedly against them. But, as you saw in the preceding chapters, some of them make it despite the odds. As one entrepreneurial leader from a large outsourcing business told me, "You have to get used to the door getting slammed in your face once in a while; but if you know how to come back in a different way, it doesn't get slammed quite as hard."

Once a company makes the strategic decision to identify and cultivate greater numbers of entrepreneurial leaders, it must decide whether to try to build them from the internal ranks of managers that it already has or go outside to get them. This is the fundamental buy-or-build question. Some interesting issues play into this decision. On one hand, people already inside the organization have survived and know how to play the game. They understand the politics, they know how to stay out of trouble, and they have developed an internal network of colleagues who help them do their jobs in spite of the organizational barriers that often get in the way of performance. So, the good news is that many managers who have been around a while come with some good organizational software already wired in. The bad news is that you don't know who could actually be more entrepreneurial unless you somehow create a seedbed in which more-entrepreneurial leadership can be identified, developed, and reinforced.

Some companies decide that it is best to buy entrepreneurial leaders from the outside, and so they search for them in other companies, based on proven track records. Nestlé, for example, was trying to get their new Nespresso coffee and coffee machine business off the ground. After several struggling years, it brought in an outside entrepreneur who was able to kick-start the business and get it going down the right path. But it had to replace this individual after about 2 years because it needed someone who was good at growing a stable business, not just starting it up.[1]

Some companies have tried to bring in outside start-up entrepreneurs to shake things up, but often with very disappointing results. Start-up entrepreneurs usually dislike large company settings. Often, they are not very good leaders or managers, and they have a notoriously low tolerance for what they consider to be stupid rules and regulations that slow down decisive action taking. They generally don't last very long, and both they and the hiring organization usually give a large sigh of relief when they decide to separate.

Companies are left, then, with trying to identify and develop entrepreneurial leaders from within their own organization or recruiting tried-and-true entrepreneurial leaders from another established company.

Hi-Pots: The Anti-Entrepreneurs?

In my work with large companies that have decided to develop more-entrepreneurial leaders from within their current manager cohort, they often start with a list of high potentials (hi-pots), assuming that they will have the best chance of success in becoming entrepreneurial leaders. Most large organizations have some sort of list or chart with the names of young managers whom they believe have high potential to move quickly up the ranks of the organization and into senior-level positions. Once these folks are identified through performance appraisals or assessment centers, or they receive special recognition for good work on projects or assignments, they are often put through accelerated training programs and stretch job assignments and are fast-tracked up the organization. So, it's not a huge leap of faith to suppose that hi-pots would make the best entrepreneurial leaders.

In working with companies that have hi-pot programs, we often find a very curious phenomenon that is difficult to explain at first but seems obvious upon further reflection. Some of the most high-potential managers in large companies are often the least entrepreneurial. If you think about a mega insurance company, for example, the high potentials often are those who are identified as playing by the rules, being good soldiers, doing excellent work at their assigned jobs, gradually working their way up over the years, and definitely not telling superiors that they have a better idea on how to grow the business. John Kelley (in the miner profile in Chapter 6), in contrast, was the perfect example of an entrepreneurial leader who succeeded so well in changing the business and getting results in such an environment that his company fired him.

Now, you might argue that insurance companies should not want more entrepreneurs due to their risk-averse natures, but look at Progressive Insurance. It is a model of innovation and entrepreneurial thinking. It was the first insurance company to offer to put GPS systems in its customers' cars, so that its customers were only charged for the driving they did. The GPS system tracks a driver's habits and routes, and they are charged accordingly. City driving is more expensive than country, and speeding is more expensive than near speed limit driving. Progressive is one of the fastest growing companies in the auto insurance industry due to its entrepreneurial orientation. And its name says it all.

Fidelity Investments also has a culture and history of entrepreneurial thinking. While it rewards good soldiering, it often is on the lookout for managers who challenge the status quo and who are willing to take a risk. And many of these managers are rewarded for their efforts by getting the opportunity to run the new businesses they envisioned. Fidelity knows that not all of these people will be successful as entrepreneurial leaders, but they are given a chance to prove their mettle.

Uncorking the Bottle

I no longer try to predict who can or cannot be a successful entrepreneurial leader. The only real way to find out is to give people the skills, confidence, and knowledge to be a successful entrepreneurial leader and then give them the opportunity to try it. From this seedbed emerges the latent entrepreneur. The seedbed can be created by on-the-job development or by structured educational experiences. IBM, GE, and Intel, for example, like to put young managers in job assignments in which they are required to develop and utilize entrepreneurial skills. Siemens and Mott's put people through an entrepreneurial education program to prepare them for playing the entrepreneurial leader's role.

Intel, for example, has a specific organizational structure called Corporate Business Development (CBD),[2] whose avowed mission is to "make Intel do what it does not want to do." CBD is essentially an internal venturing group. It has seed money to incubate new ideas and business opportunities that would fall outside of Intel's core businesses. These ideas are allowed to take shape, at least for a while, under the CBD umbrella, where they are protected, nurtured, and developed.

At the end of 2 years, these seedlings have three possible futures: They could be picked up by an Intel group to be integrated into the core business. They could be spun out or off as separate businesses to be sold or developed. Or they are shut down. The interesting part of this model is that Intel will tap the shoulder of one of their managers whom it wishes to develop and will give her a tour of duty at CBD as a "corporate entrepreneur." These newly minted corporate entrepreneurs get a chance at the wheel, to see if they can be entrepreneurial. They are given coaching and mentoring by senior executives within and outside of CBD, and they have a chance at a significant promotion if they are successful. So, Intel uses a combination of careful selection, on-the-job training, coaching and development, and immersion to find out which of its managers can be entrepreneurial leaders. It is also interesting to note that, in contrast to start-up entrepreneurs, who conceive their babies and thus have passion for them, at Intel, the new corporate entrepreneurs are often handed someone else's baby and asked to adopt and develop a love for it. The passion for the start-up entrepreneur comes from creating the baby; an Intel entrepreneurial leader's passion comes from spending time with the baby and knowing that their career advancement may depend on how well they love and care for it.

IDG provides another example. As we saw earlier from the John Kilcullen profile, IDG tries to hire individuals with a lot of drive and a point to prove, and then gives them a chance to create a business. Like Intel, it devotes seed capital to this process and is willing to make a number of small bets in order to test the validity of both the new business ideas and the people who are going to get a chance to bring them to fruition. It doesn't know if these managers can be successful entrepreneurs until it gives them a chance in a managed risk situation.

The Importance of Education

Another way to uncork the bottle is through very applied educational experiences in which entrepreneurial leadership is a targeted and expected outcome of the experience. As I said earlier, many companies come to us for that magic elixir in the form of some educational capsule. We now have had more than 10 years of experience in the process of trying to educate corporate managers into becoming entrepreneurial leaders. Companies like Siemens, Sodexho, Mott's, Nationwide Insurance, Ford, Mercury Computer, and others have asked us to design and run these kinds of educational programs or experiences.

One approach that has worked extremely well for many of our client companies is to combine educational inputs with real-world opportunity-development projects. Even if someone has some natural entrepreneurial tendencies, they still need to have good skills in managing the opportunity process and sound business acumen as well. An aspiring entrepreneurial leader with no financial acumen or influencing skills not only has a tremendous uphill battle trying to play this role, but can be dangerous to himself and others. If he doesn't understand the importance of managing cash flow, how to reach the customer with some unique value proposition, or the opportunity's cost of capital, then he may get himself and his company into trouble very quickly.

Fortunately, most people have an intuitive understanding of some of these concepts if they manage their own finances at home and have to influence a banker for a loan, but they need to have a more sophisticated understanding when working on developing company opportunities. The money is not theirs, and the impact of a failed venture can have broad ramifications for employees and even for the company brand. Entrepreneurial spirit and sound business skills must go hand-in-hand. High-spirited entrepreneurial leaders without business discipline are cowboys likely to get quickly gunned down, while skilled managers without the entrepreneurial spirit often are good stewards, but not likely to create huge new businesses.

An Entrepreneurial Cauldron

If it is not easy to predict who can and cannot be an entrepreneurial leader until they try, then it's necessary to provide opportunities for trying and developing at the same time. The best way to discover and develop entrepreneurial leaders is to provide a live-action, real opportunity within the company. This has a twofold purpose: to identify and develop potential entrepreneurial leaders and to help the company learn how to accommodate them. I am totally convinced that most motivated managers can act in much more entrepreneurial ways if their organizations let them. The problem is that those companies that most need entrepreneurial leadership, and that come to us for help, have the most well-developed entrepreneurial antibodies. Often, the process of developing entrepreneurial leaders highlights the organization's cultural and structural barriers that must be changed if new value creation is to be sustained over time. Otherwise, the organization will create the potential—but not the realization.

We have found that these types of entrepreneurial educational programs, if well structured, turn into powerful organizational-change programs as well. Mott's provides an excellent example of one of these types of programs.

The Mott's Model: Entrepreneurial Leadership Training in Action

Mott's Corporation is a well-respected foods and drink mixers company with headquarters in Stamford, Connecticut. When Mott's was acquired by Cadbury Schweppes, it was under intense pressure to increase shareholder value to meet very aggressive growth goals. It decided to embark on a management development program with our Executive Education division aimed at developing entrepreneurial leaders from within the company who could identify and develop significant new business opportunities. Not only did Mott's want to create new businesses, it also wanted to use the educational process to help bring about a change in the somewhat conservative business culture of Mott's.

We worked together to develop an action- and learning-based entrepreneurial leadership development program. As the faculty director and program designer, my goal was to work closely with Mott's in not only the educational and training aspects of corporate entrepreneurship, but to help the company find real opportunities that would ultimately result in new products, expanded growth, and increased shareholder value.

Developing a Template

Working with Mott's was a great experience, because we were able to further hone and refine our entrepreneurial leadership development template, which I now believe generalizes to a number of other organizations trying to rekindle their entrepreneurial spirit. We started building this template when first working with Siemens, and we have found it to be an excellent generator of innovation and new business creation for many organizations. It works because the education is intertwined with real-time opportunity identification, development, and capture. Using this model, we were also able to see how entrepreneurial leadership education can be used as a potent tool for inducing organizational change. To learn more about the details of this educational template, refer to Appendix A of this book. But for now, let's explore some of the basics of this program and the assumptions under which such a program might work.

The template follows the opportunity process. The first module consists of participants learning about entrepreneurship, innovation, and some of the marketing and financial skills that are necessary to identify an opportunity. They then go back to their organizations to look for new business opportunities, based on what they have learned in Module 1. This approach is very similar to the program that Shahrom Kiani, mentioned in Chapter 5, went through in the Siemens General Manager's Course. After a period of time, usually 2 months, participants come back for Module 2, in which we help them further refine and hone their ideas—or actively discourage them from continuing with their ideas. The purpose of Module 1 is idea generation; in Module 2 we determine if the participants' ideas are actually good business opportunities that should be pursued. Between Modules 1 and 2, we are able to differentiate among people in terms of their passion, their understanding and application of opportunity-identification tools from the first module, and the amount of time they have actually dedicated to pursuing a new business opportunity.

Participants then return to their organizations for another 2 months. When they return for Module 3, they arrive with a business plan. In this module, we help them refine—and often rewrite—these plans, before they make a formal presentation to senior management to see if they can get funding and support. Between-module coaching is also a component of the program, and we look for organizational barriers that can derail the company's desire for developing more entrepreneurial orientation. When we find these barriers, we escalate these issues to upper management to see if they are willing to remove them. If not, then we challenge their seriousness about greater entrepreneurial orientation and suggest they stop investing if they are not serious. At each module's end, we make a "go, no-go" decision on the continuation of the program. Or, the company might decide to repeat a module if it is not happy with what it is getting in terms of opportunities.

We started with a list of key assumptions to help guide our efforts. These assumptions function as the ground rules for program development and execution and can serve as a guideline for other companies embarking on this kind of "build" approach.

1. Entrepreneurial behavior is not an end in itself but a means to new-product and new-business development.
2. A joint design team, consisting of our faculty and management, oversees both the program and the implementation of entrepreneurial activities within the company.
3. The first program serves as a pilot and includes a cross-section of the company. In Mott's case, the design team believed that the program participants would be skewed to field or marketing personnel, who were perceived to be closest to the marketplace, customers, competitors, and opportunities. But, as we have seen, internally focused entrepreneurial action also can contribute greatly to a company's growth.
4. The program follows a "learn as we go" approach. Many attempts at instilling entrepreneurial behavior within a cor-

porate setting fail because those charged with identifying, developing, and capturing new business opportunities are either the wrong people or they are the right people but the organizational barriers to innovation and entrepreneurial thinking eventually wear them down or wear them out. Often, appropriate support mechanisms are not in place, and the culture and current reward systems may actively discourage innovation and risk taking.

With Mott's, the team agreed that we would probably not know the critical breakpoints until we reached them. Therefore, in addition to having the fundamental purpose of new-value creation, the program was conceived of as a change tool. Senior management agreed that, when barriers arose, the organization would test its resolve and seriousness about entrepreneurial leadership by assessing these barriers and then taking actions aimed at overcoming or surmounting them. Senior management also agreed that their inability or unwillingness to remove these barriers would be a signal to stop investing in entrepreneurial training, since it would be clear that the organization was not really serious about developing entrepreneurship within the company.

5. The company agrees to make significant resources available for following good opportunities, including money, time, materials, and talent.

6. Senior management also agrees to take a venture capital–style staged-investment approach when working with start-up businesses and the entrepreneurial leaders who found them. After each educational program module, the outcomes are assessed against the planned objectives. If the anticipated results are being achieved, the company then invests in the next stage of educational development. If outcomes are not in line with expectations, then the company can take a different approach or choose to stop investing in the rest of the project. Entrepreneurial ideas are treated in the same way. Seed money is used to nurture good ideas. More money and resources follow only those ideas that show promise.

7. Participants in the course are carefully recruited and screened, but recruitment is not restricted to high-potentials because, as mentioned earlier, in a conservative organization these people are not necessarily more entrepreneurial. Several elements are key to this process:
   · Participants are chosen from a cross-section of the organization.
   · Volunteerism is encouraged.
   · Participants are interviewed by members of the design team before selection is finalized.
   · Participants are supported in opting out of the program at any time if they do not feel that they are cut out to be entrepreneurial leaders.
8. Senior management agrees to play an active leadership role in helping the program succeed. That is, members of senior management act as sponsors to one or more of the potential entrepreneurial leaders or teams. This helps in the resolution of problems or barriers that arise in trying to turn ideas into opportunities and opportunities into reality.

We have used this educational model with several clients, and it seems appealing on several fronts. First, the work involves real opportunity identification and capture. If one or more of these opportunities comes to fruition, it will more than likely pay for the cost of the program many times over. We don't have to guess about who might become more entrepreneurial, since we are observing this firsthand. Companies don't have to invest unless they get results, and it forces senior management to "walk the talk" about greater entrepreneurship. If they are unwilling or unable to remove the barriers to greater innovation and entrepreneurial orientation, then they had better not continue down this path.

It's Never Too Late—The Story of Dieter

As I mentioned earlier, a lot of debate always arises about whether entrepreneurs are born or made, and I am sure this debate will continue. But the evidence that I have seen in these educational programs makes me very optimistic about the ability to educate motivated managers to think and act like entrepreneurs.

Perhaps my most memorable experience in trying to teach managers to be entrepreneurial leaders came in 1995, when I faced about 38 international managers from a global IT company. It was the first day of class, and things seemed to be going well. About mid-morning, I broke the class into smaller groups and sent them off to analyze a case study that looked at a successful entrepreneurial leader. In addition to discussing the case, I instructed each group to develop a brief presentation of the key learning points from the case and asked them to jot down these points on either a flip chart or a transparency for presentation.

Everyone went to their assigned break-out rooms except for Dieter, a 52-year-old German engineer. He stood over my desk, rocking back and forth on his feet, with his hands clenched behind his back. He was not smiling and seemed quite annoyed with me. When I asked him how I could help, he said in very stern terms, "Professor, which one do you want?" I replied, "Which one of what?" He said, "Do you want the presentation on a flip chart or a transparency?" I said, "Dieter, I don't care. Whichever one you like." He said even more sternly, "No! You are the professor. You must tell us!"

I was dumbfounded. No manager at his level had ever asked me this question, and he was in a class to be an entrepreneurial leader. We did some research to find out how Dieter got in this class of supposedly hand-picked managers. It turned out that his boss wanted to get rid of him, but firing someone at his age was a little complicated. His boss's clever alternative was to send Dieter off to our program, knowing that he would be away from the office for at least 6 weeks and preoccupied with course demands for even longer.

In the first module, Dieter said nothing and contributed nothing. He sat there, obviously miffed, with his arms crossed. He obviously had a dilemma: He did not want to be in the course, but he also didn't want to fail or be seen as failing, and he knew he had to make a presentation to the top brass of the company at the end of the course.

When the second module started, Dieter seemed the same, but he did come in with an idea and reluctantly presented it to the group. As it happened, he found that another participant had a similar idea, so they hooked up. At the end of the second week of this module, Dieter was perceptibly different. He was talking, his arms were no longer crossed, and he seemed more animated.

By the final week of the program, Dieter and his partner presented a very well-thought-out business plan and got backing from the board. He was one of the few participants who, along with his partner, actually developed a successful new business within his company.

What happened? Somewhere along the line, he got switched on—something that none of us could have predicted. Dieter has made me eternally optimistic about the ability of people to learn to act more entrepreneurially. According to people who knew Dieter, he had never shown a hint of entrepreneurial drive before coming to our program. He was seen as just biding his time until retirement.

So, it's never too late, and some people just need the right mix of ingredients to bring out the entrepreneurial potential within.

Entrepreneurial Leadership Can Indeed Be Learned

In working with Dieter and literally thousands of other managers, we have developed a good understanding of what can and can't be learned regarding entrepreneurial leadership. Identifying and shaping ideas can be learned, as can selling these ideas to others. Creating and communicating a compelling vision of an opportunity can be learned. Blending the roles of leader, manager, and entrepreneur can be learned. And, of course, the business planning process that helps differentiate good ideas from good opportunities can also be learned.

We have many great examples of managers who never considered themselves creative or innovative, but who found significant new business opportunities as a result of their entrepreneurial training. A Siemens manager, for example, found a unique way to stop credit card fraud through fingerprinting technology. A team from the Venezuelan national oil company, PDVSA, identified a huge commercial market for a waste product that they formerly threw away. A Mott's employee identified a way to start a spin-out business based on Mott's back-office competencies. Shahrom Kiani and Alfred Weichselbaum, profiled in Chapters 5 and 7, respectively, are great examples of the power of formal entrepreneurial education in enabling the development of entrepreneurial leadership capabilities that result in significant value creation. Kiani discovered a new market in law enforcement for his letter-reading scanners, and Weichselbaum found that stirring the pot of innovation within his unit could uncover a number of employee-driven cost-saving and value-creation ideas.

None of these opportunities would have been discovered had these participants not been exposed to an environment in which ideas were not only encouraged and supported but challenged as well. The ability to think creatively and to be innovative is a human condition. Some people exhibit these tendencies naturally, while others need a catalyst for these inherent capabilities to emerge. Education and, particularly, coaching turned out to be two of the most important ways in which innovation and creativity were stimulated to emerge. The entrepreneurship training's most effective aspect was to give participants the tools, techniques, and discipline to distinguish between a good idea and a good opportunity. And it gave them the self-confidence and motivation to try.

As I stated earlier, one of our most surprising results, and one that we had not predicted, was that we were not able to forecast with any reasonable certainty which managers would emerge as the most entrepreneurial. Neither background, education, nor past successes were good predictors of entrepreneurial leadership success.

But Does It Really Make a Difference?

Finally, however, the question is whether a real return on investment can be gained in such educational endeavors. Do any new, truly entrepreneurial ventures come to fruition that justify both the program's expense and the manager's time away from other potentially more productive and certain activities? Ultimately, will increased entrepreneurial behavior actually lead to the capture of higher margin, durable new business opportunities by the company?

Let's look at what success means. One end of the continuum is a change in the manager's behavior that fosters more innovation, creative problem solving, and circumvention of red tape. In this scenario, the manager is not really a corporate entrepreneur in terms of creating a new business venture, but she is now much more appreciative of the importance of new ideas, and subsequently acts to create a more innovative culture for her employees. This is the work of the accelerator—practicing behaviors that are easily learned and require no resources. But, as we saw in Chapter 7, these behaviors can have a significant impact on customer satisfaction, employee satisfaction, and financial margins.

At the other end of the spectrum is the creation of a completely new business that is durable and generates a great deal of money for the organization, much like the returns venture capitalists seek. This is the work of explorers, like John Kilcullen (Chapter 5). In the middle are miners, like Alfred Weichselbaum (Chapter 7) and integrators like Denise Prince and Don Cotey (Chapter 8). They create organizations that create value, so there are many fingerprints on the successes—but financial successes they are. All the people profiled in this book have created significant economic value for their respective organizations. Some got these ideas through formal entrepreneurial education, some got it because they came with the internal wiring, and some got there because the organization tapped them on the shoulder and said, "Have we got an opportunity for you!" But all of them had or developed the capabilities for spotting, pursuing, and capturing new business opportunities while successfully navigating their own organization's structures, systems, and politics.

Summary

It is important for companies to be optimistic about their ability to either find people with entrepreneurial leadership tendencies within their corporate ranks or to develop these people through focused management-development experiences. The challenge for these companies then is to provide the infrastructure and support mechanisms that continually reinforce this kind of behavior.

Chapter Ten

The Problem with Culture Change

The problem with companies wishing to rekindle their entre-preneurial heritage is that they have done a lot of things over the years to kill it. This often happens by accretion: The company grows. It adds processes and people, rules and regulations, structure and organization. All these things, while clearly important, also tend to stifle creativity, independent thinking, and accountability.

So, how do companies reverse this process? First, they don't do it overnight, and they usually don't start all over again, because it would scare the hell out of the investors. They need to begin with a clear entrepreneurial strategy.

Some companies, such as Siemens and GE, attack the bureaucratic culture. This attack often takes the form of some comprehensive culture-change program involving creating a fresh company vision, heavy emphasis on communicating and selling that vision, and often some reorganization. To be sure, this tends to be a pretty blunt instrument. A lot of folks grow old waiting for a culture to change, and then, just as it starts to change, some other visionary comes along and wants to leave their mark by changing the culture *again*. GE is one of the better examples of culture change. It spent a lot on training and development for their managers, gave them increasing freedom and accountability to run their businesses, and took out multiple layers of bureaucracy. And still it took GE 10 years.

Many of today's companies can't take years to reorient themselves. They simply don't have the time or the energy to do this, especially in increasingly turbulent and unpredictable environments. So they turn to other means or mechanisms. Mott's took the view that it would change its culture by using a cadre of entrepreneurially trained leaders to find out exactly where the barriers to greater innovation and entrepreneurial thinking lay. This is a much finer instrument than overall culture-change programs. The Mott's approach says, Let's not presuppose all the things that could stop entrepreneurial leaders from succeeding in growing the business. Let's send them out into the Mott's world and see what they bump into. We will then use this knowledge to pinpoint the necessary changes. This kind of focused change has several advantages: It's easier to sell growth programs than to sell change programs. And, line managers drive the process in pursuit of their bonus, which makes them rather motivated.

Starting with Opportunity Sets

The starting point for Siemens, Mott's, and Sodexho, which were looking for a more-entrepreneurial culture, was not with culture but with the search for opportunities—which they believed would in turn also change their cultures. This approach has a great deal of intuitive appeal. Opportunities are highly focused and, since they create value, they generally get people's attention and support, especially that of senior management. In addition, time spent pursuing new business development is hard to argue against.

Culture-change programs usually start from the inside. We have all gone through the attitude surveys, the external consultants, and executive team "show-and-tells." Often, employees come out of the culture-change experience more confused than enlightened and, while most senior managers are pretty adept at creating some compelling arguments for change, they are not so good at the follow-through.

I have gone through numerous change initiatives with large companies, and they often end in either failure or mediocre success. Then things change or someone else comes in with a different point of view and the cycle repeats itself.

When companies start with opportunities, it leads them down a different and perhaps more efficient path. Real opportunities in the marketplace often require changes in the organization for these opportunities to be captured. Opportunities tend to be discrete and concrete, thus easy to visualize and rationalize. As Bill Isaacson, one of our explorers in Chapter 5, started to get 3M into the optical lens business, it became clear that 3M had to make some changes if it wanted to be successful in this market. It needed more investment in research, partnering, and distribution.

GM's development of the Saturn company is another good example of opportunity-driven change. The opportunity was for GM to make an economy car that would challenge and win against the increasingly strong Japanese competitors. But GM knew that it would take too long for its entrenched culture, politics, and bureaucracy to change to support Saturn's new approach. To be competitive, it literally had to spin out Saturn in order to make it a success. They then brought some of the lessons learned at Saturn back into GM. And it was easier to sell to employees since they now had proof of concept. It's interesting to note that, as GM has increasingly brought Saturn under the smothering GM umbrella, it has started to suffer from what GM had initially planned against.

DaimlerChrysler presents another good example of using opportunities to help change the company. It knew that it was missing a tremendous opportunity in the burgeoning sport-utility vehicle (SUV) market, but had no offering. When it embarked on the Mercedes M-Class model, it created a new manufacturing facility in Alabama[1] and populated the project team with outsiders from Lexus, Toyota, GM, and Ford. It also gave the group a lot more leeway in decision making than was typical for DaimlerChrysler. It tested new ways of manufacturing the cars and new pay systems. Yet, the group maintained close ties and communications with the parent in Stuttgart. Stuttgart went into the venture with the express purpose of not only building a world-class SUV, but of using the Alabama experience to bring changes back to the parent company.

For both GM and DaimlerChrysler, these new opportunities were "stretch" opportunities. By this I mean the opportunities forced both companies to change some things in their strategy, organization, processes and procedures, and cultural values. So, instead of culture change leading to new opportunities, new opportunities led to, and in most cases forced, organizational change.

When Corning was about to close down its Serengeti Eyewear Sunglasses Division, an entrepreneurial leader named Zaki Mustafa, whom I mentioned earlier, went to the board with a plan to save the company and make it profitable.[2] Mustafa, who had worked for the division, felt that Corning had been too product-focused and that the business was failing due to poor marketing, anemic customer focus, and inefficient asset management. He finally convinced the board to let him try to save the division, but they insisted in having an oversight committee to watch his every move.

They OK'd Mustafa's request to head up the company, but the board wanted to maintain hierarchical control. Mustafa knew that, if this cultural value of "disempowerment" remained, he would ultimately fail in his bid to save Serengeti. An all-day meeting with the board ensued, in which they insisted on the oversight committee and he refused to accept it. He finally left the board meeting and went back to his office to pack his belongings, believing he would be fired for refusing to accept the current hierarchical control. He was about ready to leave when the board called him back in and agreed that there would be no oversight committee.

As Mustafa gained more insight into Serengeti's missed opportunity, he realized that he did not need to have Corning do the manufacturing. He outsourced this function, saving the company a lot of money. He also built his own IT system, since Corning's system actually slowed down his ability to be customer-focused and have timely market data. In addition, he changed the culture of Serengeti to a team-orientation, in which others were empowered to satisfy the customer, no matter what. Serengeti became a major success for Corning. This opportunity changed some cultural values of the parent company as well as its approaches to asset management and customer service.

Xerox, as many people know, has gone through some very difficult times. This well-known brand, like many large slow-moving companies, eventually succumbed to the weight of its own bureaucracy. Market problems, slow product development, inane politics at the board level, and accusations of fiduciary mismanagement may have irreparably tarnished this company. But Xerox actually invented much of today's computer logic. It invented the mouse and the basis for much of a PC's operating system architecture, but left its inventions unpatented—to the vast benefit of the then-fledgling Microsoft and Apple.

Subsequently, having failed to exploit its own inventions due primarily to its rigid structure, Xerox spun out a new organization called Xerox New Enterprises (XNE).[3] This organization produced some very good early wins in creating new businesses, but the political arm-wrestling among Xerox corporate executives over who would control XNE eventually killed it. In the case of Xerox, as with almost all stretch opportunities, these opportunities created pressure on the organization to change things in order to capture the opportunity. Smart organizations use this pressure to focus change efforts and to highlight barriers that need to be removed. Some companies, like Xerox, have good intentions, but the pressure for change in its case rattled too many executive-level cages.

Two Models for Change—Top-Down versus Opportunity

Most gurus in change management recite the mantra that change must start at the top of the organization and cascade down to lower levels. As I said earlier, this can take a long time. And top-level jobs are not as stable as they used to be, so it is not uncommon to see many changes start at the top, but then the top is changed and many of the change initiatives go by the board.

The nice thing about opportunity-induced change is that the leaders who induce it can come from any level. In the 3i

Siemens program (mentioned in Chapter 7), in 2005, more than $375,000 has been given out in awards to employees who thought up innovative ways to deploy their manufacturing assets. Bill Isaacson and John Kelley (profiled in Chapters 5 and 6, respectively) were in the middle of their respective organizations. Entrepreneurial leaders can and often do bring about organizational change even when they are not at the top. Some of the reasons for their successes are obvious:

· Value-creation opportunities that create pressure for internal change are an easier sell than cultural change. Instead of costing the company money, they are meant to make the company money.
· Entrepreneurial leaders are focused on changing things that will enable the specific opportunity; thus, these changes may be narrower—and therefore more doable—than an overall company-change effort.
· Most employees can relate to, and often get excited about, doing things differently if that can grow the business. They are much less excited and cooperative if they believe the change effort is really a smoke screen for cost cutting and a reduction in workforce.

A Hard Look in the Mirror

Opportunities are not hard to spot. Capturing them is the hard part. If an organization runs into itself in trying to capture a new opportunity and fails, this is usually a compelling argument to change something.

In Figure 10.1, I have shown you the typical model that most people believe is the accepted approach to change, from the top down.

In Figure 10.2, on the other hand, we see the model for opportunity-induced change. We start with a specific external focus and as we try to capture the new opportunity we find out what organizational changes need to be made in order to capture it.

Going after new business opportunities often tests the company's capabilities, resources, and resolve. It is not uncommon

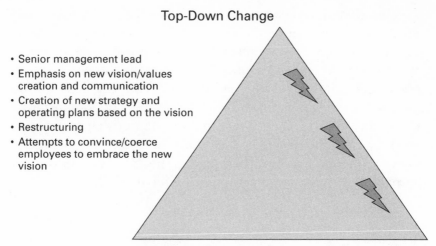

Top-Down Change

- Senior management lead
- Emphasis on new vision/values creation and communication
- Creation of new strategy and operating plans based on the vision
- Restructuring
- Attempts to convince/coerce employees to embrace the new vision

FIGURE 10.1   The conventional wisdom of top-down change.

for the pursuit of new opportunities to both push and pull the organization into new strategic orientations. The pursuit of significant new business opportunities is actually an excellent test of adaptability and survivability. If a company sees a significant new opportunity and is unable to marshal the resources or command the speed to make it happen, then this can be a wake-up call that creates pressure for change. The company has an

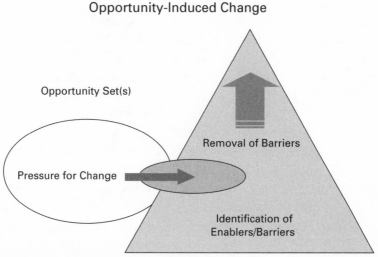

Opportunity-Induced Change

Opportunity Set(s)

Pressure for Change

Removal of Barriers

Identification of Enablers/Barriers

FIGURE 10.2   Opportunity-induced change.

excellent chance to analyze and diagnose what must happen to capture the opportunity in a much more precise manner.

The continuous and disciplined drive for new business opportunities keeps an organization sharp. It forces closeness to markets, allows for the assessment and development of entrepreneurial skills and attitudes, and forces the organization to keep a reserve of funds "just in case" something really good comes along. And it helps the organization undergo precise change "surgery," rather than using the general exploratory approach that most large companies typically follow.

Summary

While probably hundreds of books on change and change management exist, it is important to keep in mind that change must be compelling for people to move from what they believe are safe waters to unknown waters. When the ship is sinking, everyone runs to get off, but that doesn't mean they know where to go to be safer. When the organization is sailing smoothly, even if unwittingly heading into a hurricane, most people remain pretty contented unless they can be convinced of the imminent danger. Thus, the real challenge for today's organizational captains—if the organization is to survive and thrive in turbulent times—is to create the vision and motivation for people to change. As we can see from all the star performers who have fallen off the Fortune 500 Top 100 list over the last 30 years, this is no easy undertaking. Getting an entire organization to change its culture is almost impossible without major and often painful surgery.

Perhaps the best way to keep the ship running smoothly while allowing it to change direction quickly comes from spotting new opportunities for trade in new places. Entrepreneurial leaders are constantly on deck, keeping watch for new ports of trade and suggesting new routes. Some of these new ports can offer enticing trade opportunities but take the ship in a different, potentially more prosperous direction. Risks exist, of course, but the alternative is that senior staff sits around the captain's table debating how to first change the attitudes of sailors and get them all to agree to change course. The entrepreneurial captain would most surely get closer to the port of opportunity and send out a few small entrepreneurial leaders to test the waters, and then move pretty quickly to a port that has high potential. The crew is much more likely to come along because they see some proof that this port is a place of real opportunity. Thus, organizational change might be more successful if the organization spends less time worrying about culture and spends more time pursuing strategically important opportunities, which in turn force culture change.

Chapter Eleven

Building the Entrepreneurial Organization

A large and successful food services business came to us a couple of years ago and asked for advice and help in infecting their managers with more of the entrepreneurial spirit they once had. Their entrepreneurial founder believed that his company had become bogged down in structure, policies, procedures, and risk averseness and was not as innovative or entrepreneurial as it needed to be to compete effectively in an increasingly difficult world. So, we designed a program to teach its managers to act more like entrepreneurial leaders. The outcome of this educational program was to be the identification, development, and capture of real new-business opportunities.

Since working with this company and many others seeking a renewal of their entrepreneurial spirit, I now use a new phrase in my lectures: "Be careful what you ask for, you might get it!" As a result of the program, this food services company asked for and got a cadre of motivated entrepreneurial leaders, who identified a number of new business opportunities, not just ideas. Our program got rave reviews from both the participants and the company's executives, but was cancelled—due to its success! While the company was able to implement some important innovations, it was not prepared for the huge flow of good ideas that came from the participants. What both we and they discovered is that the organization must be ready and able to handle people who think and act like entrepreneurs and the opportunities that situation creates. We know we can identify and develop these people. We know these people can identify significant new business opportunities for their respective organizations. And we know that organizations intent on developing greater entrepreneurial leadership must think carefully about how they intend to handle these people and integrate them and their opportunities back into the company. Getting people all dressed up with no place to go is an exercise in futility and a waste of money as well, unless it awakens the organization to what it must do differently the next time.

This company is a very good company, and it had the best of intentions, but it was not prepared for the excitement, motivation, and entrepreneurial productivity the program engendered. It is not alone in this. We often warn our clients that they really need to plan thoughtfully before creating more entrepreneurial activity. The payoffs, as we have seen from the profiles in previous chapters, can be enormous, but the organization must be ready to deal with the power of the creative mind and the energy of the impassioned heart. When people get "switched on" to play the entrepreneurial leader role, they need some place to apply that newfound energy and focus. The organization must be prepared to deal with this reality. Thus, having an entrepreneurial strategy and structures, processes, and procedures that support such activity is a must.

Don Cotey Jr.'s profile in Chapter 8 is an excellent example: IBM wanted more entrepreneurial activity and was smart enough about it to understand that it had to treat new businesses much differently from mature ones if the internal start-ups were to survive.

Placing Your Bets

At the end of the day, companies wishing to be more entrepreneurial have to place a bet. They either bet on entrepreneurial leaders to help overcome slowness, lethargy, and bureaucracy, or they "bolt on" formal structures and processes to counterbalance large company inertia. Mott's, Siemens, and Sodexho, for example, placed their bets on developing more entrepreneurial leaders through targeted entrepreneurial development programs. If enough of these people are identified and developed, then they should have an impact on the organization in terms of both business development and culture change. Intel and P&G, on the other hand, bet on formal structures and processes, like incubators, opportunity-identification groups, and corporate business development departments. These companies don't want to upset the apple cart and make a lot of organizational changes, but prefer instead to add another structure to overcome the bureaucracy and slowness of their current structures. While it might sound silly, I have seen this approach work.

"Bolt-on structures" are new organizational devices that are added to an organization's existing structure to overcome some of its weaknesses. For example, P&G's Corporate New Ventures (CNV) group, which I mentioned in Chapter 4, was created specifically to help increase cross-organizational innovation. The P&G brand structure was so focused on its individual brands that the company lost opportunities to share technological innovation among its brands. For example, before this new structure was in place, it had taken P&G 10 years to migrate its clothing softener over to its paper products brands. CNV was created in part to help find these synergies and exploit them.

But, to sustain a more entrepreneurial culture over time, both people and processes must be examined, and the organization must be brutally honest about what needs to be changed if it is serious about rekindling its entrepreneurial spirit. IDG, for example, bets on both structures and entrepreneurial leaders. It keeps the business units small and the corporate staff very lean, and is great at recruiting and developing talented entrepreneurial leaders who are then given a great deal of freedom (and accountability) to run their businesses. From my perspective, the IDG model represents the best of both worlds. It helps develop entrepreneurial leaders, but it also has some entrepreneurial wiring in place that will support and sustain this type of leadership when it is practiced.

I realize that many organizations do not yet have this wiring, and sometimes it can take years for the electricians to finish the job. But competition doesn't wait for years to attack, so companies need to do something now. As we have seen, developing cadres of entrepreneurially oriented leaders and sending them out as missionaries in their own organizations can help. However, bolt-on structures can also help.

Antibodies and Antidotes

Rekindling a burned-out entrepreneurial spirit is not easy. Large organizations often have very well-developed and highly resistant strains of entrepreneurial antibodies that can overwhelm and destroy attempts at rekindling entrepreneurial spirit. Companies must understand what these antibodies are and prepare antidotes to them. So, let's take a look at some of the more common antibodies we have seen and what companies need to do to neutralize them.

The Alice Malice: It Doesn't Matter Which Road You Take

Perhaps the biggest antibody facing companies wishing to rekindle their entrepreneurial spirit is that they really don't know what they mean by "entrepreneurial." To paraphrase the Cheshire Cat in the Alice in Wonderland fairy tale, "then either road will take you there." This was the cat's response to Alice being lost and asking advice as to which of two roads to take. When he asked Alice where she was going, she said that she did not much care. Thus, his answer. Many companies just want to be more entrepreneurial, but have not really come to grips with which road to take.

It is quite fascinating and frightening to hear people use the word *entrepreneurial*, thinking they know the meaning, when in fact they actually differ a great deal when asked the details. If a company is not clear on what it means by the term, then it is bound to run into trouble. I worked with one company for a year just trying to get top management to agree on the meaning of corporate entrepreneurship. To some, *entrepreneurial* means growth, to others it means thinking like an owner or creating a new business within the business. One of the major reasons I developed the entrepreneurial leader typologies was to help companies get greater definition about what they want when they say "more entrepreneurial."

For example, if a company finally agrees that more explorer behavior is desired, then it will probably want to think about how to structure a new business or venture within the existing business. If, on the other hand, the company finally defines *entrepreneurial* as accelerator-style entrepreneurial leadership behavior, then this would mean something quite different. No venture capital fund would be necessary, but it would probably want to train these people in what behaviors to exhibit on the job and try to measure how well they practice these behaviors. Alternatively, if the company identified "more entrepreneurial" as mining behavior, then this would imply yet another approach to rekindling the entrepreneurial spirit.

Having first a clear definition and then creating support mechanisms that are tailored to this definition is much more effective and efficient than simply asking for "more entrepreneurial spirit." It helps frame and define the concept and undoubtedly leads to better results in the end. If top management cannot agree on which fork to take, then they are better off not taking any path at all.

The 5C Virus: Checkers Checking Checkers Checking Checkers

Perhaps one of the biggest obstacles to more entrepreneurial behavior that I have seen in large companies is the amount of time, energy, and staff devoted to control—or should I say overcontrol. In Chapter 4, I mentioned that IDG, a company that is incredibly successful at serial entrepreneurship, had only 19 corporate headquarters staff for 14,000 employees. This is an extreme case, to be sure, but Pat McGovern made a conscious decision in trying to replicate his entrepreneurial spirit by purposefully keeping HQ staff to a minimum. Every company needs control, but IDG's view is to hire smart people with something to prove, give them a lot of support, push them for aggressive results, pay them well, and hold them accountable. There are several possible explanations as to why companies seem to need "checkers checking checkers checking checkers." One is that they must not have good people working for them or they would not have to watch them all the time. Or, they have good people but either don't realize it or don't trust them. Another interpretation is that being watched all the time has sapped them of their natural entrepreneurial tendencies or has attracted people who are risk averse and thus enjoy the control.

Whatever the interpretation, micromanagement and focus on control mechanisms inhibit entrepreneurial leadership. As you saw from the entrepreneurial profiles, some of these folks are pretty good at getting around and through such mechanisms. But even the successful ones will tell you how difficult it is to build new business when you are constantly filling in data for people who are not creating economic value. IBM discovered that some of its highest potential new businesses were being killed in the first year because they could not meet financial and performance metrics that were typical of IBM's mature businesses. When IBM started using different management and control systems for different types of businesses they got some spectacular successes, as noted in the Don Cotey case from Chapter 8.

As one of my client companies was trying to increase its entrepreneurial orientation, it simultaneously instituted a complex new budgeting and control system. This system literally took a month out of everyone's year just to fill in the forms with the requested information. In frustration, one of our entrepreneurial leaders sent an e-mail to the head controller that outlined the costs in labor and lost business as a result of filling in these forms and asked if this was the intention of the data collection. (You'll read what happened shortly.) As often happens, the people in the control function were just trying to do a better job of control, but the result was actually the inhibition of value creation.

Another of my clients is in the software solutions business. Although the company is very successful, it realizes that to grow, it must develop better management skills among its managers, particularly those in the middle of the organization. The company wants these managers to take on more responsibility and act more like owners of the business, not just stewards, and it has spent a great deal of time in developing a new strategy and values to help guide these middle managers. But it also has a policy that senior management must personally approve any capital expenditures over 80 euros. Now, you can see a slight problem: hundreds of thousands have been spent on consultants to help the organization increase speed, agility, and personal ownership, yet a rule like this remains in place and even has its defenders. Absurd? Perhaps. But this sort of thing is all too prevalent in many companies. If this organization really wants to send a message about ownership and personal accountability, it should take this rule out immediately and let every manager above a certain level have more discretion regarding spending. Removing this rule would probably have greater impact on how managers view their future roles than a thousand PowerPoint presentations about the new corporate values.

The 5C virus is a very stubborn one and, without the right attention and treatment, it can become deadly to any organization. (You may remember the story in Chapter 1, about the book publisher that had a rule against shipping books by air.) This virus comes on slowly over the years, and the checkers who check checkers sincerely believe that the way to run the business better is to make sure nothing gets overlooked and nothing is left to chance. Checkers thus spawn other checkers, who create more processes and control mechanisms, eventually checking the creativity and risk taking out of the organization—along with the entrepreneurial spirit.

In companies looking to become more entrepreneurial, one of the first things that must happen is an examination of the layering on of processes, procedures, and forms. Is it going to continue to slavishly rely on and defend these processes in spite of the desire for greater entrepreneurial leadership? Does it really need all this data and information? Does anyone actually look at it or use it? Clearly, all employees can justify what they do, but not all they do is justifiable. Companies that truly want to increase their entrepreneurial quotient must wage a continuous and unrelenting war on bureaucracy and complexity. They also need a pipeline directly back to senior management regarding the roadblocks that entrepreneurial leaders encounter in trying to identify, develop, and capture new business opportunities. The Mott's entrepreneurial development program I described in Chapter 9 had this kind of feedback loop built in at the very beginning of the program.

Managers at all levels can fight bureaucracy, especially if they show the cost-to-benefits ratio in economic terms. The manager I mentioned earlier, who detailed the lost productivity involved in the budgeting process, got an immediate audience with both the controller and the CEO to discuss how they might modify some of their requests for data. CEOs who desire greater entrepreneurial leadership and business growth must focus as much on removing the handcuffs as they do on capitalizing the business.

The Check's in the Mail Syndrome

Everyone listens to that famous global radio station WIFM (What's in it for me?). Some entrepreneurial leaders ply their trade simply because of the personal enjoyment they get from playing that role. I found several of these people at one of my transaction processing clients, even though the company is not overtly supportive of this behavior. When I asked them why they do it, they said it was because it is fun. When I asked if their entrepreneurial successes had really helped their career, most had mixed experiences. Some said that it had helped a little, while others thought it might have actually gotten in the way of faster advancement. So why do they do it? Because it's fun.

This type of motivation is fine for those people who have entrepreneurial leadership already wired in, but it is not enough to induce it in potential entrepreneurial leaders, nor to sustain it over time. Often, managers will be asked to play the role of entrepreneurial leader and are told by upper management, "Trust us. We really want you to do this, and we will take care of you." This is a little bit like being told the check's in the mail. If we want managers to step up and step out as entrepreneurial leaders, it is not unreasonable to expect them to ask, "What's in it for me?"

With some exceptions, most companies wanting greater entrepreneurial spirit have not really thought this question through; they expect "trust us" to suffice. Yet, it is essential to have both a formal strategy of entrepreneurship and a commensurate structure for reward and recognition. For an entrepreneurial leader like Denise Prince (see Chapter 8), who has helped create several successful external ventures with more to come, receiving a Montblanc pen and a letter of commendation probably won't do the trick. At some point, she might reasonably expect an equity stake or stock in one of these ventures, not just a merit increase based on the current corporate pay structure. Geisinger is actually discussing now how they should go about doing this. P&G and Intel offer the potential of a two-step promotion for a successful entrepreneurial leader. And, in these two competitive organizations, a two-step promotion is hard to come by. But many of the companies that come to us for entrepreneurial leadership training have not really thought through how they will reward people differently for practicing entrepreneurial behaviors. Stepping off the standard career path to pursue a risky, perhaps unsuccessful venture requires a reward that makes the risk worth taking.

Peer Fear Infection

What I call "peer fear infection" is a particularly cunning little malady and one that can sneak up very quickly on the best of entrepreneurial leaders. John Kelley, the miner at VariTrust profiled in Chapter 6, was undone primarily by his peers. Because of his leadership skills and his success in turning around VariTrust's Annuity Service Center, John got a reputation as a creative and entrepreneurial guy. He was often called on to give speeches to other companies about how VariTrust had grown its business through his inventive rearrangement of assets. Several other insurance companies used his center as a benchmark. In short, all this attention and the changes John was instituting annoyed his peers, and they conspired to get even. John blamed himself for some of this fallout, because he had not really considered or involved his peers in what he was doing. Entrepreneurial leaders sometimes revel in an "I'll show you" attitude, which clearly does not help the situation. Also, John's boss, who was his mentor in all of this, did not really do the necessary blocking and tackling for John with his peers. Instead, he spent most of his time making sure that his own boss was on board and protecting John just enough so that he could demonstrate "proof of concept."

His peers' feelings and behaviors are quite understandable, and I even have some sympathy for them. It's no fun when the new kid on the block comes along and rewrites the role of manager to that of entrepreneurial leader and then gets a really big win out of it. It upsets the apple cart, especially the conventional wisdom about how good, obedient soldiers are the ones who get promoted.

So, organizations attempting to promote more entrepreneurial behavior must advertise this openly. They must state it in their strategy, and they must measure it in their performance reviews. We often hear the adage "What gets measured, gets done!" This is not always the case with entrepreneurial leaders, but observing, measuring, and supporting this type of behavior promotes the frequency of its occurrence.

In one of the corporate entrepreneurship programs I taught, I encountered a manager from a large European financial services organization. When I asked him about his job, he said he was the company's "stealth entrepreneur." I had never heard this term before, nor have I heard it since. I asked him what this meant. He replied that he had been told by the CEO that he had the unwritten title of stealth entrepreneur and that he would be given a good sum of money that was not earmarked for anything in the budget. He was to keep this fund a secret and scout the organization for innovative and interesting new business ideas. If he liked them, he was at liberty to dispense some seed capital to support these initiatives. But he was never to tell anyone how much he had or where he got it. The CEO's fear was that, once this money was located, everyone would try to claim it.

On one hand, I like the CEO's approach; he understood the politics that can result from having a formal depository of funds for innovation. Everyone wants a piece. It's no wonder that internal venture funds in large organizations so often fail. So, this was the CEO's very clever attempt to keep such a fund alive—by keeping it secret. While I applaud his creativity, however, he was also setting up his stealth entrepreneur for some heavy peer fear. He will eventually be found out, seen as special, and targeted for a few arrows in the back by his colleagues. I wish him well.

The Overdose

The "overdose" is a particularly fatiguing ailment. At first, it doesn't sound that dangerous, but on further reflection it can be a killer. We often find overdosing in large companies that believe entrepreneurial leadership should be in addition to, rather than part of, the manager's job. By this, I mean senior management often wants more entrepreneurial orientation, but only after hours. It's treated as something you do *in addition* to your daily work, so you are paid for your regular job but expected to moonlight as an entrepreneurial leader. Thus, the company gets twice the productivity at half the price—theoretically.

Most people who work in large companies are pretty busy. Perhaps they are not always creating value, but they are busy nonetheless. It is not uncommon to find people putting in 10-hour days. If most of this work is just fighting fires or filling out forms, then little time is left over for creative thinking. John Kilcullen, described in Chapter 5, often comes to my classes to help teach the case study about him. While he delivers a number of powerful messages about being a successful entrepreneurial leader, one of his most poignant messages concerns the need for time for creative thinking. When you are always doing, it is tough to be creative. So, John talks about the importance of delegating, of going for walks, of exercise, of spending time with the family, and making sure you take a vacation. This helps clear the mind and allows it to function at its creative best.

I can hear you saying, "Great idea, but I'm too busy." I have two responses. The first is that, if you are not thinking creatively, then someone else is and will beat you to the next opportunity. The second comes from an excellent article I read in the *Harvard Business Review* entitled "Reclaim Your Job."[1] I often assign this article to managers who claim they never have enough time to do the important work because they are so busy doing the unimportant work, like filling in forms. The authors make a key point (one actually made well before the article by the Eagles, the long-lived rock band, when they sang, "So often times it happens that we live our lives in chains/And we never even know we have the key"[2]): Managers are not really managing when their job controls them. They need to control their own work, and subsequently their own destiny, by prioritizing and making sure that they work on the important stuff. Management is such an amorphous and ambiguous job that how we play the role depends both on who *we* are and how *we* define the role. If we believe the job is in charge of us, then it is. If, on the other hand, we believe that we are in charge of the job, then we are. It's not about work-load, it's about interpretation.

So, one way to build more entrepreneurial thinking into your job is to think more entrepreneurially. Nobody can stop you from thinking. They may try to stop some of your acting, but in many companies, especially large ones, this can take some time. Even more beneficial, however, would be senior management's overt statement that more entrepreneurial thinking will not only be appreciated, it is expected and will be measured and rewarded.

In addition, senior management must be prepared to let people spend some time working on innovation. 3M is best known for this, but other companies could learn to emulate it. If an entrepreneurial leader's idea is really good, then management has to be prepared to take the person off her current job and make the pursuit and capture of the new opportunity the person's primary job. Again, Don Cotey's profile in Chapter 8 exemplifies this organizational mindset. IBM made the capture of the life sciences business opportunity his major focus and job responsibility, rather than a sideline. And he wasn't asked to do this in addition to his day job; it became the primary focus and *purpose* of his day job.

Booster Shot

We have discovered entrepreneurial leaders at all organizational levels, many of them in the middle. These folks are not tied up with shareholders or analysts like those at the top; they make things run on a day-to-day basis. They often see opportunities and have the guts to go for them, but they might need "a shot of help" from people in power, to increase antibody resistance just long enough to prove that their opportunity is real. In many of the companies with whom we work, we suggest the development of "power mentors." Some companies already use such a system, but other companies could greatly benefit from the antiviral therapy.

Power mentors are usually senior-level managers who are well-known and respected in the organization and, most important, have had some well-known entrepreneurial wins in their backgrounds. These wins do not actually have to be recent. Some of these power mentors have not had a win for years, but they still have the entrepreneurial leader tag hung around their neck—they are part of the organization's entrepreneurial folklore. They are not hard to find. Ask several people in any large organization to point out one or two of these people, and they can do so. These folks are perfect mentors for budding entrepreneurial leaders. They have been there, done that. They can run interference for the fledgling entrepreneurial leader, advise him on how to get around barriers, counsel him on how to get the right players on his side, and sometimes shelter him from uninformed *no!* responses and those who enjoy stifling creativity just for the fun of it.

Although entrepreneurial leaders can succeed without such mentors, it is a much harder job. Natural entrepreneurial leaders often find power mentors on their own, but companies wishing to become more serial and systematic about entrepreneurial behavior should formalize this process. If you have a good idea and you can find someone who is credible, well-known in the company, and with enough juice to help you succeed, then you are off to a good start. In addition, you have the start of a team. Sometimes, these mentors have to discourage bad ideas, but even this advice is extremely valuable. It keeps entrepreneurial leaders from going over the edge on things that really won't pan out.

Once found or assigned, these power mentors must practice a particular kind of coaching that you don't hear about in typical coaching books or models. I have discovered this type of coaching to be immensely helpful to the development and success of corporate entrepreneurial leaders. I call it "catalytic coaching." I know that this term seems like another one of those pesky oxymorons, but it is the only term I could think of that describes this incredibly important entrepreneurial leader–development tool.

Coaching is usually seen as something that is supportive, learner-centered, and nonconfrontational. Catalytic coaching also involves listening and support, but utilizes a very tough and systematic line of questioning, to see if the would-be entrepreneurial leader has an idea or an opportunity and whether she has passion for it. If we don't see passion, we state this and ask why. If the idea isn't strong, we might say, "Get another idea, one that you love." We will also challenge the individual to see if she really has spent the time and energy required to differentiate an idea from an opportunity. We might ask questions like, "How do you know people will buy it?" "Have you asked any potential customers?" "How many, when, what were their demographics?" If she hasn't done her homework, then we will suggest that she go back to the drawing board, because she only has an idea, not an opportunity.

If we don't understand the opportunity, its unique value proposition, and the customer target, then we tell her so. This is clearly unconventional coaching. While it is a little bit "in your face," it's meant to challenge, test, motivate, and assess the would-be entrepreneurial leader's mettle, passion, knowledge, and seriousness about her opportunity and her willingness to fight for it.

In addition, we challenge a leader to think bigger about his idea, to ask "What if you did this or that? Couldn't it be a bigger opportunity?" Or, "Why would you want to spend your time doing this? It doesn't look very promising or interesting. Could you make it more interesting?" Surprisingly, the coach does not need to know a lot about the details or technical underpinnings of the idea; they just have to ask the right questions. Some of the best new businesses we have helped spawn out of our workshops on entrepreneurial leadership got their real kick from this type of coaching. And it allows us to start separating good ideas from good opportunities and good entrepreneurial leaders from not so good ones.

In some ways, catalytic coaching mirrors what venture capitalists often do when vetting the various proposals that are put before them. Thus, you can see that a company's use of power mentors who are well-versed in the art of catalytic coaching can do a lot to help in the development of greater entrepreneurial thinking and acting throughout the company. If the company embarks on a formalized entrepreneurial development program, then each would-be entrepreneur should be assigned, wherever possible, to an identified power mentor. This also sends a strong signal that the company is serious about rekindling its entrepreneurial spirit.

Summary

Large companies are never perfect "host organisms" for entrepreneurial infections, and they can never be entrepreneurial in the way they were at the beginning of their existence. But they can reasonably hope to rekindle the spirit in more modified ways and more targeted areas. Expecting every manager to be an explorer would not only be folly, it could jeopardize what is already good and working. You just need enough! And you need to be savvy enough to manage the paradoxes of large and agile, planful and opportunistic, controlled and adventurous. This management of paradoxes allows a company to rekindle and sustain greater entrepreneurial orientation while keeping the good stuff. In the next and final chapter, I will give you two metrics that will help you analyze how ready the organization—or a part of it—is for greater entrepreneurial leadership and how ready individual managers are to play a more-entrepreneurial role.

Chapter Twelve

Organizational Readiness

Over the course of this book, I have tended to paint all large companies with the same brush. I have made the case that, when we think of large companies, we often think of negatives like *corporate, rule-bound, slow, encumbered, lethargic, risk-averse,* and *old boys' network.* To be sure, stereotypes often have their origins in fact, and the same is true with large companies. Many are slow, many are risk-averse, and the fact that fewer and fewer of my crack MBA students want to work for large companies must say something in general about many of their environments. But not all large companies are like this. GE, Intel, IDG, Siemens, and others have had some successes in counterbalancing the stereotype.

If a company is large and has been able to maintain or rediscover its entrepreneurial underpinnings, then congratulations are in order. It would probably not seek help in rekindling its entrepreneurial spirit, since the flame has never really gone out or it was able to reignite the spark by itself. But for those companies that seek help, it is important for them to get some sort of baseline or starting point. How bad are they, really, in killing or extinguishing their entrepreneurial flame, and do they already have some surviving entrepreneurial leaders kicking around who could serve as role models or "power mentors" in the future?

To help companies get a baseline, I developed two survey instruments: one to measure the organization's overall entrepreneurial orientation and the other to assess a manager's entrepreneurial leadership orientation. The first instrument, the Entrepreneurial Orientation Survey (EOS) in Appendix B, has already been validated within a number of companies. The second, the Entrepreneurial Leadership Questionnaire (ELQ), in Appendix C, is a new survey instrument based on the four entrepreneurial leadership typologies discussed in Chapter 4. The ELQ measures the degree of entrepreneurial behavior shown by the company's managers, as seen by their direct reports and others. It is a 360-degree feedback instrument focused on entrepreneurial leadership. In the following pages, I provide you with the rationale for these surveys, some sample questions for each dimension, and some sample output of the results. I have not included all the survey questions, due to their proprietary nature, but you will have enough information to start your own analysis.

I use these surveys prior to many of our educational intervention programs to help companies better prepare their strategies for creating and sustaining entrepreneurial spirit. In general, the lower the scores on these surveys, the more the company may be in need of rekindling its entrepreneurial heritage and the more difficult it will be, requiring efforts on many fronts. Because the surveys allow various ways of stratifying the information, companies can examine their standing by level of management, by division, business unit, or geography to determine where and with whom they want to start. But first, let's talk about the EOS, its background, its rationale, and its results.

Entrepreneurial Orientation Survey

The EOS (Appendix B) was built on my research into what entrepreneurial companies look like, especially regarding some key metrics of entrepreneurial orientation. Because our clients wanted their organizations to be more entrepreneurial, I needed to know what factors separated entrepreneurially oriented companies from those that were less so. Depending on an organization's entrepreneurial orientation, it may or may not make sense for the company to try to find and develop entrepreneurial leaders. As I said earlier, companies ill-prepared for entrepreneurial behavior must be careful what they ask for, because they might get it. Thus, understanding where your company is strong and where it is weak in its entrepreneurial orientation is a good place to start. The EOS diagnosis provides this starting point. A discussion of which roads are best traveled to remedy the situation can then follow.

In doing my homework, I talked with my colleagues; interviewed business leaders, consultants, and professionals at other business schools; and read the literature to see what these companies did to be described as entrepreneurial and innovative. I was able to summarize this research in something I call the 7 Fs of entrepreneurial orientation. These 7 Fs formed the basis for the EOS.

The 7 Fs

To be described as high in entrepreneurial orientation or opportunistic, a company must score relatively well on the following dimensions. These are not meant to be exhaustive, but they are diagnostic enough to provide a baseline:

- Fast
- Flexible
- Focused
- Friendly
- Frugal
- Far-reaching
- Futuristic

Clearly, companies that score low in these categories will have much more difficulty in capturing opportunities. Opportunities exist in windows of time, and these windows can close, often very quickly. Interestingly, my research with large companies suggests that such companies still have the ability to spot new business opportunities. Their real challenge is whether the organization possesses the other characteristics of entrepreneurial orientation that will allow them to actually *capture* the opportunity. Managers in these companies are often frustrated, because they see what could be but can't get their organization off the dime quick enough to do anything about it. Appendix B shows each of the seven "F" dimensions, with sample questions relating to each one.

Fast.   Speed is clearly a competitive advantage in capturing opportunities. The first company to market with a new product is usually the most successful. Speed means fast decision making, fast resource allocation, and fast delivery. Thus, an organization that builds itself around speed is essentially creating a competitive advantage, with or without a clearly differentiated product.

One excellent example of the value of being fast is a Massachusetts company that manufactures steel-reinforced rubber hoses.[1] Rubber hose is hardly an exciting product, and it is pretty tough to differentiate one hose from another. This lack of differentiation creates a commodity market space in which competitors slog it out in the trenches by price cutting and subsequent cost cutting.

This company was no different from the rest of these commodity kings. In some ways, in fact, it was worse. For one thing, its delivery times were horrible, creating a cadre of infuriated customers. Some salespeople had actually segmented the list of angry customers into groups with titles like Irritated, Slightly Angry, and Really PO'ed. Worse, this list actually included most of the company's customers. It seems that the inability to deliver goods on time fostered an abiding anger toward the company from its customers. And, since switching costs are usually low in a commodity business, dissatisfied customers were leaving in droves.

Finally, a new general manager came on the scene and took immediate action—or more accurately, several actions. He reengineered the production floor to make it more efficient, streamlined operations, and created a "SWAT" team that could deliver special orders within 24 hours. Most important, he listened to his employees' suggestions for reinventing the company around the core value of speed.

As the success of Federal Express tells us, customers will gladly pay for speed, and this company's customers were no exception. Its new emphasis on speed—finally resulting in the capacity to deliver product faster than anyone in the market space—allowed the company to capture significant, high-margin growth opportunities in a price-cutting marketplace. Let's face it: If a Boeing 747 sits on a runway because it lacks one rubber hose, the airline doesn't give a twirling propeller where the hose was born. It is only important that the hose arrives in time for takeoff.

Flexible.   In today's marketplace, flexibility is as important as speed. The ability to move people and resources quickly to capture a new market opportunity is essential to success. Too often, in large companies, designated functions, division of labor, and the eventuality of bottlenecks make it hard to keep a company's resources—and especially its human resources—fluid and available for new opportunities. Opportunity-capture demands that companies break down boundaries. It requires internal cooperation and collaboration. But when you look inside many companies, you find rigidly drawn borders between departments and divisions, and ultimately between people.

One of the biggest reasons that large organizations get caught and surpassed by the competition is a lack of agility. They have lost the ability to move people and resources quickly enough to stave off multiple small attackers. Being large doesn't necessarily mean that a company can't be agile. It just means that large companies have to constantly evolve mechanisms for building and maintaining agility while simultaneously creating processes and procedures to ensure order. Some good examples of large but agile companies exist: ABB, General Electric (GE), and AVCO Financial Services among them.

Despite its current problems, ABB Corporation has been an exemplar of a large but flexible organization. It is global and diverse, yet it manages to react quickly to market opportunities. It does this through a culture of cooperation, with flexible working structures, such as temporary task forces and teams. The company moves managers around the world, allowing staff to develop far-reaching, international management skills. ABB has organized much of its business along a business-unit structure and, perhaps most important, it has a miniscule corporate staff. I visited ABB corporate headquarters in Zurich a couple of years ago and was quite surprised at the unassuming nature of both the headquarters and the senior managers. The company is determined to be lean, agile, and extremely responsive to its operating businesses.

GE is another company that seems to have learned how to manage size and agility. When Jack Welch first came to GE, he described the company as extremely bureaucratic and slow moving. The company had layer upon layer of bureaucracy, and managers spent their time fighting for their corporate perks, while protecting their positions and status at all costs. Welch first cleaned house by vacuuming away layers of middle management personnel and unnecessary bureaucracy. But he didn't stop there. He actually promoted agility by breaking the business down into small business units, while giving line managers decision-making power and profit-and-loss responsibilities. Managers of small business units—who operate close to the ground in the marketplace—often are able to recognize and defend against threats from small predators, and they are first to see and seize new business opportunities.

AVCO Financial Services (recently absorbed by Citigroup), a large consumer finance company, is another example of a large but agile organization. Over the years, the company found a unique way to build agility into its necessarily complex and bureaucratic structure—the company dealt with finance and its attendant regulations around the world, after all. AVCO's marketing and product development folks often test marketed novel ideas in Australia. They learned that the adventurous Aussies are inclined to try anything once, even sometimes multiple times, despite some pain, thus providing a good testing ground for new ideas. And the Land Down Under was so far away from corporate headquarters in Irvine, California, that the corporate kahunas at HQ had little control over these experiments. If an idea worked in Australia, developers migrated it to the UK, then to Canada, and eventually to the States. Although large and operating under a number of federal reporting and conduct policies, the company developed agility by building an outpost of creativity. (As an aside, the company was also smart enough to buy those little upstarts who wanted to nibble away at its niche markets.)

Focused. As we have said, companies must plan and create structure, or they can sink into a quagmire of chaos. At the same time, however, they must be open to important opportunities that enter their field of vision. These days, so many opportunities appear on the horizon that the ability to focus on a few—and the right few—has become critical. No organization can afford to expend the time and resources required to chase every opportunity that comes its way. So, while remaining flexible and agile, an organization must develop a clear focus, choosing opportunities that fit logically into the corporate jigsaw puzzle. Focus and flexibility must go hand-in-hand in 21st-century organizations.

3M Corporation offers the perfect example of a company that has developed a focused but flexible approach to its business. Its core products are adhesives. But the company's development of Post-it Notes prompted a reevaluation of its core business. It had traditionally been focused on tape. But it was flexible enough to realize that its real underlying competence was in building the "stickiness" into the tape. By making this slight change in mindset, the company was able to refocus its business and create a host of new products and markets for its core capabilities. Its original focus allowed the company to become successful, while its flexibility allowed it to see possibilities and modify focus. This an inherent paradox for 21st-century organizations: planning and flexibility become inextricably intertwined partners.

Friendly. Another important trait we found in entrepreneurial companies was friendliness. Young, start-up companies know instinctively that they must be friendly to internal and external customers and to employees. Without the enthusiastic support of these three constituencies, a new company has little chance for success. And, if a large, established company hopes to survive in the current environment, it must also craft a new identity as a friendly organization. Think of today's airlines, most of which are in trouble, and ask how they would score on customer friendliness. Not well, from my extensive travel experiences. I wonder if some relationship exists between their customer friendliness orientation and their financial results?

Customer friendliness is not new. It's something we business school professors have been preaching for years. But opportunity-focused companies put a new and interesting spin on the concept. They are equally as interested in determining where customers are not being satisfied as they are in understanding what is currently making consumers happy. They understand that some of the best opportunities grow out of these gaps—or "white spaces"—in customer satisfaction.

The second kind of friendliness necessary for an opportunity-focused organization is internal customer friendliness. The Japanese really developed the notion of internal service. We all talk about the importance of external customer service, but the Japanese were the first to identify internal customer service as a requisite to external customer service. If cross-organizational service is poor, external service also will be poor, especially on the delivery side. Without good internal service, a company spends its time training clerks and others actually interfacing with customers to apologize and try to make up for lack of delivery on promises. Eventually, customers tire of listening to excuses and find someone who is a master at delivering on promises, not just a master at delivering excuses.

I recently bought a new phone from newly constituted mobile service provider. The phone was very cool, state-of-the art, Internet-enabled, with Windows included. I really liked the phone, but it had some serious problems. I had to send it back for repairs after the first three months. Early adopters often have these sorts of problems, so I was not overly concerned. But after dealing with my new service provider, I could have torn my hair out. I called Customer Service, they sent me to Warranty and Repair, they sent me back to Customer Service, who sent me back to Warranty and Repair. Sound familiar? All the people were polite and friendly and apologized, but they weren't talking to each other. I was doing the integrating—and not very successfully.

To make matters worse, my particular phone was on back order and neither Warranty nor Customer Service could give me any date as to when that phone would be back on the market, let alone in my increasingly sweaty little hands. So I said, "Send me a different phone until the new one comes out again." "Sorry, we can't do that" was the reply. "We can only send you the original type of phone, which you bought for $399." "OK," I said, "then give my money back, since we have a contract for you to supply me with a new phone, and you cannot deliver on your end of the bargain!" "Sorry, sir. We can't do that either. It's against our policy." So, now I'm thinking small claims court.

Fortunately, since I was writing this book at the time, I decided to try and outsmart and outmaneuver the company's bureaucracy with their own bureaucracy. A sort of corporate judo, if you will. I would utilize their own power against them. I was aware that this company had a 30-day return policy on any new phone you purchased from them, no questions asked. Since my phone was 3 months old, I was not able to return it or get a refund. So, in my last conversation with the Customer Service representative I said, "What if I do the following: Since you cannot guarantee when my original phone will come to me, why don't I buy a new phone from you every month until mine comes? I will return your phone on the 29th day, you give me my money back, I will buy another new phone, use it for 29 days, and return for a refund etc., until my original phone gets repaired." There was a steely silence on the other end of the phone and the company rep said, "I don't see any policy against that, so I guess it would be a good solution." Good for me perhaps, but what are they going to do with all the used and returned phones? I doubt that they will be able to resell them and certainly not for new-phone prices.

All of us have experienced similar treatment. It is aggravating, costly, inefficient, and unfriendly. Unfriendly to their own internal people as well as to me. And, it certainly was not entrepreneurial. This story is illustrative of why scoring low on friendliness as a marker should be a wake-up call. Some companies are actually measuring internal customer service and holding departments with poor ratings accountable for improving them. Most opportunity capture requires internal coordination to satisfy the customer.

Employee friendliness certainly seems to have gone out of fashion in recent years. In this culture of constant downsizing and widespread outsourcing, it seems an anachronism to talk about employee satisfaction. But here's the truth: Unhappy, insecure employees make rotten interfaces with customers. Entrepreneurial start-ups understand this very well, and so they work very hard to keep employees happy. New-media and Internet companies are famous for their ping-pong tables, lunch-hour dance lessons, and generous compensation packages—most often with stock equity as a part of the deal. Equity as part of a compensation package is wise on a couple of levels: First, it certainly makes for a happier employee, and second, it makes an employee feel invested in the company.

I find it interesting that we are so surprised these days by good service. On a recent trip to California, I rented a car in Irvine and dropped it off in Los Angeles. I asked the counter person at Hertz if there was a drop-off fee. She assured me that there would be no fee because LA and Irvine were so close. Hertz is extremely efficient in billing, so my bill arrived at my home before I did. I noticed immediately that, despite the associate's assurances, the $50 drop-off charge had been added.

We all know the drill from here: Another bad customer experience story is about to unfold. I found the 800 number on the bill and called customer service. I anticipated that I would encounter a polite, well-trained customer service representative who would apologize for the misunderstanding but do nothing to help. Anticipating this situation, I was ready and armed to the teeth with an offensive strategy.

I informed the rep that I wanted to talk directly to her supervisor. "But, sir," she said, "perhaps I can help, I'm the customer service representative." "That's exactly the problem," I responded. "Representative, nothing! Give me a decision maker!" "But sir, please, let me try and help," she pleaded. "All right, but we are wasting time. Here is the problem," I said, explaining the situation. "I'm very sorry, sir, I will take that off your bill immediately," she answered. I was speechless. She had just taken the wind out of my once-billowing sails. I sheepishly thanked her and hung up.

I like telling this little story. The Hertz service rep had obviously been empowered to make the decision. She truly wanted to help me, and she was persistent.

Big companies must learn what start-ups already know. Unhappy employees do not give good service or creative ideas. As a result, the company either does not get or does not listen to the potential for opportunities—the white space of employee dissatisfaction. They see complaining customers as a pain in the butt, and usually don't care to convey this information back to the company managers, who probably wouldn't listen anyway. Motivated, empowered, engaged employees are often closest to real opportunity sets, and they want to pass on what they learn.

So, the F of *friendliness* can pay substantial dividends to an organization interested in innovation and corporate entrepreneurship. Not only does it create satisfied customers inside and outside the organization, but it creates a chain of intelligence that naturally flows into and through the organization, which can lead to new opportunities.

Frugal.   Frugality is not cheapness. Being frugal means spending one's money wisely in service of one's strategy. You may think I'm stating the obvious here, but an examination of a company's corporate strategy and an analysis of its financial strategy may reveal some striking incongruities. A company that says its success hinges on customer service but spends a disproportionate amount of money on R&D does not have a financial footprint that matches its avowed strategy. Thus, it is unlikely to ever achieve what it says it desires.

I am currently working with a large, international mining company. It has recently changed its strategy from being capacity-driven (filling the mills) to technology-driven (leading by technological innovation). The company has spent a lot of money on consultants to help it reach the conclusion that this is the way to go in its market space. It has also rolled out a number of communications and training initiatives to reinforce this new order.

Then, as if out of the blue, the company's executive committee in Asia allied with a competitor to increase capacity for a product that the company has repeatedly said would not constitute the company's future. This investment was significant, meaning that other initiatives more in-line with the new corporate strategy are now on indefinite hold. This is truly a case of disconnected focus and frugality. No wonder both the stock markets and the employees are confused about the worth of this company.

For entrepreneurial companies, frugality also means a consistent focus on keeping costs under control while taking advantage of new opportunities for growth. Entrepreneurs and entrepreneurial companies must focus on the top line—revenue—not just the bottom line. I am always dumbfounded when I hear that a company requires across-the-board cuts. Across-the-board budget cuts can only mean that senior management has no focus. Five percent across the board might sound fair, but it is incredibly stupid. Entrepreneurial companies know that they should cut costs in low- or no-opportunity areas while simultaneously investing in high-potential growth opportunities. This is what I mean by frugality—spending and cutting wisely.

Entrepreneurial companies also put some elasticity in budgets and forecasts by planning for unforeseen opportunities. Some even create internal venture capital funds to spur innovation in interesting ideas.

Far-Reaching.   The next F refers to markets and distribution. Opportunistic companies realize that the world is a global one and don't restrict their efforts to local geographies. This approach allows them some elasticity if market conditions worsen in one or two of their markets but not in others. Local companies often get killed when they depend on one or two local customers, no matter how large the accounts. Defense-dependent companies learned this lesson all too well when the federal government began slashing defense budgets in the late 1980s. There could hardly be a bigger customer than the U.S. government, but many companies that depended solely on government work were quite literally and quite suddenly defenseless. Fortunately, the Internet now allows even the smallest mom-and-pop operation global reach. Small, opportunistic companies understand the importance of this concept and typically reach out to many different customers and markets.

Futuristic.   Customer friendliness only tells you about current customers, not future ones. Thus, a flaw in a lot of customer-focused companies is that they rely on current customer feedback. They must do this of course, but they must also consider customers who are not even on their radar screens. These are the customers they do not yet have for the products and services they don't yet supply. Now, that may sound impossible, but this kind of anticipation of new markets is critical if a company is to successfully compete in the marketplace of the future. Sometimes, a company actually creates new customers and markets when it develops a new technology or product.

Vinay Chowdhry, founder of Qualicon (a DuPont subsidiary), represents an excellent example of discovering needs that customers don't even know they have and using this knowledge to not only start a new company but to create a new industry as well. Gaurab Bhardwaj, one of my colleagues, works closely with Vinay, and they coined the term "anticipatory entrepreneurship" to describe this phenomenon. Vinay worked at DuPont and spent a lot of time with people in the food-processing industry looking for potential products that DuPont might develop for this industry. He found that industry insiders wanted fast analysis of bacteria, such as *Salmonella*, on food so that they could make appropriate and timely production decisions. But, as he listened more deeply, he discovered that these potential customers didn't actually trust existing test methods because of high error rates. So, creating faster test methods alone would have produced data that still would not have been trusted. This led Vinay and his colleagues to develop high-quality bacterial analysis instruments that gave accurate and timely results. Using Qualicon's products, food-processing companies could now protect against bacterial contaminations and thus provide safer and higher quality food items to consumers. Thus, the birth of Qualicon as the global gold standard for food testing.

Using the EOS to Assess Company Readiness

The EOS survey has been slightly modified from the original 7 Fs assessment. It now includes a "General" section, which encompasses the tightness of financial and budgeting control, as well as a section that asks respondents to describe their own entrepreneurial orientation (see Appendix B). As you will see, the EOS asks two fundamental questions: "How do we rate ourselves now?" and "What would we like our rating to be?" It is very valuable to find out if most people in the organization desire more entrepreneurship, or if only a couple of senior executives think that is valuable. If a discrepancy in ratings occurs, then it tells these executives that they need to undertake a huge PR campaign to persuade others that this is the path the company wants and needs to take.

The 7 Fs I defined earlier describe the opportunity-focused organization—one that is ready and able to pounce on new business opportunities. *Friendliness, future* orientation, and global reach (*far-reaching*) allows enterprises to identify opportunities; speed (*fast*) and *flexibility* allow them to aggressively pursue these opportunities. *Frugality* ensures that resources are available to help capture the opportunity. And finally, *focus* keeps a company from going off the deep end and becoming so entrepreneurial and ranging so far afield that it goes out of business.

Sample EOS

You will find sample questions from the EOS in Appendix B. Due to its proprietary nature, not all the questions or the scoring key has been provided, but you will get a good idea of what sort of questions we ask.

Note that the EOS was not designed to provide answers about *how* a company can be more entrepreneurial, but to provide a baseline for discussing and prioritizing entrepreneurial focus and action.

Spider Web Sample Output from the EOS

Figure 12.1 presents the output of the EOS for one of our clients. This will give you an idea of some of the data generat-

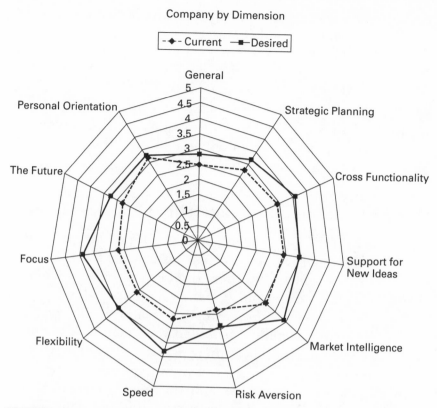

FIGURE 12.1   Spider web sample output from the EOS. Copyright: Impact Strategies, 2001. Licensed to Babson College.

ed by this instrument. In the figure, the solid line measures the average score across the company on desire for more of the entrepreneurial dimension, with the dotted lines measuring the current state. As this sample diagram shows, the people surveyed see their company as average in these dimensions and desire only a little improvement in most areas, with the greatest needs in speed, focus, market intelligence, and frugality. The profile of this company seems average in most dimensions, and it does not want a lot more—thank you! But the survey output makes clear which areas need to be improved.

This profile is a breakdown of the company in general. When we broke the questionnaire down by division, it was clear that some divisions needed a lot more help than others.

For example, one division was in the highly volatile telecommunications market, and it was clear from the diagram that they were below 3 on almost all the EOS dimensions, although they wanted to be at 4. Another division of this company was in a relatively slow and predictable market, and the results showed the current and desired EOS measures to be almost identical. This suggested that the company did not need or want to be much more entrepreneurial in this division, and this also squared with senior management's view.

The Entrepreneurial Leadership Questionnaire

I designed the ELQ to roughly map the four Entrepreneurial Leadership Typologies that I discussed in Chapter 4. In addition, I have added another dimension called General Entrepreneurial Leadership (GEL), which are behaviors that cut across all categories of entrepreneurial leaders. The ELQ (Appendix C) is generally distributed via e-mail to a sampling of a manager's subordinates, their peers, and their boss, who then rate this manager on each of the survey items in terms of both importance to the rater and the frequency with which they observe their manager practicing this behavior. Those individuals who fill in the ratings remain anonymous to the manager, and only summary data is reported back.

If, for example, a behavior is very important to subordinates, but the manager is not practicing it, then the manager has the option to increase his frequency of performance. On the other hand, the manager might find that he is practicing this behavior frequently, but raters don't think it is important. In this case, the behavior either needs to be less frequent or the respondents need to understand that it is more important than they think. Thus, the manager might be advised to start communicating this message.

In some cases, both the manager and their direct reports may not think a particular behavior is important, and so the manager is not doing it very much. Because all the behaviors are related to entrepreneurial leadership, this finding would tell senior management that they have a significant challenge ahead of them in trying to change the culture if they want more entrepreneurial orientation.

While I don't usually report back data on individual managers to the company, the data can be cut and categorized by groups of managers, by level, by geography, and by function, thus allowing the organization to pinpoint those areas in which it wants and clearly needs more-entrepreneurial activities. For example, low importance and low frequency might be just the findings you want for a control function, but not for new product development or for marketing. But, cases may arise in which controlling should act in more entrepreneurial ways.

The ELQ also has a special section that allows employees to rate senior management as integrators. Remember, integrators are generally at the senior level and are responsible for developing enterprise-wide entrepreneurial spirit. This data is very helpful for the executive group that says it wants to rekindle that old entrepreneurial spirit. Low ratings for those executives might indicate that the problem begins with them. They will probably have to figure out how to "walk the talk" before they ask others in the organization to do the same.

In Appendix C, you will find a sampling of ELQ questions and a scoring key. Nothing stops you from copying it and giving it out to your subordinates in order to rate you. I would caution you, however, to use someone outside the organization to collect and collate the data, to guarantee the confidentiality of the data and the anonymity of the respondents. Otherwise, I suspect you will not get very valid data, if any at all. (Although I have included only a sampling of questions, they are enough to give you the idea.)

The ELQ, like the EOS, is a diagnostic tool that helps organizations plan a strategy for rekindling their entrepreneurial spirit. Without this diagnosis and planning, as the Cheshire Cat reminded us, it won't matter which road you take.

Summary

Over the years of helping companies try to rekindle their entrepreneurial spirit, I have come to realize the tremendous importance of defining terms. I recently taught a course in which *innovation* was the central theme and participants had been drawn to the program because their respective organizations were struggling with how to become more innovative. I was the third presenter, and I was struck by the fact that everybody nodded when the other faculty members used the word *innovation*. When it came my turn to speak, I said, "Before I start, I just want to see if we are all talking about the same thing." So, I asked four participants to give me their meaning of the word. As you might expect, there were four different definitions.

This definitional problem is the same that I face when I use the word *entrepreneurial*. Getting folks in an organization to agree on terms like *innovation* and *entrepreneurial* is the starting point for the rekindling of entrepreneurial spirit. Throughout this book, I have tried to put some clarity around the concept of entrepreneurial leadership. As you have seen, having organizational managers lead from an entrepreneurial perspective can pay handsomely. But, as you have also seen, it is a tremendous challenge. It not only requires the identification and development of the right people, it also requires critical support mechanisms if more entrepreneurial activity is to be scalable and sustainable.

The EOS and the ELQ are aimed at helping companies get a baseline analysis on the people side and the organizational support side of entrepreneurship before they rush into anything. These instruments also serve to develop a common language and common understanding of some of the concepts put forth in this book.

My hope for all who have read this book is that it helps you make more informed decisions. No magic bullet or secret formula exists; if either of them did, it would probably not be as effective as well-thought-out and well-informed human judgment. At the end of the day, better leadership, better management, and increased entrepreneurial activity only come from people agreeing and working together in the creative process that is at the heart of the entrepreneurial spirit.

Entrepreneurial Leadership Development Program Template

I have found the following template to be highly effective in developing entrepreneurial leaders while simultaneously leading to new business development. This template follows the three key stages of opportunity development, using just-in-time educational inputs from faculty to help the entrepreneurial leaders move their opportunity from idea to reality.

- Module 1. Opportunity identification
- Module 2. Opportunity development
- Module 3. Opportunity capture

Figure A.1 shows the "flow" of a typical entrepreneurial leader–development program. The term *selection* in the figure refers to how potential entrepreneurial leaders are chosen. Sometimes they are assigned to the class based on their managerial positions, such as general manager, and sometimes participants have had to apply and go through a rigorous screening program.

The following is a brief description of the purpose, rationale, and objectives of each of the key entrepreneurial modules

The Babson Entrepreneurial Leader–Development Program

FIGURE A.1   Entrepreneurial leader–development program.

that we typically employ in our entrepreneurial leadership training programs. We have found that the between-module coaching of our potential entrepreneurial leaders is extremely important. This is where we really get insight into the organizations' entrepreneurial barriers and antibodies.

Module 1: Opportunity Identification

In the body of this book, I discussed the difference between good ideas and good opportunities and the skills necessary to differentiate the two. Module 1 of the program combines entrepreneurial thinking and general management skills such as finance, marketing, and operations. Participants are asked to look carefully at themselves and their own personal characteristics to see if they truly want to try their hands as entrepreneurial leaders. We encourage program participants to drop out of the program if they decide it is not for them, assuring them that no stigma will be attached. The goal is for participants to be able, at the end of the module, to begin to look for real entrepreneurial growth opportunities for their organization. This does not mean simple iterative increases in the core business or line extensions, but opportunities in the platform and breakthrough categories.

Coaching Between Modules 1 and 2

We encourage individual coaching and mentoring for participants during the period between Modules 1 and 2. Ideally, coaching should be done by both faculty and individuals at the participant's company. The purpose of the coaching is to get people to focus on real opportunities. This "catalytic coaching" (see Chapter 11) can help participants avoid those business-as-usual ideas that are often the first ones people seek.

Module 2: Opportunity Development

The purpose of Module 2 is to take those opportunities identified in Module 1 and begin to develop and shape them into realities for the company. In Module 1, we look for lots of ideas and divergent, creative thinking. In Module 2, we begin to assess and evaluate these ideas against key metrics such as market demand, proposed customer value, potential scale and scope, and financial viability. Some opportunities, as they are increasingly vetted, become unattractive. When this happens, we typically congratulate the entrepreneur for not spending any more money and ask him to go back to the drawing board and seek out another opportunity, join another participant's team, or withdraw from the program.

Participants with viable opportunities are asked to start the business planning process. Module 2 begins by looking at the importance of the entrepreneur, the entrepreneurial team, and the resources required to bring an opportunity into reality. Each participant is asked to identify key team skills and competencies and develop a recruitment strategy for getting these people interested and involved in pursuing the opportunity with him. We also examine organizational strategy, structure, and systems as they related to new-product, new-business, or new-value proposition development to make sure that we have some of the infrastructure necessary to support high-potential opportunities.

Coaching Between Modules 2 and 3

The business plan development of the opportunity is the principal focus for between-module coaching following Module 2. Business plan development consists of a description of the opportunity, the rationale for pursuing it, market research and analysis, needed resources, timetables, financial investment, forecast, cash flow analysis, an implementation plan, and an analysis of key stakeholders and the strategies needed to involve them. We also insist that program participants talk to potential customers before completing this plan. As we saw from Shahrom Kiani's profile in Chapter 5, the customer is critical in ensuring that you have a real opportunity, not just a neat idea. Remember that Shahrom not only got customer interest, he got customer resources to help him further shape his team's proposed opportunity.

Module 3: Opportunity Capture

In the final module, participants further hone and refine their business plans in preparation for presentation to interested parties. Typically, top management is interested, but we have had potential customers and partners come to these presentations as well. In Module 3, we also address the development of a vision and a marketing campaign for selling the opportunity to others both inside and outside the organization. Entrepreneurial leaders must be able to capture the attention and emotion of those from whom they are trying to win resources. At the end of this session, we expect crisp, polished business plans and a lot of passion.

Module 3 also stresses the leadership aspect of entrepreneurial leaders. All leaders must be able to vividly—and credibly—describe and communicate the vision of their opportunity. Entrepreneurial leaders need excellent "visioning" skills to capture and effectively communicate their opportunity to both internal company people and customers. Influencing skills, communication capabilities, and the ability to present fact-based arguments are all requisites for successful entrepreneurial leaders. During previous modules, but particularly during this module, we assess individual participant's strengths and weaknesses in this area and provide coaching and further skill development when necessary.

Post-Module 3 Implementation

Perhaps the most significant part of any of our entrepreneurial leadership programs is what happens after the end of Module 3. Here, opportunities are selected, investments are made, barriers to implementation are identified and overcome, and entrepreneurs are chosen and given accountability for implementing their ideas. If the organization does not provide complete and dedicated support during this phase, then it is unlikely that the development program will have any effect. In fact, it may make things worse, in that the company now has newly created entrepreneurial leaders who are frustrated in their ability to actually implement what they have worked so hard to develop. And they are primed to practice these skills elsewhere.

Most of the time, we identify these problems before this point, especially if the company agrees to our staged investment advice. We can take partial responsibility for helping design and monitor the appropriate support mechanisms, but companies like Mott's, Siemens, Sodexho, and others ultimately are accountable for providing the appropriate infrastructure and support. Some companies do this well; others fail miserably.

Despite the lack of support structures, some entrepreneurial leaders still manage to get through, and one $250 million dollar success isn't too bad out of 25 or 30 people. But the company will probably not realize the value creation that it could have garnered had it been more disciplined in preparing the ground for the entrepreneurial leader's reentry. And, of course, monitoring should be ongoing if these managers are to continue applying their newfound entrepreneurial skills.

Entrepreneurial Orientation Survey (EOS)

The following are sample questions from the EOS. Due to its proprietary nature, not all the questions nor the scoring key has been provided, but you will get a good idea of what sort of questions we ask.

The Entrepreneurial Orientation Survey (EOS)

Name _____

Organization _____

Business Sector_____

Country _____

The purpose of this survey is to understand and assess the key dimensions of Corporate Entrepreneurship. In the following sections, you will find a number of questions that cover a range of organizational domains. Unlike other surveys, you are asked to *not* think too much. We are interested in your immediate reaction to each question. Go with your first reaction!

As you answer these questions, please use the frame of reference of your organization "in general." We realize that departmental and specific divisional or unit analysis may be different.

You may also find that we have not covered some areas which you think are important aspects of an entrepreneurial orientation. If you think we have missed anything, you will find space at the end of the survey for your comments.

Please circle the number (1–5) that best fits your agreement/disagreement with the following statements about your company in general.

In *general*, my company:

	Strongly Disagree	Disagree	Unsure	Agree	Strongly Agree
1. Adheres to tight budget controls.	1	2	3	4	5
2. Rewards managers for cost cutting.	1	2	3	4	5
3. Keeps a pool of funds available for new business opportunities.	1	2	3	4	5
4. Makes money available for really good ideas.	1	2	3	4	5
5. Requires several layers of approval for obtaining out-of-budget investment money.	1	2	3	4	5

Regarding *strategic planning*, my company:

	Strongly Disagree	Disagree	Agree Somewhat	Agree	Strongly Agree
1. Utilizes a formal strategic planning process.	1	2	3	4	5
2. Lets strategy evolve based on trends in the marketplace.	1	2	3	4	5
3. Expects managers to stick closely to the yearly plans and budgets.	1	2	3	4	5
4. Doesn't have a clear strategy.	1	2	3	4	5
5. Relies heavily on outside consultants for developing strategy.	1	2	3	4	5

Regarding *cross-functionality*, my company:

	Strongly Disagree	Disagree	Agree Somewhat	Agree	Strongly Agree
1. Has very few cross-functional silos (interdepartmental barriers).	1	2	3	4	5
2. Has departments which willingly share ideas and information with each other.	1	2	3	4	5
3. Encourages cross-functional discussion and problem solving.	1	2	3	4	5
4. Formally rewards cross-functional cooperation.	1	2	3	4	5
5. Rotates employees through different functions as part of a formal employee development process.	1	2	3	4	5

Regarding *support for new ideas*:

	Strongly Disagree	Disagree	Agree Somewhat	Agree	Strongly Agree
1. Management generally encourages us to think up new and different ways of doing things.	1	2	3	4	5
2. There is one major function in our organization, which is primarily responsible for innovation and new business development.	1	2	3	4	5
3. We have a suggestion method in place, which works well in capturing employee ideas.	1	2	3	4	5
4. The organization does not take kindly to challenging the way things are done around here.	1	2	3	4	5
5. We often meet informally to discuss new business ideas.	1	2	3	4	5

Regarding *market intelligence*:

	Strongly Disagree	Disagree	Agree Somewhat	Agree	Strongly Agree
1. The customer is king in our organization.	1	2	3	4	5
2. Unless you are in sales or marketing, there is very little encouragement to meet with customers.	1	2	3	4	5
3. The company routinely gives customer satisfaction surveys and publishes the results internally for all of us to see.	1	2	3	4	5
4. Senior executives rarely visit customers directly.	1	2	3	4	5
5. Most of our employees know who our closest competitors are and how we stack up against them.	1	2	3	4	5

Regarding *risk aversion*:

	Strongly Disagree	Disagree	Agree Somewhat	Agree	Strongly Agree
1. Our company is proud of its conservative heritage and orientation.	1	2	3	4	5
2. We are careful not to make mistakes.	1	2	3	4	5
3. We are not afraid to invest in new ventures on an intuitive gut feeling rather than based on careful analysis.	1	2	3	4	5
4. People generally have a lot of latitude in the organization to try new things and fail.	1	2	3	4	5

	Strongly Disagree	Disagree	Agree Somewhat	Agree	Strongly Agree
5. We talk a lot about the need for greater risk taking in our organization, but the reality is people who try and fail don't last very long.	1	2	3	4	5
6. We prefer to grow in a planned and controlled manner.	1	2	3	4	5

Regarding *speed*:

	Strongly Disagree	Disagree	Agree Somewhat	Agree	Strongly Agree
1. Customer complaints are handled quickly and efficiently.	1	2	3	4	5
2. Problems do not get solved quickly.	1	2	3	4	5
3. Managers have a great deal of autonomy in making decisions.	1	2	3	4	5
4. Customers describe us as a fast-moving company.	1	2	3	4	5

Regarding *flexibility*:

	Strongly Disagree	Disagree	Agree Somewhat	Agree	Strongly Agree
1. We rely heavily on task forces and temporary teams to solve problems.	1	2	3	4	5
2. When we see a new business opportunity we are slow to allocate resources in pursuit of the opportunity.	1	2	3	4	5

Regarding *flexibility*:

	Strongly Disagree	Disagree	Agree Somewhat	Agree	Strongly Agree
3. We frequently move people around to different functions and departments in order for them to gain a broader perspective on our business.	1	2	3	4	5
4. People are expected to go through the proper channels in getting their job done.	1	2	3	4	5
5. We are pretty informal regarding titles and levels in the organization.	1	2	3	4	5

Regarding *focus*:

	Strongly Disagree	Disagree	Agree Somewhat	Agree	Strongly Agree
1. We do few things, but do them well.	1	2	3	4	5
2. We are a fragmented organization; the right hand seldom knows what the left hand is doing.	1	2	3	4	5
3. Senior management has a clear vision as to where we are going and how we are going to get there.	1	2	3	4	5
4. If you asked two different people what our strategy is, you would probably get two different answers.	1	2	3	4	5
5. We are quite willing to spend money, as long as it's for the right things.	1	2	3	4	5
6. Even the man/woman on the shop floor knows the company's vision.	1	2	3	4	5

Regarding *the future*:

	Strongly Disagree	Disagree	Agree Somewhat	Agree	Strongly Agree
1. We consider ourselves a "cutting-edge" company.	1	2	3	4	5
2. We do not invest a lot of resources in R&D efforts.	1	2	3	4	5
3. Our company likes to try to create totally new markets based on innovative products that customers do not even know they need yet.	1	2	3	4	5
4. We tend to be followers rather than leaders in our product/service offerings.	1	2	3	4	5
5. Employees are not generally rewarded for experimentation in our company.	1	2	3	4	5

Personal Orientation

Please rate *yourself* on the following questions.

	Strongly Disagree	Disagree	Agree Somewhat	Agree	Strongly Agree
1. I have often had fantasies of starting and running my own business.	1	2	3	4	5
2. I do not consider myself to be a rebel.	1	2	3	4	5
3. The quickest way to get to the top is to do your job to the best of your ability.	1	2	3	4	5
4. I often daydream at work.	1	2	3	4	5
5. I love to challenge the status quo.	1	2	3	4	5

Please rate *yourself* on the following questions.	Strongly Disagree	Disagree	Agree Somewhat	Agree	Strongly Agree
6. I dislike rule breakers.	1	2	3	4	5
7. It is very important for me to have a fair, predictable compensation package.	1	2	3	4	5
8. I would give up my current salary and benefits package for a much lower salary and an equity position in a high-potential, yet risky start-up.	1	2	3	4	5
9. I am much more comfortable in a relatively structured environment	1	2	3	4	5

Entrepreneurial Orientation Survey (EOS)

My Company

In this section, please check the answer which best describes your feelings about your organization in general.

1. In terms of overall market performance, compared to our competitors I would describe us as:
   ☐ Exceptional performers
   ☐ Above average
   ☐ Average
   ☐ Below average
   ☐ Poor performers

2. In terms of empowerment, my company is:
   - ❑ Exceptional
   - ❑ Above average
   - ❑ Average
   - ❑ Low in empowerment
   - ❑ Very low in empowerment

3. In terms of innovation, we are:
   - ❑ Very experimental
   - ❑ Somewhat experimental
   - ❑ Average
   - ❑ Not very experimental
   - ❑ Extremely conservative

4. We believe in:
   - ❑ Compensating people relative to their performance
   - ❑ About average with our competitors
   - ❑ Somewhat below our competitors' compensation packages
   - ❑ Poor compared to our competitors

About Me!

Please answer the following questions about yourself as honestly as you can. No one will see these results except Babson researchers, and we guarantee the anonymity of your responses.

	Strongly Disagree	Disagree	Agree Somewhat	Agree	Strongly Agree
1. I am more proud of my technical accomplishments than I am of my leadership of people.	1	2	3	4	5
2. I would prefer running a well-organized, integrated organization over a creative, disorganized organization.	1	2	3	4	5
3. Most people in our organization would describe me as a maverick.	1	2	3	4	5
4. I pride myself in being politically astute.	1	2	3	4	5
5. My peers would generally describe me as a creative loner.	1	2	3	4	5
6. I believe entrepreneurs are born, not made.	1	2	3	4	5
7. I believe entrepreneurs can learn a few things, but have to have a lot of the right stuff.	1	2	3	4	5
8. I believe entrepreneurs are successful as a result of both personality characteristics and learning.	1	2	3	4	5

9. I believe entrepreneurs can learn a lot about how to be an entrepreneur.

1   2   3   4   5

10. I believe entrepreneurs are mostly a product of learning and experience, not personality.

1   2   3   4   5

Comments: _____

Entrepreneurial Leadership Questionnaire (ELQ)

The purpose of the following questionnaire is to assess the importance to you of various behaviors that your direct supervisor may practice and the extent to which he/she actually practices these behaviors. The questionnaire is completely anonymous. Your responses will be aggregated with the responses of your boss's other direct reports in order to be scored (at least three direct reports must fill in this questionnaire for each boss).

Please rate the importance to you of each behavior on a five-point scale, with 1 being very unimportant to 5 being extremely important.

Then rate each behavior on the frequency with which your boss actually practices this behavior on the job: 1 indicates almost never, while 5 indicates almost always.

Importance Rating (I)	1 Not at all important	2 Somewhat important	3 Important	4 Very important	5 Extremely important
Frequency Rating (F)	1 Almost never	2 To some extent	3 Frequently	4 Often	5 Very often

1. Spends time on new business development.
   (I) 1 2 3 4 5   (F) 1 2 3 4 5

2. Points out the competition's weaknesses and how we could exploit them.
   (I) 1 2 3 4 5   (F) 1 2 3 4 5

3. Listens to and acts upon customer complaints.
   (I) 1 2 3 4 5   (F) 1 2 3 4 5

4. Challenges us to think about new and better ways to do our work.
   (I) 1 2 3 4 5   (F) 1 2 3 4 5

5. Encourages the bending/circumvention of company rules when they get in the way of achieving business goals.
   (I) 1 2 3 4 5   (F) 1 2 3 4 5

6. Assertively communicates to upper manager regarding how things could be run better.
   (I) 1 2 3 4 5   (F) 1 2 3 4 5

7. Looks for creative ways to manage, use, or rearrange company assets and resources.
   (I) 1 2 3 4 5   (F) 1 2 3 4 5

8. Passionately looks for new ways to grow the business.
   (I) 1 2 3 4 5   (F) 1 2 3 4 5

9. Motivates us to think of innovative ways to beat the competition.
   (I) 1 2 3 4 5   (F) 1 2 3 4 5

10. Effectively sells new business ideas to upper management.
    (I) 1 2 3 4 5   (F) 1 2 3 4 5

11. Supports our suggestions for improving the business.
    (I) 1 2 3 4 5   (F) 1 2 3 4 5

12. Gets things done even if it means going around the system.
    (I) 1 2 3 4 5   (F) 1 2 3 4 5

13. Communicates a vision of how the organization could be better in the future if we were to make certain improvements.
    (I) 1 2 3 4 5   (F) 1 2 3 4 5

14. Encourages us to challenge the status quo.
    (I) 1 2 3 4 5   (F) 1 2 3 4 5

15. Makes sure that we keep the customer in mind when making changes to our organization.
    (I) 1 2 3 4 5   (F) 1 2 3 4 5

16. Tells us where we stand vis-à-vis the competition.
    (I) 1 2 3 4 5   (F) 1 2 3 4 5

17. Pushes us to innovate in how we do our work.
    (I) 1 2 3 4 5   (F) 1 2 3 4 5

18. Actively identifies, develops, and goes after new business opportunities.
    (I) 1 2 3 4 5   (F) 1 2 3 4 5

19. Makes sure that we have the right team of people in place to successfully capture these new opportunities.
    (I) 1 2 3 4 5   (F) 1 2 3 4 5

20. Displays enthusiasm for us learning new skills.
    (I) 1 2 3 4 5   (F) 1 2 3 4 5

21. Quickly takes a different direction when results aren't being achieved.
    (I) 1 2 3 4 5   (F) 1 2 3 4 5

22. Encourages others to take the initiative and action for their own ideas.
    (I) 1 2 3 4 5   (F) 1 2 3 4 5

23. Motivates people to think about how to do their work in new and interesting ways.
    (I) 1 2 3 4 5   (F) 1 2 3 4 5

24. Allots time to helping others find ways to improve our products and services.
    (I) 1 2 3 4 5   (F) 1 2 3 4 5

25. Creates a climate that encourages continuous improvement.
    (I) 1 2 3 4 5   (F) 1 2 3 4 5

26. Willingly moves ahead with a promising new approach when others might hold back.
    (I) 1 2 3 4 5   (F) 1 2 3 4 5

27. Promotes an environment where risk taking is encouraged.
    (I) 1 2 3 4 5   (F) 1 2 3 4 5

28. Identifies, encourages, and protects rebels who might think and act differently than the majority of employees.
    (I) 1 2 3 4 5   (F) 1 2 3 4 5

29. Encourages others to outwit and outmaneuver the company's bureaucracy.
    (I) 1 2 3 4 5   (F) 1 2 3 4 5

30. Quickly utilizes different approaches to overcoming obstacles when the initial one doesn't work.
    (I) 1   2   3   4   5   (F) 1   2   3   4   5

31. Creates an environment where people feel free to try new things.
    (I) 1   2   3   4   5   (F) 1   2   3   4   5

32. Challenges us to creatively discover ways to do more with less.
    (I) 1   2   3   4   5   (F) 1   2   3   4   5

33. Demonstrates an entrepreneurial orientation at work.
    (I) 1   2   3   4   5   (F) 1   2   3   4   5

34. Pushes the organization to be fast, flexible, and adaptable so that we can react quickly when new business opportunities arise.
    (I) 1   2   3   4   5   (F) 1   2   3   4   5

35. Actively fights the encroachment of bureaucracy in the company.
    (I) 1   2   3   4   5   (F) 1   2   3   4   5

36. Utilizes an extensive network of people throughout the organization that is willing to help if called upon.
    (I) 1   2   3   4   5   (F) 1   2   3   4   5

37. Analyzes work flow, resources, processes, and procedures to see how we can do our work better, faster, and cheaper with better impact for the customer.
    (I) 1   2   3   4   5   (F) 1   2   3   4   5

38. Expects us to constructively identify and solve cross-organizational problems and issues.
    (I) 1   2   3   4   5   (F) 1   2   3   4   5

39. Willingly listens to suggestions from others about how to do things differently.
    (I) 1   2   3   4   5   (F) 1   2   3   4   5

40. Support us in fighting for changes which will improve the way the company works.
    (I) 1   2   3   4   5   (F) 1   2   3   4   5

The following survey items should only be rated in reference to your views of Senior Management. Senior Management refers to the CEO or top manager of the organization and his/her team of direct reports. Clearly there are individual differences among senior managers so please refer to what you believe most of them do. If the behaviors are too varied among the Senior Management team, then rate each item with just the CEO/Top Manager in mind.

41. Strives to build an innovative culture within our company.
    (I) 1   2   3   4   5   (F) 1   2   3   4   5

42. Encourages entrepreneurial thinking and risk taking.
    (I) 1   2   3   4   5   (F) 1   2   3   4   5

43. Reacts quickly to remove organizational barriers that get in the way of doing business.
    (I) 1   2   3   4   5   (F) 1   2   3   4   5

44. Encourages open communications and idea-sharing across organizational units and functions.
    (I) 1   2   3   4   5   (F) 1   2   3   4   5

45. Keeps the organization informed and updated on industry trends and competitor strategies.
    (I) 1   2   3   4   5   (F) 1   2   3   4   5

46. Actively encourages business improvement suggestions throughout the organization.
    (I) 1   2   3   4   5   (F) 1   2   3   4   5

47. Takes action to implement many of these suggestions.
    (I) 1   2   3   4   5   (F) 1   2   3   4   5

48. Keeps the organization focused on its core strategy but also supports new business initiatives.
    (I) 1   2   3   4   5   (F) 1   2   3   4   5

49. Puts aside money outside of the normal budget process in order to fund and support innovative ideas.
    (I) 1   2   3   4   5   (F) 1   2   3   4   5

50. Encourages employees to challenge their decisions.
    (I) 1   2   3   4   5   (F) 1   2   3   4   5

ELQ Scoring Key

The questions on the survey map to the five dimensions of entrepreneurial leadership:

· GEL—general entrepreneurial leader behaviors
· E—explorer behavior
· M—miner behavior
· A—accelerator behavior
· I—integrator behavior

Simply add the rating associated with each question under each dimension to get the overall scores for both importance (I) and frequency (F). Normally, this is done by computer, but you can do a self-rating to see where you fall in your own estimation.

GEL	Explorer	Miner	Accelerator	Integrator
5 I F	1 I F	6 I F	4 I F	13 I F
12 I F	2 I F	7 I F	11 I F	28 I F
26 I F	3 I F	15 I F	14 I F	34 I F
27 I F	8 I F	32 I F	17 I F	36 I F
29 I F	9 I F	37 I F	20 I F	41 I F
30 I F	10 I F	38 I F	21 I F	42 I F
33 I F	16 I F	40 I F	22 I F	43 I F
35 I F	18 I F		23 I F	44 I F
39 I F	19 I F		24 I F	45 I F
			31 I F	46 I F
				47 I F
				48 I F
				49 I F
				50 I F

Add up the scores under each dimension for each question on both importance and frequency, and then look at the table below to get an idea into which category your scores fall. Please keep in mind that your self-ratings may be different from how others see you.

Score Range	GEL	Explorer	Miner	Accelerator	Integrator
High	34–45	34–45	26–35	42–55	53–70
Medium	23–33	23–33	18–25	31–41	36–52
Low	9–22	9–22	17–24	11–30	14–35

Notes

Chapter One

1. Gifford Pinchot III, *Intrapreneuring* (New York: Harper & Row, 1985).
2. T. Amabile and D. Whitney, *Corporate New Ventures at Procter & Gamble* (Boston: Harvard Business School Press 1997).
3. M. Porter, *Competitive Strategy: Techniques for Analyzing Industries and Competitors* (New York: Free Press, 1980).
4. G. Bennett Stewart III, "EVA Works—But Not If You Make These Common Mistakes," *Fortune*, May 1995.

Chapter Two

1. J. Kotter, "What Effective Managers Really Do" (Boston: Harvard Business Review Press, Mar. 1, 1999).
2. E. Ghiselli, *Explorations in Managerial Talent* (Pacific Palisades, CA:, Goodyear Publishing, 1971).
3. D. Geroy, A. Bray, and D. Venneberg, "The CCM Model: A Management Approach to Performance Optimization. *Performance Improvement Quarterly* 2005;18 (2):19.
4. K. Blanchard and P. Zigarmi, *Leadership and the One Minute Manager: Increasing Effectiveness through Situational Leadership* (New York: Blanchard Management, 1985).
5. W. Bennis, *On Becoming a Leader* (Reading, MA: Addison-Wesley, 1989).
6. D. Garvin and J. West, *Serengeti Eyewear: Entrepreneurship within Corning* (Boston: Harvard Business School Press, 1993).
7. D. Gookin, *DOS for Dummies* (New York: Hungry Minds, 1999).
8. E. Tyson, *Investing for Dummies* (New York: Hungry Minds, 2003).
9. R. Westheimer, *Sex for Dummies* (New York: Hungry Minds, 2001).
10. J. Pearce, T. Kramer, and D. Robbins, "The Effects of Managers' Entrepreneurial Behavior on Subordinates," *Journal of Business Venturing* 1997;12 (2): 147–160.

Chapter Three

1. J. Lange, "Entrepreneurial Myths," Babson Executive Education Presentation, Corporate Entrepreneurship open enrollment program (May 2003).
2. Spinelli, Steven, Babson Executive Education Presentation. Corporate Entrepreneurship open enrollment program, 2003.
3. J. Timmons, *The Entrepreneurial Mind* (Andover, MA: Brick-House Publishing, 1989).

Chapter Four

1. "VeriTrust Annuity Center" (Babson Case Study, revised 2005).
2. T. Amabile and D. Whitney, *Corporate New Ventures at Procter & Gamble* (Boston: Harvard Business School Press 1997).

Chapter Six

1. John Kelley is not this leader's real name. His name, the names of his fellow employees, and company and division names have been changed. All events related in this case are real.

Chapter Seven

1. J. Pearce, T. Kramer, and D. Robbins, "The Effects of Managers' Entrepreneurial Behavior on Subordinates," *Journal of Business Venturing* 12, no. 2 (1997): 147–160.
2. Siemens, *Idea Management: The 3i Program* (internal document, Siemens, October 2000).

Chapter Eight

1. The Horizons model designated businesses in one of three categories: Horizon 1 was mature businesses providing profits and cash flow. Horizon 2 was businesses experiencing accelerating growth. And Horizon 3 was emerging businesses that were still in the developmental stage. H3s could be designated as EBOs.
2. In 2000, IBM had six sectors, containing a total of 17 industry verticals.

Chapter Nine

1. K. Rashani and J. Miller, "Innovation and Renovation: The Nespresso Story," Harvard Business School Press, Case # IMD046, 2000.
2. R.A. Burgelman and R.S. Bamford, "Intel Corporation: The Hood River Project (A)," Harvard Business School Press, Case # SM49A, 1997.

Chapter Ten

1. W. J. Bruns Jr., C. Knoop, and A. St. George, *Mercedes-Benz in Alabama: Lessons from the Field* (Boston: Harvard Business School Press, 1989).
2. D. Garvin and J. West, *Serengeti Eyewear: Entrepreneurship within Corning* (Boston: Harvard Business School Press, 1993).
3. Arthur M. Blank Center for Entrepreneurship, Babson College, Babson Park, MA: 2000.

Chapter Eleven

1. S. Bruch, "Reclaim Your Job." Repr., Boston: *Harvard Business Review*, 2004.
2. *Already Gone*, The Eagles, 1974.

Chapter Twelve

1. Film. *Speed is life: Get fast or go broke.* Tom Peters. Video Publishing House, Schaumburg, IL: 1991.

Index

Note: Boldface numbers indicate illustrations.